The Executive Politics and Governance series focuses on central government, its organisation and its instruments. It is particularly concerned with how the changing conditions of contemporary governing affect perennial questions in political science and public administration. Executive Politics and Governance is therefore centrally interested in questions such as how politics interacts with bureaucracies, how issues rise and fall on political agendas, and how public organisations and services are designed and operated. This book series encourages a closer engagement with the role of politics in shaping executive structures, and how administration shapes politics and policy-making. In addition, this series also wishes to engage with the scholarship that focuses on the organisational aspects of politics, such as government formation and legislative institutions. The series welcomes high quality research-led monographs with comparative appeal. Edited volumes that provide in-depth analysis and critical insights into the field of Executive Politics and Governance are also encouraged. Editorial Board Philippe Bezes, CNRS-CERSA, Paris, France Jennifer N. Brass, Indiana University Bloomington, USA Sharon Gilad, Hebrew University Jerusalem, Israel Will Jennings, University of Southampton, UK David E. Lewis, Vanderbilt University, USA Jan-Hinrik Meyer-Sahling, University of Nottingham, UK Salvador Parrado, UNED, Madrid, Spain Nick Sitter, Central European University, Hungary Kutsal Yesilkagit, University of Utrecht, the Netherlands

More information about this series at
http://www.palgrave.com/gp/series/14980

Tobias Bach • Kai Wegrich
Editors

The Blind Spots of Public Bureaucracy and the Politics of Non-Coordination

palgrave
macmillan

Editors
Tobias Bach
Department of Political Science
University of Oslo
Oslo, Norway

Kai Wegrich
Hertie School of Governance
Berlin, Germany

Executive Politics and Governance
ISBN 978-3-319-76671-3   ISBN 978-3-319-76672-0   (eBook)
https://doi.org/10.1007/978-3-319-76672-0

Library of Congress Control Number: 2018940770

Cover illustration: D. Trozzo / Alamy Stock Photo

Printed on acid-free paper

This Palgrave Macmillan imprint is published by the registered company Springer International Publishing AG part of Springer Nature.
The registered company address is: Gewerbestrasse 11, 6330 Cham, Switzerland

Acknowledgements

This idea for this book developed in the context of a research project addressing the 'administrative factor' in explaining the financial crisis at the beginning of the twenty-first century. In the process of developing its analytical framework, presenting and discussing draft chapters, and inviting contributors, it gradually developed a life of its own. It became a book about how day-to-day decision-making in public organizations is subject to different types of attention biases. Those biases may lead to major disasters, but they may also have less severe, though far from trivial, consequences, such as inducing organizations to avoid coordination with other organizations. The contributions to this book address those attention biases and their effects for various types of public organizations in different policy sectors and national contexts. We believe this diversity is extremely helpful in addressing questions of the 'why didn't they see it coming?' type, which are typically raised after major disasters and government blunders. At the same time, the issues raised in this book also appeal to the broader agenda of providing a theoretically informed, but realistic, account of organizational life in a political context.

The book project started to take shape during a workshop entitled 'The Blind Spots of Public Bureaucracies' at the University of Oslo's Department of Political Science in November 2016, where most contributors to the book presented first drafts of their chapters. Initial ideas for what has become the book's introductory chapter were presented at the panel 'The Administrative Dimension of Financial Market Regulation' at the IPSA (International Political Science Association) World Congress in Poznań in July 2016, and we presented a more full-fledged version at the Executive

Politics and Governance group at the Political Studies Association's international conference in Glasgow in April 2017. We thank the participants of those events for their feedback, which helped us to sharpen our arguments. In particular, we would like to thank Tom Christensen, Martin Lodge, Paul 't Hart, and Jan-Hinrik Meyer-Sahling for their constructive feedback on different versions of the introductory chapter. Martin Lodge also commented on the book's final chapter.

There are more people we would like to thank. We would not have engaged in editing this volume without our academic mentor Werner Jann, who introduced us to organization theory and the importance of bounded rationality for decision-making. He taught us that a good theory about public organizations also needs to help answer very practical questions and illustrate ways for improving decision-making. We hope that the approach put forward in this book fulfils both criteria. We also thank Jessica Leong Cohen for her invaluable assistance in preparing the final manuscript. This is a book about organizations, and we should not forget to thank the German Federal Ministry of Education and Research for funding the project State, Risk and Society (STARS) and the Department of Political Science at the University of Oslo for funding the author workshop. Kai Wegrich wishes to thank the Harvard Kennedy School's Ash Center for Democratic Governance and Innovation for hosting him during his sabbatical in Fall/Winter 2017/18 (during which time the manuscript was finalized).

Oslo, Berlin   Tobias Bach
April 2018   Kai Wegrich

CONTENTS

Part I   Conceptual Foundations   1

1   **Blind Spots, Biased Attention, and the Politics of Non-coordination**   3
    Tobias Bach and Kai Wegrich

2   **Accounting for Blind Spots**   29
    Martin Lodge

3   **Blind Spots: Organizational and Institutional Biases
    in Intra- and Inter-organizational Contexts**   49
    Tom Christensen

Part II   Blind Spots and Attention Bias   69

4   **Professional Integrity and Leadership in Public
    Administration**   71
    Wolfgang Seibel

5   The Alarms That Were Sent, but Never Received:
    Attention Bias in a Novel Setting   87
    Helge Renå

Part III   Bureaucratic Politics: Reputation, Blame, and Turf   111

6   Why Cooperation Between Agencies is (Sometimes)
    Possible: Turf Protection as Enabler of Regulatory
    Cooperation in the European Union   113
    Eva Heims

7   Blame, Reputation, and Organizational Responses
    to a Politicized Climate   133
    Markus Hinterleitner and Fritz Sager

8   Passing the Buck? How Risk Behaviours Shape
    Collaborative Innovation   151
    Krista Timeus

9   Media and Bureaucratic Reputation: Exploring Media
    Biases in the Coverage of Public Agencies   171
    Jan Boon, Heidi Houlberg Salomonsen, Koen Verhoest, and
    Mette Østergaard Pedersen

Part IV   Achilles' Heels and Selective Perception   193

10   Central Banks and Banking Regulation: Historical
     Legacies and Institutional Challenges   195
     Jacint Jordana and Guillermo Rosas

11 **Why Do Bureaucrats Consider Public Consultation Statements (or Not)? Information Processing in Public Organizations**   217
    Simon Fink and Eva Ruffing

Part V   Implications   239

12 **How to Deal with the Blind Spots of Public Bureaucracies**   241
    Tobias Bach and Kai Wegrich

Index   263

Notes on Contributors

Tobias Bach is Associate Professor of Public Policy and Administration at the University of Oslo, Norway, and fellow at the Hertie School of Governance, Germany. His research focuses on the structure and organization of government and executive politics in a comparative perspective.

Jan Boon is a postdoctoral researcher affiliated with Aarhus University, Denmark, and the research group Public Management & Administration at the University of Antwerp, Belgium. His research focuses on reputation management in the public sector.

Tom Christensen is Professor of Public Policy and Administration at the University of Oslo, Norway. He has published extensively on public sector reform and institutional change from a comparative perspective.

Simon Fink is Professor of the Political System of Germany at the University of Göttingen, Germany. His research interests are policy diffusion, research and technology policy, and Europeanization.

Eva Heims is Lecturer in Public Policy at the University of York and Research Associate of the Centre for Analysis of Risk and Regulation (LSE). Her main research interests are the executive politics of regulation and comparative public policy and administration.

Markus Hinterleitner is a postdoctoral researcher at the KPM Center for Public Management at the University of Bern, Switzerland. His research concentrates on the drivers of elite and organizational decision-making and the effects of decision-making on policy.

Jacint Jordana is Director of the Institut Barcelona d'Estudis Internacionals and Professor of Political Science and Public Administration at Pompeu Fabra University, Spain. His recent publications examine the diffusion of regulatory institutions, the comparative development of domestic public policies, and policymaking in policy networks.

Martin Lodge is Professor of Political Science and Public Policy at the Department of Government and Director of the Centre for Analysis of Risk and Regulation (CARR) at the London School of Economics and Political Science, UK. His key research interests are in the areas of executive politics and regulation.

Mette Østergaard Pedersen is a PhD fellow at the Department of Management, University of Aarhus, Denmark. Her research interests are motivation, values, leadership, and reputation management in the public sector.

Helge Renå is a PhD candidate at the Department of Administration and Organization Theory at the University of Bergen, Norway. His research interests are organizational sense- and decision-making in unsettled settings, and assessment standards in evaluations and investigations of crisis responses.

Guillermo Rosas is Associate Professor of Political Science and a research fellow at the Weidenbaum Center on the Economy, Government, and Public Policy at Washington University in St. Louis, USA. His research focuses on the economic consequences of political regimes and effects of political institutions on political elite behaviour.

Eva Ruffing is a senior researcher at the University of Hannover, Germany. Her research topics are the interplay between European and national administrations, focusing on agency autonomy, policy influence, and structural adaptation, and public participation in administrative decision-making.

Fritz Sager is Professor of Political Science at the KPM Center for Public Management at the University of Bern, Switzerland. He is specialized in administrative studies and theory, policy research and evaluation, organizational analysis, and Swiss politics.

Heidi Houlberg Salomonsen is an associate professor at the Department of Management, Aarhus University, Denmark. Her main research is on strategic communication in public sector organizations, top civil servants and ministerial advisers in central government organizations, and public leadership.

Wolfgang Seibel is Professor of Political and Administrative Sciences at the University of Konstanz and Adjunct Professor of Public Administration at the Hertie School of Governance, Germany. He has held guest professorships at the University of California at Berkeley and Stanford University, USA, and at the Central European University, Hungary.

Krista Timeus is a postdoctoral researcher affiliated with the Institute of Governance at ESADE Business and Law School, Barcelona, Spain. Her work focuses on public sector innovation and urban governance.

Koen Verhoest is a research professor at the research group Public Management & Administration at the University of Antwerp, Belgium. His research interests are the governance, autonomy, and coordination of public sector organizations.

Kai Wegrich is Professor of Public Administration and Public Policy at the Hertie School of Governance, Germany. He is a political scientist with research interests in executive politics, regulation, public sector reform, and innovations in policymaking.

LIST OF FIGURES

Fig. 6.1	Four cooperation outcomes of the politics of (non-) cooperation	118
Fig. 7.1	The causal mechanism between elite polarization and public service delivery	135
Fig. 9.1	Predicted probability of multiple threats as function of negative reputational history, based on model 1 (multiple threats (1) vs. no threats (0))	184
Fig. 9.2	Predicted probability of multiple threats as function of negative reputational history (only articles with threats), based on model 2 (multiple threats (1) vs. single threats (0))	185
Fig. 9.3	Predicted probability of response as function of article length (only articles with threats)	186
Fig. 10.1	Institutional separation between central banks, regulatory agencies, and ministries	201
Fig. 10.2	Banking agencies: regional evolution (1920–2015)	202
Fig. 10.3	Banking agencies: central banks versus regulatory agencies	203
Fig. 10.4	Banking agencies: creation and autonomy year (1920–2015)	205
Fig. 10.5	Financial regulation Fragmentation Index (1971–2015)	209
Fig. 11.1	Grid demand planning procedure in Germany (simplified overview, scenario framework consultation not shown)	222

LIST OF TABLES

Table 1.1   Four biases in organizational attention   11
Table 2.1   Blind spots and unintended consequences   35
Table 2.2   Worldviews, Achilles' heels, and blind spots   40
Table 3.1   Blind spots and organization theory perspectives: arguments and examples   63
Table 4.1   Institutional requirements and logics of action   76
Table 5.1   Distribution of output and activity indicators in annual performance contracts, 2004–11   95
Table 8.1   Codes and categories from interview data   161
Table 9.1   Reputational dimensions   183
Table 9.2   Logistic regressions models   184
Table 9.3   Relationship between article characteristics and response likelihood   186
Table 11.1   Participants in the consultations   224
Table 11.2   Influence of submissions by actor type   225
Table 11.3   Determinants of FNA decision   226
Table 12.1   Mechanisms, antidotes, and limitations of de-biasing organizations   247

PART I

Conceptual Foundations

Blind Spots, Biased Attention, and the Politics of Non-coordination

Tobias Bach and Kai Wegrich

Introduction: Organizational Life in a Political Context

The laundry list of contemporary bureaucratic malaises is as long as it is predictable, with common complaints ranging from cost inefficiencies and inflexibility to presumed aversions to entrepreneurship and 'customer' orientation. When buried among these items, coordination problems—whether despite or due to their pervasiveness—might be easy to overlook. The individual citizen lost in a bureaucratic maze, shuffled from one office to another, seemingly without end, epitomizes one such problem of (poor) coordination in the public sector. But while this kind of coordination problem is certainly embarrassing and has spurred an entire folklore

T. Bach (✉)
Department of Political Science, University of Oslo, Oslo, Norway
e-mail: tobias.bach@stv.uio.no

K. Wegrich
Hertie School of Governance, Berlin, Germany
e-mail: wegrich@hertie-school.org

© The Author(s) 2019
T. Bach, K. Wegrich (eds.), *The Blind Spots of Public Bureaucracy and the Politics of Non-Coordination*, Executive Politics and Governance, https://doi.org/10.1007/978-3-319-76672-0_1

3

about the insufficiencies of bureaucratic organizations (Goodsell, 1985), coordination problems within and between bureaucracies hardly stop here.

Although the lion's share of coordination problems do not end in large-scale disaster, more than a handful of major blunders on the part of public organizations can be related to problems of inter-organizational coordination. Those blunders—and the chain reactions some ignited in their wake—have cost numerous lives, as in the case of the US intelligence agencies' failure to piece together information that might have prevented 9/11 (National Commission on Terrorist Attacks upon the United States, 2004; Parker & Stern, 2002). An example on a smaller scale, though with no less of a tragic end, is the German police authorities' protracted failure to link serial killings of mostly immigrant citizens in different parts of the country to an underground right-wing terrorist group (Seibel, 2014; this volume). And even the 2007–08 financial crisis can be partially explained by certain facets of organizational behaviour, including a lack of coordination between regulators due to 'policy groupthink and shared blind spots' (Gieve & Provost, 2012, pp. 62–63) and regulators' one-sided attention towards specific tasks (Gilad, 2015).

Although diverse, these examples illustrate three points. First, they identify organizational factors as the main causes of coordination problems and biased attention and hence speak to established literatures on pathologies of information processing in formal organizations (Parker & Stern, 2002; Pidgeon & O'Leary, 2000; Wilensky, 1967). Second, they both highlight blunders and failures and reveal coordination problems in day-to-day decision-making in organizational life. Indeed, the idea of a clear analytical distinction between success and failure in public policy seem rather elusive, as success and failure are subjective and contested categorizations (Bovens & 't Hart, 2016). Third, whereas solutions seem to be available for some of those problems (such as one-stop shops to ease citizens' encounters with administrative specialization), finding straightforward answers to other questions, such as how to reorganize intelligence services (Hammond, 2007) or how to draw lessons from government blunders (Bovens & 't Hart, 2016), are more challenging tasks. Any attempt at addressing the source(s) of failure is likely to entail new challenges. In other words, we are facing administrative dilemmas that are inherent to organizational life (Hood, 1974; Wilensky, 1967). These themes lie at the core of this book, which puts a spotlight on the organizational foundations of biased attention and coordination problems in the public sector.

The study of coordination within and between public organizations and problems related to achieving coordination occupies a prominent place within the scholarship on organizational dysfunction, especially since coordination appears to be normatively desirable but inherently difficult to realize in practice (Bouckaert, Peters, & Verhoest, 2010; Metcalfe, 1994; Scharpf, 1994; Wegrich & Štimac, 2014). The need for coordination within and between organizations is a consequence of specialization 'through which the organization reduces a situation involving a complex set of interrelated problems and conflicting goals to a number of simple problems' (Cyert & March, 1963, p. 118). At the same time, specialization leads to a multiplication of organizational goals through the development of local rationalities or the well-known 'tendency for the individual subunits to deal with a limited set of problems and a limited set of goals' (Cyert & March, 1963, p. 117). The above-mentioned examples are illustrations of different types of biased attention and coordination problems, sometimes causing inefficiencies and annoyance, sometimes leading to drastic failures.

This book addresses various phenomena that tend to be considered irrational or pathological behaviours of public bureaucracies. The 'blind spots' that figure prominently in this book are a distinct type within a larger universe of biases in organizational decision-making leading to potentially dysfunctional effects, or to accepted negative effects in the case of administrative trade-offs and dilemmas (Hood, 1974). As we argue in more detail below, those biases emerge from intentionally rational behaviour of bureaucratic organizations operating in political contexts. We study these biases with respect to their implications on coordination within and between organizations and in particular the absence or rejection of coordination, as illustrated by previous examples and which we clumsily call 'non-coordination'. The aim of the book is to provide theoretical tools and empirical insights that address the conditions for effective coordination and problem-solving by public bureaucracies using an organizational perspective. And while one might argue that blunders have received undue attention compared to success stories in the coordination of public sector organizations, we consider a grounded understanding of the inevitable biases in organizational behaviour in a political context as critical for understanding not only what goes wrong but also how things could work out positively.

The book's distinct contribution is looking beyond cases commonly considered to be major policy failures and government blunders by focusing on everyday decision-making and coordination within and between public organizations. That said, several contributions take disasters as their starting point, yet they provide theoretical insights that are relevant for a better understanding of how public organizations work on a day-to-day basis (see the chapters by Seibel and Renå). We seek to advance this purpose by developing a typology of four distinct biases in organizational attention and decision-making that engender coordination problems or the outright absence of coordination (non-coordination): selective perception, inherent weaknesses, bureaucratic politics, and blind spots. These four biases reflect recent advances in public administration scholarship such as bureaucratic reputation theory (Carpenter & Krause, 2012; Maor, 2015) and blame avoidance (Hinterleitner & Sager, 2016; Hood, 2011) as well as established theorizing on the drivers of organizational behaviour, especially approaches emphasizing the boundedly rational nature of organizational decision-making (Jones, 2017; Simon, 1947) and an institutional perspective on organizations (Selznick, 1957; Wilson, 1989). Those theoretical contributions have already been somewhat influential in and of themselves, but public administration scholarship has yet to consolidate these perspectives and develop a broader agenda that tackles the permanent challenge of supposedly rational organizational behaviour exerting centrifugal forces on individual organizations and organizational units. We think this is a more than appropriate agenda at a time when the reality of power dispersion often meets unrealistic expectations regarding the potential—and logic—of collaboration and coordination.

Selective perception, inherent weaknesses, bureaucratic politics, and blind spots have three aspects in common. First, they are instances of *organizational behaviour* rather than individual misconduct or exploitation such as corruption and patronage. While it is ultimately individuals who make decisions, we are interested in how organizational roles and contexts shape decision-making, guide attention, and create blind spots. Second, the different biases are a result of *intentionally rational behaviour* leading to biases, imbalances, and other unintended effects, rather than the result of deviations from role expectations, norms of appropriate behaviour, and formal rules. Whereas deviant behaviour and organizational failure are important issues, we are primarily interested in how 'normal' behaviour leads to unintended and potentially disastrous effects (Pidgeon & O'Leary, 2000). Third, we maintain that the *political context* of bureaucratic organizations has important repercussions on organizational behaviour. The political element in particular implies the existence of plural, competing rationalities (Cyert & March, 1963); ambiguities of organizational objectives and performance (Allison, 1997); competing evaluations of organizational performance by various stakeholders (Bovens & 't Hart, 2016); and a concern with organizational maintenance in light of multiple and often conflicting demands for accountability (Wilson, 1989).

This introduction first places these phenomena into a broader theoretical context, which revolves around the notions of bounded rationality, institutionalized organizations, and unintended and paradoxical effects of collective action. After that, we flesh out key characteristics of the above-mentioned biases in organizational attention and discuss relevant scholarship to illustrate their analytical purchase. We focus on two biases in particular—bureaucratic politics and blind spots—as those have the greatest potential for providing novel insights into the politics of non-coordination. Throughout this introductory chapter, we highlight the subsequent chapters' contributions to an improved theoretical and empirical understanding of coordination and decision-making in the public sector.

Theoretical Foundations: Bounded Rationality and Institutionalized Organizations

In this chapter, we follow a tradition in public administration, public policy, and organization research that rests on a theoretical foundation of *bounded rationality* and is interested in organizational, and governmental, decision-making (Egeberg, 2012; Jones, 2017; Simon, 1947). Bounded rationality is often discussed as a corrective concept to the assumptions of classic rational choice theory and is invariably connected to the work of Herbert Simon, who assumed that while decision makers are intentionally rational and thus set clear objectives, they have limited information-processing capacity. Hence, decision makers do not maximize their preferences but reduce their ambition and 'satisfice'; that is, they stop searching for an optimal solution when an acceptable one presents itself (see Jones, 2017, for a succinct summary).

While attention and cognitive biases are certainly relevant for understanding decision-making at the individual level, we are interested neither in individual bureaucrats' decisions nor in deviations from an objectively rational form of decision-making. Simon (1947) developed the concept of bounded rationality from the limited capacities of individuals to process information, yet he applies the concept to *organizational decision-making* ('administrative behaviour'). The main interest of the earlier debate on bounded rationality was in the ways that organizational context shapes decision-making. Simon considers formal organizations to be rationality enhancing devices, since they allow the parallel processing of issues and problems through division of labour and specialization, and their organizational integration through procedures and hierarchy. The key lesson from behavioural organization theory is that recurrent features of organizations have to be understood in connection to humans' limited attention capacities (Jones, 2017). Therefore, understanding organizational behaviour means understanding how organizations process information and what limitations they face in doing so.

For many scholars, *formal organizational structure* such as horizontal and vertical specialization is key to understanding those processes and limitations (Egeberg, 2012; Wilensky, 1967). According to this literature, formal structure channels the attention of decision makers in organizations (thereby directing attention away from other facets of a given problem or policy). A key foundational contribution to this literature is Luther Gulick's (1937) work on administrative organization, which argues that each fundamental method of departmentalization (purpose, process, location, clientele) will involve unavoidable trade-offs, especially if only one principle prevails (Hammond, 2007). Although Gulick's (1937) ideas were largely discredited after Simon's (1947) devastating critique of what he famously called 'proverbs of administration' that allegedly lacked empirical substance, recent scholarship provides a more optimistic view of Gulick's writings (Hammond, 1990; Meier, 2010). The bottom line of this literature is that organizational attention is a function of formal organizational structure, with different structures eliciting distinct behavioural effects.

However, as anyone who has ever been part of a formal organization knows, formal structures are only one aspect of organizational life, which is driven at least as much by informal values and norms. According to another intellectual tradition, *informal values and norms* are important drivers of organizational behaviour, and formal organizations gradually turn into institutions with distinct identities recognized by employees and stakeholders alike (see also Christensen, this volume). This tradition explicitly questions the importance of formal organizational structure for decision-making. In his seminal work on administrative leadership,

Selznick (1957) famously argues that organizations develop into institutions by acquiring a distinct identity or a 'distinctive competence'.

That said, an institutional perspective on (public) organizations also emphasizes that a unique identity goes hand-in-hand with a 'distinctive inadequacy': the same organization cannot be equally good at everything (Selznick, 1957). An example used by Selznick is the NAACP (National Association for the Advancement of Colored People), which had a distinct competence as a political organization able to lobby for its cause but also a distinctive inadequacy in mobilizing large numbers of street-level protesters. Likewise, in his well-known analysis of bureaucratic dysfunctions, Merton (1940) shows that goal displacement and bureaucrats' identification with impersonal rules are virtually inevitable consequences of bureaucratic organizations. The flip side of bureaucratic virtues such as precision and effectiveness is the inflexibility of bureaucracies to adapt to complex and changing realities.

In general terms, Merton (1940) suggests that any action or decision 'can be considered in terms of what it attains or what it fails to attain' (p. 562). Thus, by focusing on one aspect of a given problem, other aspects of that problem as well as altogether other problems are neglected. This neglect may take the form of a simple administrative dilemma in which pursuing one objective negatively affects another (Hood, 1974). A typical dilemma is 'multi-organizational sub-optimization' (Hood, 1974, pp. 450–452), which includes both simple ignorance of what other organizations are doing and the pursuit of conflicting objectives by different public bodies. This may not be a bad thing as such; the representation of different legitimate interests in policymaking by ministerial departments is a case in point. At the same time, division of labour within the public sector may also lead to counter-productive developments such as 'switching yards' between national and local welfare systems (Lodge & Wegrich, 2014).

These instances of coordination challenges are obviously rooted in the intellectual tradition of Herbert Simon and Luther Gulick stressing how formal structure guides organizational attention. However, neglect or disinterest in specific aspects of the organizational environment may also take the form of a blind spot or 'not seeing the not seeing' (Lodge, this volume). Those blind spots are the result of the institutional nature of organizations entailing 'interpretative frames that individuals use to generate meaning' (Barnett & Finnemore, 1999, p. 719). It is precisely those interpretative frames that result in biased processing of information as a distinct weakness of institutionalized organizations. We now turn to a more exact definition of blind spots and other biases in organizational attention in public bureaucracies.

FOUR BIASES IN ORGANIZATIONAL ATTENTION

Following from the above discussion, we focus on two distinct ways of understanding organizational behaviour. A structural perspective following the tradition of bounded rationality emphasizes how organizational design predictably channels decision-making behaviour. In contrast, an institutional perspective focuses on the gradual process of organizational 'emancipation' from the original intentions of institutional design, which results in unique norms and values that guide decision-making behaviour. These approaches use distinct analytical perspectives on organizations, emphasizing formal structure and goals ('instrument'), on the one hand, and institutional identity and uniqueness ('institution'), on the other. The purpose of this distinction is certainly not to provide an exhaustive analytical toolbox (for a more comprehensive perspective, see Christensen, this volume). For instance, alternative perspectives could address how the dynamics of decision-making in small (leadership) groups affect organizational attention (Janis, 1989) or might consider multiple explanations beyond organizational factors in the study of attention biases (Parker & Stern, 2002). That said, we believe that both formal structures and informal norms and values are essential elements of any analytical framework for understanding attention biases in organizational life.

Moreover, one can distinguish between intended and unintended aspects of organizational behaviour. This requires further elaboration, as different analytical perspectives come with different notions of (un)intentional behaviour. As mentioned above, our understanding of attention biases or blind spots in a broad, metaphorical sense is based on the assumption of intentionally rational behaviour. That said, any kind of intentional behaviour may also have unintended consequences (Lodge, this volume). A structural perspective on organizations emphasizes the intentions of those in charge of designing formal structures. For public organizations, this will usually be elected politicians using institutional design as a means to achieve policy objectives.

In contrast, an institutional perspective almost by definition assumes that the process of institutionalization has a distinct flavour of 'agency drift' away from the intentions of those initially designing an organization

Table 1.1   Four biases in organizational attention

Organizational behaviour	Analytical perspective on organization	
	Instrument, focus on structure	Institution, focus on identity
Intended	Selective perception	Bureaucratic politics
Unintended	Achilles' heels	Blind spots

(i.e. the intentions of legislatures or governments). This is, however, not the kind of unintentional behaviour we have in mind. We simply acknowledge that decision-making in institutionalized organizations may also have instrumental features, which involve the deliberate protection of organizational identity through 'administrative leadership' (Boin & Christensen, 2008; Selznick, 1957). Table 1.1 combines these two analytical dimensions into a simple matrix containing four distinct biases in organizational attention. Those biases may lead to problematic outcomes in terms of coordination and problem-solving, yet they are not organizational pathologies or policy failures per se. As the next section shows, establishing an objective standard for what constitutes a failure is inherently difficult (Bovens & 't Hart, 2016; Lodge, this volume).

Selective Perception

The notion of selective perception refers to the channelling of attention as a function of the division of labour within and between organizations (Dearborn & Simon, 1958). As Simon (1964) argued in his discussion on the concept of organizational goals, individuals in organizations are constrained by the demands and expectations associated with their role in the organization. Importantly, except for those at the highest level, organizational roles are defined by attention to subsets of the proclaimed 'official' organizational goal (such as improving transport infrastructure or public health). Any organizational subunit will be in charge of a specific aspect of the organization's overall goals, yet this does not necessarily ensure goal achievement (Cyert & March, 1963). In many ways, this is perhaps the archetypal form of organizational attention bias. Public bureaucracies usually have a clearly defined sphere of authority that guides their attention and priority setting. This is not problematic as such but is in fact necessary to ensure sufficient levels of expertise.

However, as outlined above, organizational specialization and selective perception have important implications for intra- and inter-organizational coordination (Cyert & March, 1963). In the context of public organizations (and beyond), specialization leads to pervasive coordination problems (Wilensky, 1967, pp. 48–57). For instance, different units in ministerial departments will approach the same issue from different (and similarly selective) perspectives (Scharpf, 1994). The standard research perspective related to coordination deals with deliberate attempts to achieve some level of coordination, that is, alignment and integration, between different interdependent organizational units (Metcalfe, 1994). In analytical terms, the question is whether the solutions produced by subunits within organizations or by different organizations will contribute to solving overarching problems (Cyert & March, 1963). While the literature on coordination has been continuously interested in the *difficulties* of achieving (effective) coordination, the often implicit starting point is the existence of some degree of motivation to achieve more than just independent decision-making by interdependent organizations or organizational units. The key problem around which a rich body of scholarship has developed is the problem of finding agreement in a context where coordination can only be achieved by some level of voluntary engagement of (more or less) autonomous actors (Scharpf, 1994).

In contrast, little attention has been paid to the other side of coordination, namely the issues and topics that are not even put on the agenda in inter-organizational arenas, that fall between the cracks of organizational attention, or that are even deliberately avoided or shifted around between organizations because they are associated with little credit and much (potential) blame or high costs (see the section on 'bureaucratic politics' later in the chapter). Those coordination problems may lead to issues of coordination 'underlap', as opposed to 'overlap', between different units' spheres of responsibility. While the latter is characterized by the desire of various parties to be involved in an issue when it falls within their organization's competence, the former is defined as the absence of responsibility by any one organization for the issue in question (Koop & Lodge, 2014). In policy implementation, a typical underlap problem would be a single case that does not fit into any specific category leading public authorities to take action, such as offenders that are under the age of criminal liability. In policy formulation, cross-cutting policies such as demographic change or de-bureaucratization represent issues that all departments are supposed to consider but that in fact fall between the cracks of departmental boundaries (Wegrich & Štimac, 2014).

Most current research implicitly assumes, rather than empirically tests, the effects of selective perception on organizational behaviour and coordination within and between organizations. In many ways, the other attention biases discussed below build upon the notion of selective perception. That said, recent studies on the European Commission's administration highlight how selective perception drives decision-making behaviour in the policymaking process by narrowing down different units' attention to specific aspects of policy problems and solutions (Hartlapp, Metz, & Rauh, 2013; Vestlund, 2015).[1] At the national level, in a meticulous analysis of a series of killings of mostly immigrant shop owners in Germany, Seibel (2014; this volume) shows how selective perception resulted in a protracted lack of coordination between police authorities investigating murders that had been committed in different states but with the same gun. The contribution by Fink and Ruffing (this volume) illustrates how selective perception drives the processing of information received though public consultation by a regulatory agency on the location of large energy grids. Their analysis shows that while the feedback from citizens and organizations touched upon multiple implications of a given alternative, the regulator disregarded all consultation statements while privileging an expert report on technical aspects in its assessment of various alternatives. This kind of selective attention to information can plausibly be related to the regulator's formal jurisdiction of considering technical aspects of grid planning.

Achilles' Heels

The second type of bias in organizational attention encompasses unintended effects of formal organizational structure. We define these as inherent and potentially known weaknesses, or Achilles' heels, of different ways of organizing (see also Lodge, this volume). The basic idea is very simple: any organizational form comes with particular strengths and weaknesses.[2] Hood (1998) draws on cultural theory as a way to classify organizational styles—hierarchical, egalitarian, individualist, and fatalist—and discusses how each organizational style comes with particular types of organizational failure and breakdown. Also, each style comes with its own particular logics of responding to blunders and failures, namely aiming at 'purification' of organizational styles (i.e. failure in implementing rules will call for more and more detailed rules and methods of control). The more any of the four distinct models of organization is used, the more pronounced these inherent weaknesses will become. Hood (1998, p. 18) argues that the characteristic problems linked to purification of any one model of organizing will also be more pronounced because of resistance from critics espousing other cultural worldviews.

But thinking in public administration about trade-offs and inherent weaknesses of particular organizational forms has a longer tradition and goes back at least to Luther Gulick's (1937) classification of principles of organization (by purpose, process, location, clientele) (see also Christensen, this volume). Again, the argument is that each type of specialization comes with inherent strengths and weaknesses (Hammond, 1990). This is not only true for different types of organizational specialization but also for typical institutional configurations linked to the regulatory regime of entire sectors, such as the positive state (with its tight organizational integration of different roles such as owner, regulator, and service provider) and the regulatory state, in which those roles are separated (Bach & Wegrich, 2016). Whereas the former model lacks incentives for efficient policy choices, the latter model is haunted by the spectre of regulatory capture by powerful regulatees.

As illustrated by Hammond (2007), complex policy areas usually require the application of multiple principles of organizational design within the same or across multiple organizations. This may indeed help reduce the inherent weaknesses of any form of specialization by creating a redundancy mechanism. At the same time, complex models of organization based on multiple principles will require what Hammond (2007) calls 'interagency committees', that is, horizontal, non-hierarchical structures of coordination. Any attempt to centralize decision-making in such complex systems will inevitably lead to well-known bottleneck problems of overload in terms of information processing and conflict resolution at the top of the hierarchy (Scharpf, 1994).

The contribution by Jordana and Rosas (this volume) addresses trade-offs between different organizational models of financial regulation. They observe substantial divergence with regard to the concentration of financial regulation responsibilities in central banks as opposed to the existence of separate regulators or hybrid solutions. Most importantly, they discuss the policy implications of different institutional models, such as in terms of potential trade-offs between the conflicting goals of financial stability and inflation control in central banks with regulatory powers. An important lesson is that studying the effects and trade-offs of complex institutional configurations is far from a trivial matter, and Jordana and Rosas provide important insights into potential avenues for further research.

Bureaucratic Politics

The third type of bias refers to deliberate forms of selective attention with the purpose of nurturing and protecting organizational identity. This includes organizational behaviour driven by considerations of turf protection and reputation-seeking. We use the umbrella term 'bureaucratic politics' to underline that the different approaches subsumed under this perspective consider public organizations to be political actors in their own right rather than cogs in well-oiled governmental machines steered by those at the top (Allison & Halperin, 1972). The bureaucratic politics perspective considers organizational behaviour to be driven by the desire to defend organizational interests and to endorse distinct policy perspectives (see 't Hart & Wille, 2012, for an overview and critical discussion of different streams within this literature). For instance, the 'bureau-shaping' approach understands organizational behaviour as driven by bureaucrats' motivations of increasing interesting policy work at the expense of cumbersome administrative tasks (Dunleavy, 1991). In contrast to this approach, which is in the tradition of approaches focusing on utility-maximizing bureaucrats (Downs, Niskanen), an institutional perspective on organizational behaviour emphasizes the pivotal importance of maintaining (and defending) institutional identity or distinct competences. In particular, this includes opposition against policy proposals or administrative reforms that may undermine an organization's institutional identity (Selznick, 1957; Wilson, 1989).

This kind of bureaucratic politics includes organizational behaviour driven by considerations of turf protection (Wilson, 1989), responses to reputational threats (Carpenter & Krause, 2012), and blame avoidance (Hood, 2011). When a bureaucracy's jurisdictional autonomy is at stake, when its unique competence is questioned, or when it potentially faces public blame, organizational behaviour will be driven by concerns about organizational maintenance (Bach, De Francesco, Maggetti, & Ruffing, 2016; Busuioc, 2016; Heims, 2017). In particular, concerns about institutional identity and reputation amongst key stakeholders will guide bureaucracies' decisions about engaging in particular tasks, including cooperation with other public bureaucracies. Such organizational politics of non-coordination have been one of the key insights from public administration research over the last one or two decades, although parts of the theoretical foundations (turf protection, blame avoidance) go back to the 1980s at least (Weaver, 1986; Wilson, 1989).

The perhaps most obvious manifestation of how organizations create, maintain, and defend their institutional identity is linked to the concept of organizational turf. Following Wilson (1989), turf is understood as an organization's formal jurisdiction and its internal mission or identity. To secure support for the organization both from outside (politicians, stakeholders) and inside (employees), the organization's leadership will strive for a close match between jurisdiction and mission by means of bureaucratic politics (Bach et al., 2016). An organization with many potential rivals has to constantly fight for scarce budgetary sources and qualified personnel, whereas an organization with a unique task is in a much safer haven as long as it circumvents failures and builds up a favourable reputation amongt relevant stakeholders (Carpenter, 2010; see also Christensen, this volume). To maintain support, organizations engage in turf-protecting strategies, such as fighting other organizations that seek to perform one's own tasks and avoiding cooperation with other organizations due to the potentially deleterious implications for an organization's identity and mission (Busuioc, 2016; Heims, 2017; Wilson, 1989).

The contribution by Heims (this volume) addresses the politics of non-coordination head-on. It provides a novel perspective on turf-based accounts of bureaucratic behaviour. The chapter's main argument is that the mission orientation of public organizations does not invariably lead to fervent turf protection and coordination problems across organizational boundaries. Instead, by combining the analytical dimensions of mission overlap and resource complementarity, Heims shows that the prototypical 'destructive turf protection' epitomized by Wilson's (1989) analysis of turf-related behaviour only constitutes one possible outcome of inter-organizational coordination. In other words, bureaucratic politics can take different shapes and degrees of intensity ('t Hart & Wille, 2012). Drawing on empirical examples from coordination between national and European Union (EU) authorities, Heims (this volume) illustrates an alternative outcome of 'productive turf protection' in which cooperation is beneficial for the involved organizations despite overlapping missions (see also Heims, 2017). In a related study, Busuioc (2016) convincingly shows that national authorities display very limited interest in sharing information and cooperating with their EU-level counterparts if that cooperation threatens their reputations at the national level, which is crucial for maintaining support (financial or otherwise) and motivating staff (see Parker & Stern, 2002, for an account of reluctant information sharing among police and intelligence agencies).

The chapter by Timeus (this volume) illustrates another facet of non-coordination, namely between public organizations and various actors outside the public sector. In her study of 'collaborative innovation' practices in Barcelona, she highlights the compound effects of innovation and collaboration as risk-prone activities. Her main finding is that bureaucrats' risk perceptions discourage practices of collaborative innovation unless there is an obvious and manageable benefit of collaboration, such as the sharing of financial risks. Thus, while collaboration is considered an important instrument for finding new ways of tackling policy problems and overcoming bureaucracies' blind spots (understood metaphorically as attention bias; see below for an analytical definition), Timeus's analysis suggests that a realistic account of collaborative innovation needs to consider organizational interests.

These studies provide novel and important insights into the drivers of (non-)coordination between public organizations. A related strand of scholarship highlights reputation-seeking behaviour as a deliberate form of decision-making and task prioritization (Carpenter & Krause, 2012). The reputation approach theorizes about how public organizations cultivate distinct reputations as well as how they respond to perceived threats to agency reputation (Maor, 2015). In this literature, organizational reputation is understood as a set of symbolic beliefs about the unique capabilities, obligations, and mission of an organization amongt multiple audiences (Carpenter, 2010). A reputation-centred view suggests that reputation-sensitive organizations will react differently to external signals, depending on whether those signals are compatible with their unique identities (Gilad, 2012). For instance, Maor, Gilad, and Ben-Nun Bloom (2013) find that the Israeli banking regulator reacts reluctantly if faced with allegations in areas in which it has either a strong reputation or no formal competences, whereas it reacts publicly if those allegations address areas in which the regulator has a weak reputation. The bottom line of a reputational approach is that organizational behaviour has to be understood in relation to relevant audiences.

The chapter by Hinterleitner and Sager (this volume) addresses the effects of political polarization on the allocation of attention by public organizations, combining insights from bureaucratic reputation and blame avoidance scholarship. Their chapter in particular stresses the political context of public organizations as a core explanation for potentially dysfunctional behaviour. They argue that polarization within the political realm induces preventive blame avoidance behaviour amongst public organizations. A political climate in which black-and-white solutions are predominant entails the attribution of blame for policy failures both to political opponents and to the government apparatus. As public organizations are reputation sensitive, they will use instruments of preventive blame engineering such as the redesign of policy measures (which may entail the deliberate neglect of using evidence-based policy measures) as well as limiting the type of available information on the organization's activities. Moreover, they specify important scoping conditions for such behaviours, including an organization's resource endowment and discretionary authority to alter policy implementation.

In their contribution, Boon, Salomonsen, Verhoest, and Pedersen (this volume) discuss how the media salience of public criticism, rather than the actual substance of such criticism, affects public organizations' responses to such criticisms. They argue that bureaucratic reputation theory has paid little attention to the distinct logic of journalism, for instance regarding what issues are considered newsworthy. Moreover, they theorize about media-specific drivers (as opposed to substance-related drivers) of agency responses to allegations in the news media. This contribution shows how media attention—as part of the political context of public organizations—shapes bureaucratic priority setting.

Blind Spots

The notion of blind spots is usually used to point at some problem or issue that has failed to capture the attention of governing institutions (Gieve & Provost, 2012). Thus, in a general sense, an organizational blind spot can be understood as some kind of bias in organizational attention (see Christensen, this volume). At the same time, considering its original, medical meaning as an area of the retina that is insensitive to light, a blind spot can be considered a distinct type of biased attention that is analytically different from other attention biases (see Lodge, this volume). In analytical terms, we define blind spots as limitations or gaps in attention that result from the risk perceptions and frames embedded in an organization through institutionalization processes. In contrast to deliberate efforts to establish and maintain a distinct institutional identity, we consider blind spots to be unintended consequences of public organizations' institutional features. This view of blind spots resonates with Selznick's (1957) argument about institutionalized organizations' distinctive inadequacies as the downside of their distinctive or unique competences (see also Pidgeon &

O'Leary, 2000). In addition, we include institutionalized organizations' unawareness of those distinctive inadequacies as a key element of organizational blind spots.

Blind spots are characterized by an organization's unawareness of its incomplete information processing, or 'not seeing that one is not seeing' (Lodge, this volume). Accordingly, the distinct nature of a blind spot entails an organization's inability to detect and categorize (potentially important) information, without being aware of this inability. This makes blind spots different from selective perceptions resulting from specialization, in which the selective processing of information is deliberate and guided by formal task assignments (Fink and Ruffing, this volume). The unconscious nature of blind spots also makes them different from known weaknesses of particular organizational structures, although we concede that decision makers are likely to discount those weaknesses in organizational design processes and emphasize rather the benefits of alternative organizational forms (Brunsson & Olsen, 1993). The key difference, though, is that blind spots are rooted in the institutional nature rather than formal structure of organizations. This view of blind spots resonates with the 'man-made disasters' model of technological disasters, originally proposed by Barry Turner (see Pidgeon & O'Leary, 2000, for a summary). While also considering structural conditions, this model emphasizes how normal processes of organizational life entail flawed processing of information under conditions of complex and changing environments involving multiple organizations. In order to avoid such blind spots, this approach advocates paying attention to well-known risks, and 'simultaneously stepping outside those frames' (Pidgeon & O'Leary, 2000, p. 22).

The importance of frames for the processing of information is at the core of Fligstein, Brundage, and Schultz's (2017) analysis of the US Federal Reserve System's failure to anticipate the financial crisis of 2008. The authors show how distinct professional backgrounds bias information processing and decision-making (see also Adolph, 2013). With explicit reference to the notion of blind spots, the authors argue that biased information processing in one of the Federal Reserve's key decision-making bodies resulted from dominant cognitive frames amongt central bankers.[3] Those frames systematically favoured a macroeconomic perspective on the state of the economy based on a limited number of economic indicators to the detriment of perspective, putting worrying developments within the banking and finance industry at centre stage (Fligstein et al., 2017). The professional background of the majority of the decision makers—macroeconomics—provided a distinct frame for interpreting economic development, which involved biased processing of information about the state of the economy. This type of consensus makes it hard for dissenting voices to be raised, such as those warning of potential bubbles in the housing market, without taking the risk of being shunned by the community (Janis, 1989; Roberts, 2010). Likewise, the notion of blind spots has been used to describe how a widely shared consensus about the respective functions of banking regulators (protecting consumers) and central banks (controlling inflation) resulted in a lack of coordination in addressing problems of the subprime mortgage market (Gieve & Provost, 2012). Those insights resonate with earlier scholarship on pathologies of information processing in organizations, emphasizing how stereotypes about an organization's environment 'can for years remain impervious to evidence' (Wilensky, 1967, p. 40). Likewise, accounts of disasters such as the 9/11 terror attacks identify both psychological foundations (such as overvaluation of past successes and wishful thinking) as well as political context features (such as dominant frames and overcrowded policy agendas) as explanatory factors for why decision makers failed to anticipate the possibility of a major terror attack in the US, as they were stuck in a distinct view of terrorism-related risks (Parker & Stern, 2002). The combination of different theoretical perspectives brought to bear on the same case provides rich insights, and while this chapter emphasizes structural and institutional explanations, several contributions to this volume also use a multi-pronged approach.

Seibel's contribution (this volume) is an astute account of how a certain framing of information within organizations misguided the attention of police authorities over several years (see also Seibel, 2014). He shows how police authorities in Germany simply did not consider right-wing terrorism when investigating a series of killings of small shop owners with immigrant backgrounds and instead interpreted the killings as linked to organized crime. Police authorities adopted the framing of organized crime at an early stage and selected and evaluated new information through the organized crime lens rather than reconsidering this frame. As a result, the police treated victims' families as potential offenders, and more killings could have probably been prevented. Moreover, Seibel's analysis highlights a potential trade-off between maintaining professional integrity within one's own organization and ensuring long-term institutional survival. Hence the chapter highlights an important normative aspect, namely that turf protection may eventually undermine the task accomplishment of the organization ('the limits of pragmatism'). Also, Seibel's analysis of a distinct episode highlights the importance of political context for understanding blind spots: the professionally appropriate decision to delegate the case upwards from the state to the federal level was allegedly not taken because of considerations of not spending time and energy on the issue, which boiled down to considerations of the political opportunity costs of spending 'political capital' on solving the case.

In a similar vein, scholars studying international organizations through a public administration lens have revived Merton's (1940) argument that the virtues and power of bureaucratic organizations may also turn into problems and pathological behaviours. In particular, they emphasize that relying on a particular type of expertise within an organization will 'limit bureaucrats' field of vision and create subcultures within bureaucracy' (Barnett & Finnemore, 1999, p. 719). They argue that under conditions of insulation from feedback from the wider environment, organizations will cultivate distinct internal cultures and worldviews that imply idiosyncratic ways of processing information:

> These distinctive worldviews can create the conditions for pathological behavior when parochial classification and categorization schemes come to define reality—how bureaucrats understand the world—such that they routinely ignore information that is essential to the accomplishment of their goals. (Barnett & Finnemore, 1999, p. 722)

Barnett and Finnemore (1999) identify two causes of insulation. First, if organizations are characterized by a concentration of professionals, those professionals' backgrounds can shape organizations' worldviews (see the above discussion of pre-crisis financial regulation). Second, if organizations lack effective feedback loops about organizational performance, a typical feature of public organizations, they have limited incentives to process information that questions established ways of doing things.

The case of crisis communication amongt police forces in Norway nicely illustrates this point (Renå, this volume). Renå shows, inter alia, that the decentralized nature of the police organization and the lack of external shock situations (and subsequent low status of crisis management within the police), as well as ambiguities concerning the main police organization's function in the wake of a major structural reform, explain the malfunctioning of the national alarm system within the police. What is more, a combination of the police's distinct identity as a civilian organization, its decentralized structure, and the low level of priority attached to the emergency communication system by the political and administrative leadership resulted in low levels of awareness about the national alarm system amongst local police units and officers. In terms of preparedness for major crises, the police fall squarely into Wilson's (1989) well-known category of procedural organizations that produce visible outputs but largely invisible outcomes. This leaves them short of any measure of performance except for following standard operating procedures; yet if those procedures are systematically ignored, there is not even a proxy measure for performance under 'real' conditions.

Importantly, the case illustrates that blind spots are not merely the product of professional consensus within or across organizations, but that they also result from worldviews that are cultivated as part of organizational identity. The distinct contribution of Renå's chapter is to use an organizational explanation of the lack of attention towards crisis preparedness and, more specifically, the national alarm system. The problem identified was not that the police were not working on putting such a system in place but that there was systematic 'non-attention' to this kind of exercise. To be sure, information technology experts within the police had identified and pinpointed weaknesses in the national alarm system, yet those warnings were ignored in other parts of the organization.

The close relationship between the institutionalized nature of organizations and blind spots in organizational attention is highlighted in Sharon Gilad's (2012, 2015) work on financial regulators' prioritization of tasks. Gilad suggests that public organizations with multiple tasks are vulnerable to pressure from their environments to focus on some tasks rather than others. This in itself does not constitute a blind spot, though. She further suggests that a distinct institutional identity—in her case, the British financial regulator's self-image of being a world-leading organization—may result in resource-intensive and enduring efforts (such as producing detailed guidelines) to respond to those external pressures. Gilad (2012, 2015) argues that the British regulator's emphasis on being a front runner in developing a new approach for conduct-of-business regulation spilled over to the organization's operational level, leading to an almost complete neglect of prudential regulation (overseeing firms' capitalization and liquidity). This focus was initially prompted by media reports about the mis-selling of financial products and subsequent political pressure to address this issue, yet due to the regulator's comprehensive rolling out of a customer-oriented approach to financial regulation, its efforts in scrutinizing banks for their fair treatment of customers continued well into the financial crisis.

In addition to highlighting the distinct nature of blind spots as opposed to other types of biased attention, Lodge's contribution (this volume) provides novel insights by analysing blind spots through the lens of grid–group cultural theory, which illustrates the difference between behavioural consequences of distinct ways of organizing, on the one hand, and information processing consequences, on the other. In particular, he shows how a blind spot perspective provides additional insights by contrasting them with known weaknesses of different forms of organizing linked to the four worldviews of grid–group cultural theory (hierarchical, egalitarian, individualist, and fatalist). The key difference is that the distinct blind spots of different worldviews are related to the processing of information and involve specific ways of seeing the world, as opposed to Achilles' heels that encompass inevitable performance effects of distinct ways of organizing.

Finally, Lodge discusses possible strategies for avoiding blind spots yet concludes that blind spots are an inevitable phenomenon in organizational life. This conclusion is obviously consistent with the key tenet of cultural theory (and many other analyses of institutional design): that any way of organizing has distinct weaknesses. The particular challenge of blind spots, according to Lodge, is that those weaknesses are unknown within the organization at a given point in time. The discovery of a blind spot, then, is unlikely to happen from within the organization itself. This book's final chapter will discuss potential ways to deal with blind spots and other biases in organizational attention.

CONCLUSION

These variations of biases in organizational attention or blind spots in a broad, metaphorical sense are not mutually exclusive or jointly exhaustive, but they provide a starting point for empirically exploring a particular subset of organizational failure that can be accounted for neither by classic theories of bureaucratic failure (alone) nor by approaches of policy or regulatory failure (such as regulatory capture). For example, the failure of US security agencies to detect the plot leading to the 9/11 terror attacks has been analysed, by the US Congress's National Commission, as a result of the lack of coordination between the many agencies involved (National Commission on Terrorist Attacks upon the United States, 2004). The underlying problem was that the different agencies' organizational attention was partial, and a structure integrating those partial views was lacking (see also Parker & Stern, 2002). Moreover, the focus of attention was on other countries rather than emerging non-state terror groups, a legacy of the Cold War. In this case, different types of attention biases had contributed to failure: the structurally induced weakness and the obstruction-of-vision type of blind spot, but also considerations of organizational maintenance, turf protection, and blame.

The contributions in this volume focus on attention biases and non-coordination related to public organizations at different levels of government. This focus on 'government' may seem outdated to observers embracing a broader conception of 'governance', which stresses the importance of non-hierarchical modes of policymaking such as networks and collaboration (Mayntz, 2003). However, far from disappearing, public organizations have remained key actors in the delivery of public services as well as in economic and social regulation. The four biases outlined in this chapter highlight that any attempt to understand dysfunctionalities and paradoxes in public administration requires a 'pluralist' approach that goes beyond the usual diagnoses of 'red tape and bribery' as these 'exclude some of the key processes by which projects administered by honest and intelligent officials can be self-defeating' (Hood, 1974, p. 452).

For most concepts in the social sciences, most researchers are hard-pressed to provide definitions with which everyone agrees. The same is true for blind spots. We started the process of editing this book by inviting scholars to a small workshop under the banner of blind spots. Since then, we have engaged in an intellectual journey that has brought the distinctiveness of blind spots in comparison to other explanations of 'irrational' or 'unexplainable' bureaucratic behaviour to the forefront. As the adept reader will recognize, we did not impose any strict definitions on the authors and accept some degree of conceptual pluralism. This is not the least important because, as for instance becomes clear in Seibel's contribution, much can be gained from multiple theoretical perspectives on organizational life. We see the analytical framework put forward in this introductory chapter as a means of highlighting distinct explanations of how and why organizations do (not) act upon certain kind of information or chose (not) to cooperate with others. Those explanations have their roots in established theorizing but also in more recent efforts at understanding in particular regulatory authorities, central banks, and EU-level agencies as a kind of 'new kids on the block', as well as long-established bureaucracies like police authorities or local governments engaging in collaborative efforts or trying to deal with external pressures in terms of populism and media frenzies. In the last chapter of this volume, we discuss how our analytical framework can generate novel insights into administrative reforms and their limitations, and we sketch directions for further research.

NOTES

1. The study by Hartlapp et al. (2013) uses the theoretical language of 'bureaucratic politics' yet in essence tells a story of selective perception that is biased towards the problem views and solutions of the unit in charge and patterns of negative coordination as elaborated by Scharpf (1994).
2. Hood (1998) uses both 'blind spots' (p. 18) and 'Achilles' Heel or characteristic path of collapse' (p. 27) when referring to those inherent weaknesses of different models of organization in public management.
3. Another mechanism discussed by Fligstein et al. (2017) is organizational conditions that promote 'positive asymmetries', or the idea that actors in specific social settings bias information towards best-case scenarios.

REFERENCES

Adolph, C. (2013). *Bankers, bureaucrats, and central bank politics: The myth of neutrality*. Cambridge, UK: Cambridge University Press.

Allison, G. T. (1997). Public and private management: Are they fundamentally alike in all unimportant respects? (1980). In J. M. Shafritz & A. C. Hyde (Eds.), *Classics of public administration* (4th ed., pp. 383–400). Fort Worth: Harcourt Brace College Publishers.

Allison, G. T., & Halperin, M. H. (1972). Bureaucratic politics: A paradigm and some policy implications. *World Politics, 24,* 40–79.

Bach, T., De Francesco, F., Maggetti, M., & Ruffing, E. (2016). Transnational bureaucratic politics: An institutional rivalry perspective on EU network governance. *Public Administration, 94*(1), 9–24.

Bach, T., & Wegrich, K. (2016). Regulatory reform, accountability and blame in public service delivery: The public transport crisis in Berlin. In T. Christensen & P. Lægreid (Eds.), *The Routledge handbook to accountability and welfare state reforms in Europe* (pp. 223–235). London: Routledge.

Barnett, M. N., & Finnemore, M. (1999). The politics, power, and pathologies of international organizations. *International Organization, 53*(4), 699–732.

Boin, A., & Christensen, T. (2008). The development of public institutions: Reconsidering the role of leadership. *Administration & Society, 40*(3), 271–297.

Bouckaert, G., Peters, B. G., & Verhoest, K. (2010). *The coordination of public sector organizations: Shifting patterns of public management*. Basingstoke and New York: Palgrave Macmillan.

Bovens, M., & 't Hart, P. (2016). Revisiting the study of policy failures. *Journal of European Public Policy, 23*(5), 653–666.

Brunsson, N., & Olsen, J. P. (1993). *The reforming organization*. London: Routledge.

Busuioc, E. M. (2016). Friend or fore? Inter-agency cooperation, organizational reputation, and turf. *Public Administration, 94*(1), 40–56.

Carpenter, D. P. (2010). *Reputation and power: Organizational image and pharmaceutical regulation at the FDA*. Princeton: Princeton University Press.

Carpenter, D. P., & Krause, G. A. (2012). Reputation and public administration. *Public Administration Review, 72*(1), 26–32.

Cyert, R. M., & March, J. G. (1963). *A behavioral theory of the firm*. Englewood Cliffs: Prentice-Hall.

Dearborn, D. C., & Simon, H. A. (1958). Selective perception: A note on the departmental identifications of executives. *Sociometry, 21*(2), 140–144.

Dunleavy, P. (1991). *Democracy, bureaucracy and public choice: Economic explanations in political science*. New York: Harvester Wheatsheaf.

Egeberg, M. (2012). How bureaucratic structure matters: An organizational perspective. In J. Pierre & B. G. Peters (Eds.), *The Sage handbook of public administration* (2nd ed., pp. 157–167). Los Angeles: Sage.

Fligstein, N., Stuart Brundage, J., & Schultz, M. (2017). Seeing like the Fed: Culture, cognition, and framing in the failure to anticipate the financial crisis of 2008. *American Sociological Review, 82*(5), 879–909.

Gieve, J., & Provost, C. (2012). Ideas and coordination in policymaking: The financial crisis of 2007–2009. *Governance, 25*(1), 61–77.

Gilad, S. (2012). Attention and reputation: Linking regulators' internal and external worlds. In M. Lodge & K. Wegrich (Eds.), *Executive politics in times of crisis* (pp. 157–175). Basingstoke: Palgrave Macmillan.

Gilad, S. (2015). Political pressures, organizational identity, and attention to tasks: Illustrations from pre-crisis financial regulation. *Public Administration, 93*(3), 593–608.

Goodsell, C. T. (1985). *The case for bureaucracy: A public administration polemic* (2nd ed.). Chatham, NJ: Chatham House.

Gulick, L. (1937). Notes on the theory of organization. In L. Gulick & L. Urwick (Eds.), *Papers on the science of administration* (pp. 2–45). New York: Institute of Public Administration.

Hammond, T. H. (1990). In defence of Luther Gulick's notes on the theory of organization. *Public Administration, 68*(2), 143–173.

Hammond, T. H. (2007). Why is the intelligence community so difficult to redesign? Smart practices, conflicting goals, and the creation of purpose-based organizations. *Governance, 20*(3), 401–422.

't Hart, P., & Wille, A. (2012). Bureaucratic politics: Opening the black box of executive government. In B. G. Peters & J. Pierre (Eds.), *The Sage handbook of public administration* (pp. 369–378). Los Angeles: Sage.

Hartlapp, M., Metz, J., & Rauh, C. (2013). Linking agenda setting to coordination structures: Bureaucratic politics inside the European Commission. *Journal of European Integration, 35*(4), 425–441.

Heims, E. M. (2017). Regulatory co-ordination in the EU: A cross-sector comparison. *Journal of European Public Policy, 24*(8), 1116–1134.

Hinterleitner, M., & Sager, F. (2016). Anticipatory and reactive forms of blame avoidance: Of foxes and lions. *European Political Science Review, 9*, 1–20.

Hood, C. (1974). Administrative diseases: Some types of dysfunctionality in administration. *Public Administration, 52*(4), 439–454.

Hood, C. (1998). *The art of the state: Culture, rhetoric, and public management.* Oxford: Oxford University Press.

Hood, C. (2011). *The blame game: Spin, bureaucracy, and self-preservation in government.* Princeton: Princeton University Press.

Janis, I. L. (1989). *Crucial decisions: Leadership in policymaking and crisis management.* New York: Free Press.

Jones, B. D. (2017). Behavioral rationality as a foundation for public policy studies. *Cognitive Systems Research, 43*, 63–75.

Koop, C., & Lodge, M. (2014). Exploring the co-ordination of economic regulation. *Journal of European Public Policy, 21*(9), 1311–1329.

Lodge, M., & Wegrich, K. (2014). Fiscal consolidation in Germany: Drifting away from the politics of the switching yard? In C. Hood, D. Heald, & R. Himaz (Eds.), *When the party's over: The politics of fiscal squeeze in perspective* (pp. 161–183). Oxford: Oxford University Press.

Maor, M. (2015). Theorizing bureaucratic reputation. In A. Wæraas & M. Maor (Eds.), *Organizational reputation in the public sector* (pp. 17–36). New York: Routledge.

Maor, M., Gilad, S., & Ben-Nun Bloom, P. (2013). Organizational reputation, regulatory talk, and strategic silence. *Journal of Public Administration Research and Theory, 23*(3), 581–608.

Mayntz, R. (2003). New challenges to governance theory. In H. Bang (Ed.), *Governance as social and political communication* (pp. 27–40). Manchester: Manchester University Press.

Meier, K. J. (2010). Governance, structure, and democracy: Luther Gulick and the future of public administration. *Public Administration Review, 70*, S284–S291.

Merton, R. K. (1940). Bureaucratic structure and personality. *Social Forces, 18*(4), 560–568.

Metcalfe, L. (1994). International policy co-ordination and public management reform. *International Review of Administrative Sciences, 60*(2), 271–290.

National Commission on Terrorist Attacks upon the United States. (2004). *The 9/11 commission report: Final report.* New York: Norton.

Parker, C. F., & Stern, E. K. (2002). Blindsided? September 11 and the origins of strategic surprise. *Political Psychology, 23*(3), 601–630.

Pidgeon, N., & O'Leary, M. (2000). Man-made disasters: Why technology and organizations (sometimes) fail. *Safety Science, 34*(1), 15–30.

Roberts, A. (2010). *The logic of discipline: Global capitalism and the architecture of government.* Oxford: Oxford University Press.

Scharpf, F. W. (1994). Games real actors could play: Positive and negative coordination in embedded negotiations. *Journal of Theoretical Politics, 6*(1), 27–53.

Seibel, W. (2014). Kausale Mechanismen des Behördenversagens: Eine Prozessanalyse des Fahndungsfehlschlags bei der Aufklärung der NSU-Morde. *der moderne staat,* (2014/02), 375–413.

Selznick, P. (1957). *Leadership in administration: A sociological interpretation.* New York: Harper & Row.

Simon, H. A. (1947). *Administrative behavior: A study of decision-making processes in administrative organizations.* New York: Macmillan.

Simon, H. A. (1964). On the concept of organizational goal. *Administrative Science Quarterly, 9*(1), 1–22.

Vestlund, N. M. (2015). Changing policy focus through organizational reform? The case of the pharmaceutical unit in the European Commission. *Public Policy and Administration, 30*(1), 92–112.

Weaver, R. K. (1986). The politics of blame avoidance. *Journal of Public Policy, 6*(4), 371–398.

Wegrich, K., & Štimac, V. (2014). Coordination capacity. In M. Lodge & K. Wegrich (Eds.), *The problem-solving capacity of the modern state* (pp. 41–62). Oxford: Oxford University Press.

Wilensky, H. L. (1967). *Organizational intelligence: Knowledge and policy in government and industry.* New York: Basic Books.

Wilson, J. Q. (1989). *Bureaucracy: What government agencies do and why they do it.* New York: Basic Books.

CHAPTER 2

Accounting for Blind Spots

Martin Lodge

INTRODUCTION

Public (and private) organizations are regularly criticized for their flat-footed responses (Jennings, Lodge, & Ryan, 2018). One frequent example of apparent flat-footedness is that organizations have failed to detect or act upon available information. The 'didn't see this coming' excuse points to the ways in which organizations are rudely surprised. The blind spot phenomenon is however not only about not seeing something coming. It is, strictly defined, about *not seeing that one is not seeing*. Blind spots are about limits to vision: they relate to the kind of blinkers, frames, and biases that affect the handling of information flows, and they refer to defence mechanisms to normalize potentially threatening information. In other words, blind spots are not just a likely source of failure, but they are intrinsic to any form of organizing.

Without wishing to offer an exhaustive list of types, the three illustrations below highlight some of the key features of the blind spot phenomenon:

M. Lodge (✉)
Centre for Analysis of Risk and Regulation, London School of Economics and Political Science, London, UK
e-mail: m.lodge@lse.ac.uk

© The Author(s) 2019
T. Bach, K. Wegrich (eds.), *The Blind Spots of Public Bureaucracy and the Politics of Non-Coordination*, Executive Politics and Governance, https://doi.org/10.1007/978-3-319-76672-0_2

29

- *The lack of action despite available information.* Organizations involved have filtered out or failed to recognize information, or have viewed the transfer of information to another party as unimportant. As a result, no actions are taken. Such a phenomenon occurred in the case of the UK's Bristol Royal Infirmary hospital scandal in which widely available knowledge about heightened death rates among babies after cardiac surgery was not acted upon (despite doctors suggesting that going to that facility resembled sending patients to the 'killing fields' and the 'departure lounge'; BBC News, 1999). Other examples of failure to join the dots include the English Mid Staffordshire hospital in which between 400 and 1200 patients died due to poor care (and where available information was not regarded as significant by the relevant regulator; Campbell, 2013) and 9/11 (where intelligence services did not exchange relevant information due to procedural constraints and limited attention) (National Commission on Terrorist Attacks Upon the United States, 2004; also Parker & Stern, 2002).
- *The absence of information due to the lack of measuring tools to detect changes in the environment and inside organizations.* For example, in 2012, considerable concern emerged about the extent to which a particular type of (French) silicone breast implant was prone to rupturing. In the UK, the regulator, the Medicines and Healthcare products Regulatory Agency, was accused of being surprised as its data suggested that one per cent of implants developed flaws rather than the five per cent recorded in France (Department of Health, 2012). In this case, the lack of information was due to limited information flows, especially from private hospitals (which performed 95 per cent of all operations). The blind spot here refers to the absence of detection tools, as the private hospitals were not required to report incidents such as leaking silicone implants to the regulator.
- *The inability to identify causes.* In this particular case, the blind spot refers not so much to the lack of pattern recognition identified above but to the inability to identify (latent) causes. For example, the sudden rise of BSE (bovine spongiform encephalopathy) in cows in Germany came as a surprise to German politicians and regulators, as the most likely source of contamination, food, had been banned. The surprise here was that other sources were potentially spreading the disease, namely milk substitutes that contained animal fats. A different example might be taken from ancient Rome: it has been

suggested that Julius Caesar was well aware of potential assassination plans but was likely to have been surprised to be assassinated by Brutus, someone he had previously spared from death.

As noted in the introductory chapter by Bach and Wegrich, the notion of blind spot links to the study of unintended consequences in the social sciences in general, and the study of executive government in particular. Unintended consequences are traditionally viewed as a result of ambiguities, paradoxes, side effects, and tensions (Merton, 1936). Blind spots represent a distinct sub-set of phenomena, defined by an unknown inability (not seeing the not seeing) to detect and process potentially critical information—whether it is an inability to detect, to categorize, or to identify remedies.

The blind spot therefore contrasts with *seeing the not seeing*. Such areas include, traditionally, fog of war situations or attempts at developing single quality indicators for measuring highly complex and diverse operations, such as hospitals or universities. In such cases, organizations and individuals might be said to be 'blind'. Technologies are unlikely to come to the rescue in such situations. Technological change can address some aspects of the seeing the not seeing problem but potentially increases the problems of the blind spot in terms of not seeing the not seeing. One example is the use of modern technologies, such as GPS (Global Positioning System) trackers and satellite communication tools, in modern warfare that enable soldiers in the battlefield to be controlled from afar, reducing a reliance on professional discretion. The effect of reduced 'blindness' is said to have decreased professionalism overall. Similarly, the use of satellite navigation systems in cars is said to have reduced drivers' sense of direction. In other words, tools to support the seeing the not seeing problem actually increase the potential of *not* seeing the not seeing.

This chapter is, as noted, concerned with the blind spot as defined by not seeing the not seeing. Blind spots highlight the inherent ambiguity in social life. If the world was certain and predictable, then there would be no need for perfect vision: uncertainty and 'threats' emerging from the environment would simply not exist but would already be accounted for in existing decision-making.[1] Similarly, if our own interpretation of a given situation was 'objective', then again there would be no need to study blind spots; actors would be capable of processing all information, assessing options, and developing 'optimal' solutions. The blind spot is also not about genuine uncertainty. For example, it is possible to forecast the consequences of earthquakes, but there is genuine uncertainty about the timing and intensity of particular events—and knowledge about fault lines is largely about historical events, and not necessarily about future occurrences.

Blind spots are therefore central to our understanding of executive politics and governance. They feature in the ways in which organizations and policies are designed and operated, and they also feature heavily in the way these operations are studied and evaluated. However, while blind spots are everywhere, everything is not a blind spot. It is therefore important to delineate the characteristics of blind spots. The rest of this chapter first considers the distinct nature of blind spots in contrast to other types of phenomena that have been associated with unintended consequences. Then the discussion moves to a further consideration of varieties of blind spots before returning to a discussion of potential blind spot mitigators (see also the concluding chapter by Bach and Wegrich in this volume). Different theories have noted that systems are blind (or 'deaf') to outside interferences or that organizations and individuals are selective in pattern recognition of environmental and endogenous change processes. Accordingly, a range of blind spot remedies has also been put forward. These include 'heedfulness' to reduce the likelihood of encountering a 'normalization of deviance', the promotion of 'rational' tools for policy-making to regulate attention levels, and the avoidance of the cargo cult-like application of particular templates regardless of the nature of a problem (Vaughan, 2005; Weick & Roberts, 1993). None of these potential mitigation strategies is free of their own blind spots. As the blind spot is essential to any system of 'seeing' in the first place, no strategy of eliminating blind spots exists. In contrast, the sole mitigation strategy is to enhance the visibility of blind spots.

BLIND SPOTS AND UNINTENDED CONSEQUENCES

Among the central interests in the study of executive politics and public administration are failure, disaster, and organizational breakdown (Hood, 1974, 1976, 1998). One justification for this fascination in things going pear-shaped is that only when the proverbial has hit the fan will it be difficult to turn a blind eye to apparent failings. However, what counts as a perverse outcome and why depends on an observer's viewpoint. No universal agreement exists as to when a situation has become 'too bad' or when a particular policy response has been 'too tough', 'too prescriptive', or 'too weak'. Indeed, responses to failure and disaster are likely to vary depending on observers' particular viewpoint.

So far, so failing. Interest in unintended consequences and malfunction frequently focuses on social processes that involve organizational over- or under-compensation in terms of levels of attention. As noted, by concentrating on not seeing the not seeing, the blind spot does not refer to those technological or other limits to seeing that one is very well aware of (the seeing the not seeing). How can a perspective that concentrates on the blind spot advance these discussions? To address this question, it is essential to identify how the blind spot is distinct from a wider set of factors that are associated with unintended consequences.

For one, blind spots can be distinguished from the so-called Achilles' heels. Such Achilles' heels refer to vulnerabilities that are characteristic of particular organizational forms. To illustrate, in German (and Norse) mythology, Siegfried's vulnerability was not caused by a physical impairment (or not seeing that he was not seeing his vulnerability). It was the imprint of a leaf that left him short of invincibility—of which he was very well aware.[2] Similarly, particular ways of organizing have their own vulnerabilities. For example, an emphasis on hierarchical authority in organizational life is likely to generate blind rule-following. An example of such an organizational Achilles' heel is the Japanese Fukushima incident where failure reporting was said to be discouraged ('t Hart, 2013). Similarly, as has been shown in studies of reward systems, highly competitive work environments based on individual performance incentives are said to encourage behaviours that destroy any form of team working or system-wide responsibility. Equally, highly deliberative settings are prone to gridlock and conflicts over insider/outsider boundaries. Finally, an organizational context characterized by randomness and surprise is likely not just to prevent the rise of routinized neglect, as predictable control systems can be gamed; it is also likely to generate distrust and a lack of openness to information sharing.

Furthermore, a blind spot differs from the so-called toothpaste tube phenomenon according to which pressure on one part of the system will lead to spillages elsewhere (Hood, Rothstein, & Baldwin, 2001, p. 15). For example, attempts at tightening up standards by reducing discretion or enhancing reporting requirements might go hand in hand with corresponding behavioural adjustments, such as reduced reporting, so as to reduce the potential for subsequent litigation. Such behavioural adjustments represent conscious efforts to reduce vulnerability and involve efforts at cheating and gaming by active counter-learning. Blind spots might exist in the failure to identify such behavioural responses. However, blind spots differ from such creative compliance responses (McBarnet & Whelan, 1991), because counter-learning and other forms of creative compliance are the result of strategic responses by affected constituencies and not caused by blind spots as such.

Moreover, unintended consequences emerge as actors carefully police the boundaries of their organization. Organizational survival is dependent on maintaining a succinct and pivotal niche that attracts popular support. These boundaries are only to some extent defined by formal provisions. Instead, organizations will choose which activities are likely to attract support and choose to downplay those activities that are likely to incur criticism. In turn, criticism of the core activity of an organization is likely to be met by sustained rebuttals (see also Wilson, 1989). These boundary-policing activities are shaped by the reputational concerns of organizations and individuals within them. Such concern with the reception in front of 'networks of audiences' (Carpenter, 2010) does overlap to an extent with blind spots. Perceptions of one's self will give rise to selective blind spots, such as priming and selective defensive strategies (as discussed below). Nevertheless, not all reputation-driven behaviour and resultant unintended outcomes can be put down to blind spots (blind spots are arguably involved in the design of particular institutional arrangements that fail to spot the likely organizational responses).

Similarly, blind spots are distinct from the so-called self-fulfilling prophecies (Merton, 1948): once situations are defined in particular ways, they will have consequences.[3] As noted by Merton (1948), humans respond '… at times primarily, to the meaning [a] situation has for them' (p. 148). Defining situations in particular ways, such as classifying certain behaviours as 'criminal', creates a blind spot in terms of understanding the situation in different ways, as information is gathered in ways so as to ascertain criminal/non-criminal behaviours according to certain thresholds (in addition, it encourages certain reinforcing of social dynamics, such as those defined as 'criminal' behaving accordingly).

To summarize, a blind spot is a vision impairment whose existence is not apparent to the observer: the not seeing that one is not seeing. It is not a known weakness caused by a particular organizational arrangement or a conscious adaptive behaviour to deal with externally imposed expectations. One might be aware of the presence of a blind spot at an abstract level, but the day-to-day information gathering and processing is shaped by unconscious blind spots.

Table 2.1   Blind spots and unintended consequences

Unintended consequence	*Unique characteristics*	*Overlap with blind spot*
Achilles' heel	Particular organizational arrangements display inherent weaknesses	Underlying worldviews of organizational arrangements shape ways in which problems are perceived and what solutions are seen as appropriate
Toothpaste tube effect	Recalcitrant environments respond to stronger attention in one place by moving elsewhere	Inability to detect reallocation of attention
Organizational boundary management	Organizations carefully shape their jurisdiction to minimize risk to survival/maximize comfort	Reputational concerns create certain priming effects that shape responses to perceived challenges
Counter-learning	Emphasis on evading external constraint by adapting behaviours	Lack of sensitivity to detect responses
Self-fulfilling prophecy	Self-reinforcing social dynamics	Biases eliminate ways of gathering alternative forms of information

It is therefore important to distinguish the blind spot from other types of unintended consequences. At the same time, it is also critical to identify the areas where blind spots contribute to or complement other types of unintended consequences. Table 2.1 illustrates the mechanisms that are associated with various types of unintended consequences, but also notes areas of potential (but not inevitable) overlap with blind spots. Table 2.1 also highlights that blind spots deal with detection and the processing of information rather than strategic behaviours.

VARIETIES OF BLIND SPOTS

In the field of vision, the blind spot is generated by the lack of photoreceptors on the optic disc of the retina where the nerve passes through. In the social sciences, the blind spot relates to the selective perception of problems and solutions and 'blindness' to latent, but essential, features in any social relationship. Central to the understanding of a blind spot is that it involves an unconscious filtering out of information, whether it is to protect oneself from discomforting information or to confirm preconceived assumptions about likely patterns. The existence of such blinkers is therefore a limitation, but it is also essential to any form of organizing. That is, given limited processing capacity, it is not feasible to evaluate all information and potential combinations and consequences in unbiased ways. More specifically in the context of this chapter, it is about processes of information gathering and information processing.

An emphasis on not seeing the not seeing highlights the importance of implicit and unconscious processes that affect both long-term processes and immediate decisions (which might have a long-term effect).[4] Blind spots emerge as a result of certain distorting perspectives, such as the application of the organizational equivalents of magnifying glasses. Merton (1936), for example, noted how tunnel vision and an 'imperious immediacy of interest' generated a partial view of constellations and thereby influenced decision-making. In the case of tunnel vision, which causes the loss of peripheral vision, organizations will continue generating the same response, as there is no capability (or resource) to look beyond the perimeters of an organization's jurisdiction. In crisis situations, for example, it is said that organizations turn 'primitive' (as part of their survival instinct), reducing their capability to process complex information ('t Hart, Rosenthal, & Kouzmin, 1993).

Another example of tunnel vision, that is, an unawareness of the limited if not false nature of one's picture of the world, is provided by the sinking of the *Andrea Doria* in 1956 following a collision in thick fog with another transatlantic liner, the *Stockholm*. One of the contributing factors was that the radar setting of the *Stockholm* was assumed to be on a 15-mile setting, thereby giving decision-makers a sense of distance between the two ships. However, the radar was on a five-mile setting.[5] The blind spot here emerged by focusing on the display without checking the overall settings. In the area of executive government, such tunnel vision exists in the typical problem that international negotiations (in the context of regional organizations, for example) lead to time-pressured agreements among leading ministry officials of different countries without necessarily taking into consideration their domestic agenda and the viewpoints of all domestic stakeholders. In the area of regulation, blind spots are particularly notable when regulators concentrate on the monitoring of certain business activities that, due to technological change, may have migrated to other platforms. For example, inspections might continue to monitor business activities on the high street but be blind to the emergence of new internet-based business models run from laptops in suburban bedrooms.

In the case of the 'imperious immediacy of interest', the blind spot is generated by the urge to address short-term, seemingly urgent problems, leading to the neglect, if not direct attenuation, of more long-term, important problems. For Merton (1936), attempts at unbiased analysis are doomed as 'the satisfaction of the immediate interest is a psychological generator of emotional bias, with consequent lop-sidedness or failure to engage in the required calculations' (p. 902). The overall effect is that 'because a particular action is not carried out in a psychological or social vacuum, its effects will ramify into other spheres of value and interest' (Merton, 1936, p. 902). Such processes apply to both individual and collective decision-making. For example, in the case of higher education regulation, the regulatory demand on universities to meet immediate deadlines to address certain issues means that even less attention is paid to more entrenched and tricky issues.

These tunnel vision and 'immediacy of interest' examples of blind spots point to a more general magnifying glass effect in that certain aspects of information are highlighted and others, on the periphery, marginalized. At another level, blind spots are intrinsic to professional standard operating procedures. Accordingly, worldviews shared by professional practices provide implicit assumptions that filter out 'important' from 'unimportant' information; they enable immediate categorization of incoming information and form the basis for decisions as to whether to act or not. An example of such professional biases is the area of protection of vulnerable children. As the tragic circumstances of the Baby P case highlighted (where the consistent abuse of a toddler was not detected by a variety of institutions), an emphasis existed, in the case of single parenting, towards protecting the mother–child relationship rather than erring on the side of fostering or relying on fathers. This created a blind spot towards recognizing changes in the environment of the mother of Baby P, in particular the arrival of a new boyfriend (Marinetto, 2011). Learning is characterized by biased and reinforcing updating processes; due to confirmation biases, blind spots filter out information that potentially destabilizes existing belief systems. Instead, information that flies in the face of dominant beliefs is normalized away: it is seen as an opportunity to reaffirm existing understandings, allowing for a continuous 'triumph of hope over experience' by emphasizing the importance of one more heave of the same, but purer variety. In other words, learning is understood as strengthening the not seeing the not seeing by reaffirming existing ways of seeing the seeing.

The area of financial management offers further illustrations of such processes. For example, the study of pension liabilities is prone to all kinds of assumptions (such as about longevity); auditors focus on the material even though there is widespread agreement that organizational viability can only be understood by accounting for the immaterial (and even here there is a temptation for auditors to extrapolate on non-representative samples). Furthermore, 'relational distance' (Black, 1976) explains why some organizations' information is regarded as credible and others' is not. As noted, it contributes to problems of the so-called multi-organizational sub-optimization in that blind spots exist in terms of understanding and noticing what other organizations are doing, despite being in (loosely or tightly) coupled situations (Hood, 1976). For example, blind spots emerge in the context of safety management: in production chains one has to take 'on trust' that the quality of particular parts is assured. However, organizations are prone to the 'normalization of deviance' (Vaughan, 2005) in that deviations from the norm are increasingly tolerated (especially in conditions of time pressure). Subsequent parts of the production chain are likely to be blind to the internal processes elsewhere (in the absence of public outcry) and therefore are caught flat-footed to potential quality problems. Such processes shape not just the overall nature of an individual organization's way of working but the way in which information is exchanged within and across organizations, and they illustrate how a series of blind spots are essential for such practices to persist.

Similarly, in the area of performance management, where emphasis has been placed on output and outcome control, organizations are said to be increasingly treated as production-type organizations. According to Wilson (1989), 'production organizations' are those for which one can measure outputs and outcomes. However, this does not take into account performance that cannot be measured that easily. Being blind to these qualitative differences and being blind to the fact that not all organizations are of the production type means that organizations are evaluated on inappropriate criteria and meaningless information, while at the same time distorting the incentives of the regulated organization (Bevan & Hood, 2006; Ma, 2016, 2017). In this case, the templates of particular public management doctrines generate blind spots in that certain types of phenomena cannot be captured, as trust is placed in certain instruments of seeing and in assumptions about the likely responses. Similarly, the recent fashion in advocating risk-based approaches towards enforcement generates blind spots in multiple ways. One way is that understandings of risks will not be constantly challenged in terms of potential changes in the environment, such as the rise of a new type of risk. Similarly, risk-based instruments reduce attention to the potential aggregate effects of different risks coinciding. In other words, any instrument that is supposed to make performance 'visible' is associated with inherent blind spots that distort and suppress information—and thereby shape organizational attention and behaviours.

In line with this argument, underlying assumptions of particular models represent a blind spot; for example, if the assumption is that change is ultimately linear and incremental, blind spots exist when it comes to phenomena associated with non-linear change. Related to this, an emphasis on particular normative worldviews is likely to lead to blind spots regarding potential sources of self-destruction. One such example of a blind spot operating over time is the self-defeating nature of certain cultural values. Merton's (1936, p. 904) prime example was the rise of ascetic Protestantism in Europe (and its effect on the rise of science) and the consequent accumulation of wealth which established the conditions for the decline of asceticism.

This kind of distorting effect on vision is both essential (it allows for deeper insights) and problematic (it distorts perspective). A well-known blind spot is the emergence of particular worldviews that lead to biased ways of receiving information and seeking out solutions. As already indicated, egalitarians will always seek to identify problems in terms of 'too much' authority, rivalry, or distrust and therefore argue for 'more' participatory decision-making processes, including the blind spot of seeing potential advantages of others ways of organizing. Furthermore, such 'self-organizing' systems in which certain groups organize (and control themselves) are usually blind to misconduct unless prompted by external action, as examples of double agents in the intelligence community and of medical malpractice suggest.

Following grid-group cultural theory (6 & Swedlow, 2016; Lodge, Wegrich, & McElroy, 2010; Thompson, Ellis, & Wildavsky, 1990), it is possible to highlight the particular blind spots of the four fundamental ways of organizing, as suggested by this particular institutional theory. Different blind spots emerge as part of social relations—'*as people organize so they will behave*' (Thompson et al., 1990, p. 97, emphasis in original)—and accordingly, these behaviours will also be reflected in distinct blind spots: particular social relations have distinct ways of seeing what is appropriate or deviant. Developing this line of argumentation further, one can

Table 2.2 Worldviews, Achilles' heels, and blind spots

Contrived randomness	*Hierarchy*
Emphasis: make life unpredictable	*Emphasis:* enhance oversight and procedures
Achilles' heel: distrust undermines social relationships	*Achilles' heel:* gaming and over-emphasis on authority
Blind spot: understands all behaviour as gamed and social relations as low| trust	*Blind spot:* requires all behaviours to be categorized and assumes compliance
Individualism	*Egalitarianism*
Emphasis: enhance incentives	*Emphasis:* enhance group processes and decision-making
Achilles' heel: hyper-rivalry undermines social relationships	*Achilles' heel:* gridlock and boundary conflicts associated with participatory processes
Blind spot: understands all behaviours are driven by self-interest of motivated and capable actors	*Blind spot:* understands all behaviour as either in- or out-group

develop the blind spots of particular sets of worldviews in the context of organizing executive government, as provided by Hood (1998). Each of these worldviews suggests, as noted, that alternative ways of organizing have Achilles' heels. Furthermore, each worldview is not just affected by its own distinctive Achilles' heel, but also its own distinctive blind spot, relating to its views as to the capacity and motivation of actors (see Table 2.2).

So far, the emphasis has been on the not seeing the not seeing definition of the blind spot, as outlined above. In contrast to this emphasis on not seeing the not seeing in the sense of being unaware of one's own limitations, there is also a conscious choice to ensure that one *is* not seeing. This kind of blind spot is the 'turning a Nelson's (blind) eye' variant. According to legend, Horatio Nelson ignored the commands of his superior during the 1801 battle of Copenhagen by lifting the telescope to his blind eye. More generally, this variant points to the purposeful refusal to establish mechanisms that would potentially allow the detection of emerging phenomena. This variant of a blind spot has both supportive as well as self-defeating aspects. On the one hand, turning a Nelson's eye seems to encourage non-compliance. On the other hand, turning a Nelson's eye to certain developments might facilitate cooperation as long as they are built on 'broad discipline'. Cooperation is made possible if parties turn a blind eye to potential deviating behaviours. It might be argued, for example, that regional integration among groups of states follows such a pattern. The shared assumption that all parties cooperate supports further integration. Institutions that tightly control compliance are likely to have a self-defeating effect in that disputes over compliance patterns will generate discord and, ultimately, facilitate disintegration.

In sum, worldviews have particular ways of placing information in particular categories rather than others, and they respond in specific ways to observed deviations from expected norms. Accordingly, certain types of behaviour will not be 'seen', whether it is because of an inability to identify and/or understand the undesirability of this behaviour. Alternatively, certain information is seen because it is central to the reputation (or mission) of organizations. The blind spot is therefore central to priming and framing activities: by being primed to respond to certain types of information, one is simultaneously primed not to explore other types of phenomena that might have implications for organizational survival. It also includes probing into the 'primed' mission of an organization: once there has been an agreement on what an organization is supposed to do, it will not engage in processes that seek to disestablish that mission. In other words, any agreement on a set of objectives involves blind spots.

The blind spot is ubiquitous in the organizational life of executive government. A blind spot is not defined by a lack of information-gathering capacity due to resource deficits in terms of organization, authority, nodality, or finance (Hood, 1983; Lodge & Wegrich, 2012). Such circumstances are characterized by seeing the not seeing, which could be rectified with the addition of certain ingredients. Instead, the importance of not seeing the not seeing is that it is intrinsic to organizing and therefore to any form of information gathering in the first place. Without a blind spot, professional practices could not exist, categorization of 'appropriate' and 'inappropriate' behaviour could not be performed, and attention could not prioritize some objectives over others. There would be no organizational (or individual) identity. The challenge for executive government is therefore not the elimination of the blind spot (defined in terms of not seeing the not seeing). Such an ambition is, in fact, impossible. However, the challenge is how to enhance the possibilities of pluralizing blind spots so as to provide for multiple perspectives and to thereby make blind spots 'visible'.

Managing Blind Spots?

If, therefore, blind spots are essential to any form of organizing, how then can the effect of not seeing the not seeing be addressed? As noted, a call for 'more resources' is insufficient; it might address the not seeing concern, but it will not address the *not seeing* the not seeing aspect of the blind spot. Similarly, noting the importance of learning processes is insufficient, as it is likely to reinforce rather than challenge the existing ways of seeing and interpreting. Established ways of seeing and not seeing will only become destabilized in cases of extreme disappointment. However, the likely outcome of such a destabilization by disappointment is the reliance on a different set of technologies of seeing with their own respective blind spots. After all, seeing is about having authority and power, and highlighting blind spots is likely to be regarded as a poke in the eye of power.

Just as in the case of car mirrors, the way to deal with blind spots is to establish other mirrors that add perspective (but that have their own blind spots). Addressing the effect of blind spots requires mechanisms to enhance the plurality of viewpoints so as to expose blind spots. This pluralization might either occur by creating a second order reflection which reviews the kind of operations that occur at the first order level. Alternatively, such pluralization involves the integration of alternative perspectives in the decision-making process itself. In either case, the ways in which choices are made are being questioned.

One way to address a bias blind spot (the view that others are suffering from biases but oneself is not) is to impose procedural devices into decision-making in order to introduce alternative sources of information (see also the concluding chapter by Bach and Wegrich in this volume). These procedures are to force those in authority to reflect and thereby to be reminded of potential bias blind spots in their own analysis. However, procedural devices are likely to be more applicable to seeing the not seeing situations where further information is to ensure 'better' decision-making. Whether procedural devices are able to tackle not seeing the not seeing is questionable, as this requires challenging the type of information gathered and the ways in which information is gathered. Even without this particular caveat, procedural instruments have their own biases and blind spots, and whether they are being engaged with in any serious matter is highly questionable. After all, in executive government, procedural devices are usually at their most powerful when they are least politically important. Rather, once a decision is being made, choice-supportive biases will be deployed so as to justify decisions made. At the frontline, the imposition of additional procedural guidelines will be seen as additional strain and incur coping behaviours.

A different way of introducing pluralization is to rely on challenge units. Such units are supposed to explore information, challenge existing interpretations, and develop alternative scenarios. Such activities are said to be central to learning within organizations, but they usually suffer from the problem that such challenge functions are detached from 'real' decision-making and therefore are unable to engage on the job with potential blind spots. There is also the question of power. After all, dominant understandings are an expression of assumed authority and domination. Introducing such challenge units is likely to generate three outcomes—namely where such challenge functions are seen as irrelevant to the organization (by simply being ignored), as disruptive to the functioning of decision-making (as disagreements lead to continued stalemate), or as accommodating as the challenge function is made to understand dominant perspectives. In this scenario, the challenge function is simply subsumed into the dominant logic of decision-making.

It is this concern that pluralizing perspectives involves the highlighting of the blind spots of those in authority and power that has led to the adoption of the court jester in settings of absolute power (Otto, 2001). The jester was able to point to the authority's blind spots without being assumed to be a threat to the established powers; after all, their social standing excluded them from potential succession plans. The court jester was, however, traditionally utilized to deal with settings of 'absolute power' (such as imperial courts or the Vatican), not the day-to-day blind spots that have featured in the life of contemporary bureaucracy (where the iron cage of bureaucracy might have been said to have ironed out the scope for formal jesters, requiring the emergence of informal jesters in different places in the organizational hierarchy). Inflating the presence of court jesters in contemporary executive government might offer a valuable tool to address blind spots and other dysfunctional behaviours but might suffer from the same detachment effect as challenge units, and they might also be seen as overly disruptive to organizational routines and authority structures. Whether those in power would prefer to challenge their blind spots in the eye of potential media (shit)storms once the inevitable leak has occurred is also questionable.

A further suggestion to address blind spots by introducing different perspectives is to rely on 'clumsy solutions' (Verweij, 2014). Whether clumsy solutions can be designed remains an unanswered question, but the idea of a clumsy solution suggests a hybridizing of different perspectives so as to avoid dominance of particular blind spots (and other effects of single ways of organizing). Hybridizing perspectives might sound straightforward, but it requires institutional arrangements that require the investigation of information from different analytical perspectives and the bringing together of different professions and experiences.

However, this way of organizing against blind spots has its own Achilles' heels: it requires an understanding of who the legitimate participants and what the analytical perspectives are, it requires agreement on decision-making rules, and it requires some form of authority to enable an actual decision to be taken. It also requires a conscious effort to maintain such arrangements. How difficult this might be has been illustrated by examples from the so-called case reviews that feature in areas of social services. In these cases, representatives from different social (and criminal justice) services are brought together to join up the dots on particularly tricky cases (such as potential child abuse). Instead of offering the opportunity for an in-depth review, these meetings are usually characterized by fluid membership, limited attention and time, and lack of information. It is therefore inevitable that clumsy solutions will display particular biases and blind spots; in fact, these blind spots might be even more prominent, as disagreements between different factions become areas that shall not be named (so as to avoid embarrassing spats) and as the event of a joint review becomes a symbolic reassurance that blind spots have been explored. In turn, this discourages actors from considering what sources might exist for not seeing the not seeing.

In sum, therefore, as any form of organizing involves seeing the seeing, it also includes the intrinsic not seeing the not seeing. As all organization is about authoritative ways of seeing, therefore, pointing out blind spots is also about challenging those in authority. In other words, blind spots are not just intrinsic (and essential); pointing them out is inherently destabilizing to ways of seeing and the dominant ways of organizing. Any strategy for mitigating blind spots therefore is inherently also about challenging power.

So What?

Any discussion of blind spots invites ridicule. It encourages the rendition of the story of drunks searching for their keys under the lamp post as it offers more light. Once this initial scepticism has been overcome, the blind spot in the world of executive politics and governance becomes central: flat-footed responses are an everyday occurrence. Organizations are accused of being blind.

However, at the same time, blind spots are intrinsic to any form of organization. Dominant ways of seeing create blind spots; by defining the ways we see, we do not know what we do not see. Similarly, standard operating procedures invite dominant ways of seeing and therefore incur their very own blind spots. This chapter has offered a range of brief examples to highlight the extent to which blind spots feature in executive politics and governance. It should also offer a reminder to those in authority that their dominant ways of seeing are insuring blind spots that might invite their downfall. In other words, those claiming to be basing their policy advocacy on evidence-based policies should reflect on their own inherent limitations and blind spots.

Blind spots are therefore not about the flat-footed nature of organizations that can be blamed on useless individuals or lack of resources; instead, they are part of organizational life. Defining organizational boundaries and missions requires distinct ways of seeing things, which in turn establishes blind spots. All social life is therefore shaped by blind spots.

Any attempt at avoiding blind spots in updating or learning requires the presence of capacities designed to uncover blind spots and to challenge standard assumptions. Such a challenge function threatens the stability of existing worldviews and impairs the efficient running of organizations, as signals will be investigated and questioned. This, in turn, opens up the possibility for further blind spots as different worldviews and perspectives collide and lead to contestation, if not paralysis. Blind spots are therefore intrinsic to executive government: the blind spot might lead to unintended consequences and subsequent changes, only to re-emerge in a different guise. In other words, any blind spot-related problem is the outcome of a solution.

NOTES

1. Even self-driving cars suffer from problems of ambiguity in their environment, despite the claim that their ongoing processing of the environment reduces accidents by eliminating human error. For example, in the UK, trials of self-driving cars were conducted by insisting that such cars should remain unmarked, as it was feared that any identifiability would encourage 'bullying' by drivers of manual vehicles (Connor, 2016).
2. A related example can be drawn from football. An Achilles' heel is the equivalent of particular tactical choices (such as playing with a lone striker). In

contrast, a blind spot refers to the inherent vulnerability of dealing with ambiguity.

3. 'The self-fulfilling prophecy is, in the beginning, a *false* definition of the situation evoking a new behavior which makes the originally false conception come *true*' (Merton, 1948, p. 195, emphasis in original).

4. The short-term, immediate effect is the equivalent of the car driver who fails to detect a car in their blind spot. The long-term effect is the equivalent of looking into a distorted mirror that continuously filters out certain information while the environment is changing.

5. Similarly, in the 2002 Überlingen mid-air collision, one contributory factor was that the sole air traffic controller was unaware that the ground-based optical collision warning system had been switched off for maintenance.

REFERENCES

6, P., & Swedlow, B. (2016). An institutional theory of cultural biases, public administration and public policy. *Public Administration, 94*(4), 867–880.

BBC News. (1999, October 19). Ward known as 'departure lounge'. *BBC News.* Retrieved from http://news.bbc.co.uk/2/hi/health/background_briefings/the_bristol_heart_babies/478560.stm

Bevan, G., & Hood, C. (2006). What's measured is what matters: Targets and gaming in the English public health care system. *Public Administration, 84*(3), 517–538.

Black, D. J. (1976). *The behavior of law.* New York: Academic Press.

Campbell, D. (2013, February 3). Mid Staffs hospital scandal: The essential guide. *The Guardian.* Retrieved from https://www.theguardian.com/society/2013/feb/06/mid-staffs-hospital-scandal-guide

Carpenter, D. P. (2010). *Reputation and power: Organizational image and pharmaceutical regulation at the FDA.* Princeton: Princeton University Press.

Connor, S. (2016, October 30). First self-driving cars will be unmarked so that other drivers don't try to bully them. *The Guardian.* Retrieved from https://www.theguardian.com/technology/2016/oct/30/volvo-self-driving-car-autonomous

Department of Health (UK). (2012). *Poly implant prothèse (PIP) silicone breast implants: Review of the actions of the medicines and healthcare products regulatory agency (MHRA) and department of health.* London: Department of Health.

't Hart, P. (2013). After Fukushima: Reflections on risk and institutional learning in an era of mega-crises. *Public Administration, 91*(1), 101–113.

't Hart, P., Rosenthal, U., & Kouzmin, A. (1993). Crisis decision making: The centralization thesis revealed. *Administration & Society, 25*(1), 12–45.

Hood, C. (1974). Administrative diseases: Some types of dysfunctionality in administration. *Public Administration, 52*(4), 439–454.

Hood, C. (1976). *Limits of administration*. London: Wiley.

Hood, C. (1983). *Tools of government*. Basingstoke: Macmillan.

Hood, C. (1998). *Art of the state*. Oxford: Oxford University Press.

Hood, C., Rothstein, H., & Baldwin, R. (2001). *The government of risk*. Oxford: Oxford University Press.

Jennings, W., Lodge, M., & Ryan, M. (2018). Comparing blunders in government. *European Journal of Political Research, 57*(1), 238–258.

Lodge, M., & Wegrich, K. (2012). Executive politics and policy instruments. In M. Lodge & K. Wegrich (Eds.), *Executive politics in times of crisis* (pp. 118–135). Basingstoke: Palgrave Macmillan.

Lodge, M., Wegrich, K., & McElroy, G. (2010). Dodgy kebabs everywhere? Variety of worldviews and regulatory change. *Public Administration, 88*(1), 247–266.

Ma, L. (2016). Performance feedback, government goal-setting and aspiration level adaptation: Evidence from Chinese provinces. *Public Administration, 94*(2), 452–471.

Ma, L. (2017). Performance management and citizen satisfaction with the government: Evidence from Chinese municipalities. *Public Administration, 95*(1), 39–59.

Marinetto, M. (2011). A Lipskian analysis of child protection failures from Victoria Climbié to 'Baby P': A street-level re-evaluation of joined-up governance. *Public Administration, 89*(3), 1164–1181.

McBarnet, D., & Whelan, C. (1991). The elusive spirit of the law: Formalism and the struggle for legal control. *Modern Law Review, 54*(6), 848–873.

Merton, R. K. (1936). The unintended consequences of purposive social action. *American Sociological Review, 1*(6), 894–904.

Merton, R. K. (1948). The self-fulfilling prophecy. *Antioch Review, 8*(2), 193–210.

National Commission on Terrorist Attacks upon the United States. (2004). *The 9/11 Commission Report: Final report of the National Commission on Terrorist Attacks upon the United States*. Washington, DC: United States Government Printing Office.

Otto, B. K. (2001). *Fools are everywhere: The court jester around the world*. Chicago: University of Chicago Press.

Parker, C. F., & Stern, E. K. (2002). Blindsided? September 11 and the origins of strategic surprise. *Political Psychology, 23*(3), 601–630.

Thompson, M., Ellis, R., & Wildavsky, A. (1990). *Cultural theory*. Boulder: Westview Press.

Vaughan, D. (2005). Organizational rituals of risk and error. In B. Hutter & M. Power (Eds.), *Organizational encounters with risk* (pp. 33–66). Cambridge: Cambridge University Press.

Verweij, M. (2014). Wicked problems, clumsy solutions, and messy institutions in transnational governance. In M. Lodge & K. Wegrich (Eds.), *The problem-solving capacity of the modern state* (pp. 183–197). Oxford: Oxford University Press.

Weick, K. E., & Roberts, K. H. (1993). Collective mind in organizations: Heedful interrelating on flight decks. *Administrative Science Quarterly, 38*(3), 357–381.

Wilson, J. Q. (1989). *Bureaucracy: What government agencies do and why they do it*. New York: Basic Books.

CHAPTER 3

Blind Spots: Organizational and Institutional Biases in Intra- and Inter-organizational Contexts

Tom Christensen

INTRODUCTION

Researching blind spots may be done based on a framework combining different theories from organization theory, which offers different takes on this phenomenon (Christensen, Lægreid, Roness, & Røvik, 2007). The purpose of this chapter is to systematically use three such theories on blind spots: an instrumental theory based on bounded rationality (Simon, 1957), a cultural theory starting from Selznick's (1957) seminal work, and a neo-institutional theory focusing on myths and symbols (Meyer & Rowan, 1977). Adding to this, examples will be outlined and discussed to show the relevance of these theories for studying blind spots. The term 'blind spots' is in this chapter used in a broad metaphorical sense, covering most of Table 1.1 in the introductory chapter but mainly focusing on attention biases.

T. Christensen (✉)
Department of Political Science, University of Oslo, Oslo, Norway
e-mail: tom.christensen@stv.uio.no

© The Author(s) 2019
T. Bach, K. Wegrich (eds.), *The Blind Spots of Public Bureaucracy and the Politics of Non-Coordination*, Executive Politics and Governance, https://doi.org/10.1007/978-3-319-76672-0_3

First discussed is how blind spots are related to internal 'organization is the mobilization of bias' factors (Schattschneider, 1960, p. 71) and how different mechanisms sustain or undermine those factors. This means that something and someone will formally be organized in (and others, organized out), leaving many blind spots in terms of capacity, attention, problems, and solutions (March, 1981). But blind spots are also related to inter-organizational features and how different mechanisms may sustain or undermine them. When public organizations are dealing with other national or international organizations, they will not only act according to their own structures but will also have to adapt to comparable but different features in the environment, which may cause blind spots. Related to both internal and external structural conditions, both problems of underlap, where issues or tasks are defocused by many actors and negative coordination prevails, and overlap, where different units and actors are working on the same tasks, will be discussed. Increasing complexity and hybridity may also lead to blind spots (Christensen & Lægreid, 2011).

Blind spots may also be related to the dynamics of cultural development in public organizations, both inside those organizations and in their dynamic relationships to the environment (Selznick, 1957). The process of institutionalization selects certain aspects of internal and external pressure in creating a unique culture while others are defocused, meaning that there are potentially other underlying cultures or subcultures. Cultural complexity, i.e. the result of public organizations combining different types of culture, may also lead to blind spots. Adding to this, a focus on external complexity and hybridity and the use of myths and symbols (reputation management) may potentially amplify or modify blind spots (Wæraas & Maor, 2015). The three sets of independent factors—structural, cultural, and symbolic—may also come together in creating, sustaining, or modifying blind spots. An example of this is the dynamic between conscious efforts, cultural compatibility, and symbols in attempts at modern reform efforts (Christensen & Lægreid, 2001).

ORGANIZATION IS MOBILIZATION OF BIAS: SOME STRUCTURAL ELABORATIONS

Schattschneider (1960) in his seminal book *Semisovereign People* formulates the following famous insight: 'All forms of political organization have a bias in favor of the exploitation of some kinds of conflict and the suppression of others because organization is the mobilization of bias. Some issues are organized into politics while others are organized out' (p. 71).

If we generalize this statement, connecting it to any public organization, and see it from an instrumental-structural point of view (Christensen et al., 2007), what does this statement really mean? One starting point could be Simon's (1957) theory of bounded rationality and administrative behaviour. Actors in (public) organizations will overall have limitations on their knowledge, capacity, and attention, something that the structural design of a formal organization can help them to cope with and modify. The different principles of specialization and coordination, whether vertical or horizontal (Gulick, 1937), help in defining the formal roles of the different actors, thereby also easing their rationality limitations. Formal roles mean that an actor will focus on certain policies, issues, expertise, aspects, and so on seen from a certain hierarchical level, but will therefore also not focus others (Scott & Davis, 2007).

So the basic idea of formal organization is connected with different types of biases. For the single organizational member or actor, the bias is defined in the role, i.e. some type of knowledge, issues, and policies get attention, while others are organized out (March, 1994). Looking at the public organization as a whole, the overall structural design implies that certain types of knowledge and expertise, goals, policies, issues, and so on are organized into the structure while others are organized out or get less attention.

Seen from such a perspective, how can this provide insight into blind spots? Overall, one can say that structural design, implying organization of bias, creates potential blind spots, which have both intra- and inter-organizational aspects. First, if leaders in a public organization systematically design its structure through defining certain goals and measures, which may reflect law-making and political alliances that focus some matters and defocus others, this will inevitably create some blind spots, because some issues and problems will not receive much attention. Second, if the leadership decides that the organization does not have the resources to follow up on all of its goals fully, they can either modify their ambitions, or, something that is more common, they have to prioritize certain parts of goals to focus and follow up on (March & Simon, 1958). In doing this, they will defocus certain parts of the goals, certain actors, certain types of expertise, certain policies or issues, and so on, relative to central features of their domain (Thompson, 1967), which can be seen as blind spots. This means that blind spots are primarily the result of conscious actions by the leadership, including lack of knowledge behind the design of organizational structure. Internally, these blind spots are connected not only to the overall design, but also to organizational roles, or the compositions of organizational roles of the single members of the organizations.

Externally, blind spots may result from internal designs that are similar, i.e. different public organizations design their structures in similar and biased ways, so their interactions will systematically leave some aspects, issues, or policies to the side (March, 1981). This may be one explanation for the phenomenon of underlap, which 'refers to situations when a policy issue falls between the remits of different organizations so that no organization feels responsible' (Lægreid, Sarapuu, Rykkja, & Randma-Liiv, 2015, p. 931). Underlap implies that a system of public organizations systematically leaves blind spots because their built-in organizational biases are pretty much the same, for example, defocusing weak clients, women's rights, environmental concerns, economic crises, and so on.

A rather common feature of modern political-administrative systems is that they are structurally complex, meaning that they combine strong vertical and horizontal specialization, often labelled fragmentation, which is rather common for systems inspired by the New Public Management (NPM) reform wave that started in the early 1980s (Christensen & Lægreid, 2001; Pollitt & Bouckaert, 2017). Very serious fragmentation in non-overlapping public organizations, resulting from increased specialization in NPM-inspired reforms, has the potential for blind spots, underlap, and negative coordination, because attention is biased, defocusing actors, problems, and solutions (Scharpf, 1999). Another type of complexity has been inspired by the post-NPM reform wave, which started in the late 1990s, implying more efforts towards centralization and coordination (Christensen & Lægreid, 2007). This potentially creates problems of overlap but also of blind spots, since actors, knowledge, and issues that do not overlap with other organizations (because they often get less resources and attention of competitive reasons) may in fact be blind spots.

Structural hybridity is complexity combined with inconsistency, meaning that a public organization internally or a set of public organizations follow different structural principles at the same time (Christensen & Lægreid, 2011). Vertical specialization and de-specialization can be combined at the same time, like centralization and decentralization, or horizontal specialization and de-specialization. This can give the leadership flexibility (the foxhole syndrome of always having at least two exits), because leaders can please different actors without actually committing to actions, which leaves potential blind spots in the wake of convincing rhetoric. The downside of hybrid reforms and government is potential chaos, uncertainty, and ambiguity, because actors may be confused regarding the definition of problems and solutions, not to mention how decision-making processes should be organized. This latter phenomenon may also leave blind spots, more as a side effect of large challenges of structural design.

Bachrach and Baratz (1970), in their important work on non-decisions, in many ways followed up on the idea of mobilization of bias and in particular offered an insight into how the status quo can be kept in place, which may mean sustaining blind spots. They point to the fact that many traditional theories of politics and administration are about power struggles and 'who gets what, when, how' (Lasswell, 1936). They point, however, to the fact that some issues and considerations are systematically suppressed in some organizations and never reach the surface, meaning politics and policies are restricted, also implying avoiding bringing new issues onto the agenda. This indirect use of power, for example, systematically keeping some actors and issues away from decisions, may be upheld through sanctions. Non-decisions may be a powerful instrument for the leadership to keep dominant structures with built-in biases in place, resulting in systematic blind spots.

A supplementary angle is to use Gulick (1937), who points out that there is a relationship between public goals, choice of structural design, and effects. Deciding on a public goal may lead to choosing specific structures to achieve the wanted effects or results, built on theoretical and practical insights. Not all types of structures can achieve certain goals or policies, so the leadership builds in structural biases in the design of a public organization in order to achieve those goals. In this they have some discretion, since more than one type of structure can achieve a particular goal, a view pretty different from the modern slogan of reform, that 'one size fits all' (Christensen & Lægreid, 2001).

Gulick (1937) proposed four principles of horizontal specialization: purpose, process, clientele, and geography. Each of these principles implies biases or potential blind spots, because certain purposes, types of knowledge, clientele, and geographical areas are organized in, and certain others out. What is not self-evident is what purposes a civil service organization should be structured according to, i.e. this is done according to the decisions of the leadership, and different designs are possible. Process specialization may happen for some professional groups, like economists or lawyers, while others are organized with a heterogeneous expertise basis, which creates expertise biases. Some clientele groups are singled out, often after tug-of-wars, for example, in the health care system, giving them more attention, while others are too weak or have less powerful allies. Or, there are many different ways to organize specialization between government levels or between geographical units at the same level, giving some levels and units more attention than others.

If we look at the relationship between the horizontal specialization principles, there is even more evidence of blind spots (cf. Egeberg, 2012). Organizing primarily according to purpose, which is often the case in civil service, may create blind spots related to both defocusing some sectors or subsectors as well as splitting up expertise (similar expertise in different sectors), client groups (same problems for clients in different sectors), or geographical areas (geographical variety in sector problems). Organizing according to process, for example, gathering certain professional groups in one unit, may create blind spots regarding profession knowledge in decisions but could also cut across purposes, clientele groups, and geographical areas. Or organizing according to certain client groups may create blind spots regarding purpose or expertise. Focus on geographical structures may impose negative side effects on purposes, expertise, and clientele groups.

CULTURALLY GENERATED BLIND SPOTS

Philip Selznick (1957) emphasizes in his seminal book *Leadership in Administration* that public organizations are not easy to design instrumentally because they also develop according to a type of logic other than the instrumental one. Through processes of institutionalization, where a formal organization adapts to internal and external pressures (from the task environment), there are unique informal norms and values developed that add to the formal features. These, often labelled cultures or identities, will differ for every institution, since the mix of internal and external pressures is varied.

Two basic concepts are particularly important in this theory. *Path dependency* means that 'roots determine routes', i.e. there are certain important informal norms and values that are dominant when an organization is established, and these dominate the path further taken (Krasner, 1988). Said more simply, cultural traditions are important. *The logic of appropriateness* overall deals with the importance of cultural constraints, meaning that for actors in an institution to follow the cultural traditions, they have to act appropriately, which may imply different types of logics in different situations. When acting appropriately actors conduct what March

(1994) labels *matching*, meaning that they have to connect identity, situation, and decision rules, posing the overall question of 'what kind of decision rule am I, as an actor, supposed to use in this situation based on the cultural identity of my institution?'

The basic reasoning in this type of theory has, like in structural theory, to do with biases and potential blind spots. The mutual adaptation to internal and external pressures indicates an instrumental element, because Selznick (1957) focuses on the concept of *policy decisions*, which are crucial for the development of uniqueness, different from *routine decisions*. Even though an institutional leader is culturally constrained by the 'necessities of history' (Brunsson & Olsen, 1993), this must mean that a leader can to some degree choose in two regards. First, out of all the actors, their interests, and informal norms and values, reflected in internal discourses, the leader may decide to attend to some but not others, which potentially leaves some blind spots, which, for example, may be related to professional values or tasks being focused. Concerning adaption to external pressure, the leadership has potentially some leeway in choosing some parts of the environment and not others. Selznick (1949) in his book on the Tennessee Valley Authority stresses that co-opting certain critical business interests was a strategic choice with certain implications, leaving blind spots of other actors, norms, and values out of the equation, for example, what we today would label environmental issues related to the development of the Mississippi River. So overall, if one does not believe in complete historical determinism, there will be some leeway for leaders to choose the elements of internal and external pressure, and therefore the unique combination of the two factors, leaving in principle many other combinations behind, potentially representing blind spots.

Another take on this would be to start from the concept of path dependency. The point of departure here is that some informal norms and values are dominant at the birth of a public organization. But what decides that some informal norms and values are selected to lead the way for cultural traditions later on? One can argue that this is either a conscious choice by leaders or a natural selection process (Scott & Davis, 2007). Either way, this also implies that some informal norms and values existing during the formative years would not be brought forward or are at a disadvantage later on, which may represent blind spots. Furthermore, when an institution is starting down the path to the future, what mechanisms are keeping the unique cultural part dominant, despite changing environmental preconditions? Selznick (1957) indicates that the institutional leadership ('statesmanship'), through policy decisions, is continuously and incrementally adjusting the course, both leaving behind blind spots and not choosing some along the path forward.

A third take on this would be to elaborate on the logic of appropriateness and matching. March (1994) says that there are two processes going on. One is a historical development process, alluding to path dependency, that results in some dominant cultural norms and values in an organization, and one is where this process and dominant values are made relevant in decision situations, i.e. the real matching. This reasoning can be elaborated in at least three ways (Christensen & Røvik, 1999). First, it cannot be taken for granted that the historical path will bring forward a homogeneous and consistent cultural identity, because there may exist tensions and subcultures. Second, there is no guarantee that situations are easy to define as a basis for matching, i.e. the leadership and organization members may have different views on this. Third, decision rules may be many and partly ambiguous. According to this elaboration, matching could be rather problematic and not a one-to-one thing, potentially leaving blind spots related both to the historical path and to resulting identities, definition of situation, and choice of decision rules. The more ambiguity and heterogeneity, the potentially greater enhancement of blind spots—or the opposite, the more homogeneity and less ambiguity, the lower the potential for blind spots. This means that leaders may try to limit variety in definitions of situations and identities in order to focus on a narrower set of decision rules, thereby limiting biases.

The topic of cultural compatibility is rather central in the reform literature (Brunsson & Olsen, 1993). The main reasoning is that when a reform wave, like NPM or post-NPM, or single reform efforts are happening, the success of these reforms depends on the compatibility between cultural traditions and the cultural content of the reform proposal (Christensen & Lægreid, 2007). Further, if there is compatibility, reforms will rather easily be decided on and implemented. If there is complete lack of compatibility, conflicts may erupt, and the probability of acceptance and implementation is rather low. The most interesting cases, however, are when the reform is partially compatible, which often means that some elements are accepted while others are pushed back. This may open up much more room for blind spots, partly because some reform elements will be chosen and others not but also because some internal cultural elements will be kept while others will be adjusted or changed. Again, this may be decided by cultural determinism but also through the policy decisions of the leadership. More blind spots might be related to a sharper cultural profile decided by the leadership, or blind spots might be modified by making the profile broader and more encompassing.

A more elaborate version of this cultural interpretation, where rational and cultural thinking are combined, is found in the works of Kathleen Thelen. Streeck and Thelen (2005) make a distinction between the change process, which can be both incremental and abrupt, and the result of the change process, which may be characterized by either continuity or dis-continuity. This permits four possible combinations of process and result, of which one is of special relevance here, i.e. 'breakdown' and replace-ment', which is the concept used for a combination of abrupt change and discontinuity of result. To understand this potential removal of blind spots and continuation on another path, with a lot of continuity, one must understand the mechanisms that are behind the opening of the window and keeping it open for some time so that the new path is established. The mechanisms may be based in policy or reform entrepreneurships but also in the fact that a system has 'come to the end of the road' and is culturally breaking down (Aberbach & Christensen, 2001).

BLIND SPOTS GENERATED BY MYTHS AND REPUTATION MANAGEMENT

According to a myth perspective, public organizations will use myths and symbols systematically to further their goals (Christensen et al., 2007). The leadership will engage in double talk and hypocrisy, meaning that they will talk in one way and act in another (Brunsson, 1989). They hope to achieve higher legitimacy and more support through this, because it gives them more flexibility and it is not that easy for other public actors or citizens in general to make a distinction between talk and action. We may say that talk and action are loosely coupled, alluding to a lot of image building and window dressing going on (Christensen and Gornitzka 2017). This is what Erving Goffman (1990) talks about in his distinction between 'front stage' and 'back stage', where the front stage represents the social construction of reality and the back stage action is in real time (Berger & Luckman, 1967).

Double talk may imply different things. First, it may represent meaning making (March, 1994), i.e. reality is difficult to grasp and there may be different understandings and views. The leadership is therefore important for defining for other internal actors or stakeholders in the environment how one can understand reality, including public problems and solutions.

Second, it can imply a more systematic distortion and exaggeration of reality, i.e. it is claimed that a public organization may achieve goals and act in ways that are highly unlikely to happen. Either way, there will potentially be blind spots. Of the many possible definitions of situations, problems, and solution, only a few will be lifted up for exposure, while many will be left behind, often for few obvious reasons. Eventually, leading people astray will make reality obscure, also leaving a lot of potential blind spots.

A recent and more elaborated strand of literature, related to myths and symbols, deals with reputation management or branding of public organizations (Wæraas & Maor, 2015). Carpenter (2010) defines organizational *reputation* as 'a set of beliefs about an organization's capacities, intentions, history, and mission that are embedded in a network of multiple audiences' (p. 33). Reputation management is when these beliefs, ideas, or symbols are used in a systematic way to appeal to diverse audiences in order to build a reputation. Potential effects of reputation management include achieving more general support, building goodwill and slack in general (Cyert & March, 1963), but also more specific support leading to the provision of more resources (Easton, 1965). The reputation profile could be broad, which may have a bridging effect (Røvik, 2002), but this may also imply lacking sharpness and appeal (Van Riel & Fombrun, 2007). A more specific and narrow profile may have more appeal but may create more internal conflicts (Waeraas & Solbaak, 2009).

Carpenter (2010, pp. 45–46) makes a distinction between four dimensions of reputation of public organizations. First, through the *performative* dimension, various stakeholders get the impression that an organization is delivering instrumentally on outputs and outcomes according to core goals (Chapleo, Durán, & Díaz, 2011). Second, the *moral* dimension deals with whether a public organization is emotionally appealing and follows high standards, i.e. whether it is perceived as 'compassionate, flexible and honest' (Carpenter & Krause, 2012, p. 27). Third, the *technical/professional* dimension focuses on creating an image of a public organization that is scoring high on professional capacity and competence, which is a very crucial aspect of the activities of civil service on different levels (Wæraas & Byrkjeflot, 2012). Fourth, according to the *procedural* dimension, a public organization creates the impression that it follows appropriate procedural and legal requirements in decision-making, which both relates to internal activities and to dealing with users and the public in general. The reputation management studies are in many ways elaborating on the myth perspective, in particular related to Carpenter's (2010) dimensions.

Reputation management implies systematic biases and therefore potential blind spots. The whole point is to focus on some aspects of the activities of a public organization and make them sound fantastic, whether this is done as some kind of reporting on what has been done or whether the reporting is more aspirational, i.e. about what could be done—often an ambiguous distinction to the receivers of image building (Christensen & Lodge, 2016). This is very evident in the case of a narrower profile, where many activities are defocused and as such function as blind spots. Based on Carpenter's (2010) dimensions, an organization's leadership can brag about the performance of its public organization without mentioning the professional, moral, or procedural aspects. Or certain types of activities related to one dimension will be mentioned, but not others. For example, a university bragging about Nobel Prize winners or centres of excellence defocuses all other research activities that could be of good quality. Or universities with the aspiration of scoring high on diversity or having an international orientation may obscure that not much is actually happening in these fields. Even when a public organization choses to further a broad reputation profile, very seldom nuances are possible, meaning that they exaggerate and abstract certain factors of the dimensions while others are not much mentioned, leaving blind spots (Christensen & Lodge, 2016).

EXAMPLES OF BLIND SPOTS

Structurally Generated Blind Spots

One of the most famous studies in public administration is the study by Allison (1971) of the Cuban missile crisis. Two examples of blind spots in this study originate from what we can label local rationality and standard operating procedures (SOPs). It is rather important in an international crisis that the different political-administrative decision-making bodies and actors—not to mention, different parts of the security and military apparatuses—interact and coordinate closely, but that was only partly true in this case. During the Cuban missile crisis, the Central Intelligence Agency (CIA) controlled the flight paths of U-2 spying planes according to earlier experiences and crises. This meant that a lot of areas were geographical blind spots because of structural search biases, while others were well covered. When the crisis started, some members of the CIA came up with the idea that it was necessary to change the flight paths, but this suggestion was not implemented right away because the director of the CIA was on honeymoon. When the director returned and changed the path, the Soviet missiles were detected, and the conflict escalated.

Later on in the crisis, the president decided on a Marine Corps blockade. Again, SOPs dominated and distorted. The leadership of the Marines agreed with the president to establish the blockade close to Cuba in order to have more time to negotiate with the Soviet Union if their ships should sail towards Cuba. In reality, and according to Marines' SOPs, they put the blockade further out, creating a blind spot, again geographically, between the two blockade points (the chosen and the actual) that could have been potentially crucial and dangerous in a climate nearly leading to a third world war.

Culturally Generated Blind Spots

In her seminal work *Imitation and Innovation*, Eleanor Westney (1987) analyses how Japan in the Meiji period (1859–1912) systematically imitated the West, mostly Western Europe, in order to change a number of its public and private organizations. The part of the story fitting into a cultural interpretation is related to the cultural preconditions of imitation. The overall idea was that understanding the cultural context of the countries they imitated would help the Japanese actors to understand the cultural contextual preconditions in their own country. But this was a big challenge in several ways. The delegations sent abroad had not enough expertise to grasp or imagine the cultural context they imitated, partly because their own culture was so different and also partly because of the evolution of and changes within the cultural solutions they imitated. These two factors are connected to blind spots. First, Japan only imitated parts of the underlying culture, for example, professional cultures in European systems such as postal services, police organizations, and newspaper businesses. This meant that they did not culturally grasp the full picture of their imitation, leaving blind spots that could be important. Second, when they returned home to adapt the imitated solutions they had brought to Japanese administrative and business culture, this became challenging and left blind spots because they had received a distorted picture of the cultural context in the West and also faced problems of determining which part of their own culture should be adapted or kept. So they had difficulties adding to the normal challenges of cultural compatibility.

Symbols and Blind Spots

In their article titled 'Information in Organizations as Signal and Symbol', Feldman and March (1981) start from some kind of an economic man point of view regarding information and decisions. Information is a vital part of decisions and is therefore sought through seemingly rational processes to be used to evaluate alternatives and consequences. On the other hand, the authors refer to several studies showing that empirical reality is often far from this idealized picture, i.e. information may relate to symbols. Rather often, enough information has been gathered, but still leaders and stakeholders in the environment ask for more. So information as signal and symbols, as a social construction of reality, trumps the instrumental use of existing information. It is often easier for leaders to ask for more information, because saying that they have enough makes them vulnerable to criticism.

The potential effects of this division between the symbols of information and information efficiency/rationality are diverse. One effect is that making decisions could be overall more difficult because of information overload and rationality challenges, which in reality potentially leave a lot of information at the fringes, i.e. blind spots. Another is that the information that is easy to find and transform to symbols will probably get the most attention, again leaving potential blind spots.

Blind Spots Combining Perspectives

The case discussed here is a slightly modified version of the analysis made by Aberbach and Christensen (2001) of the big NPM reform leap in New Zealand in 1984. The 1970s were economically problematic for New Zealand in many ways. The country's narrow food-oriented export industry experienced problems and had to reorient after the United Kingdom became member of the European Union in 1972; a world recession happened in 1974; oil price shocks occurred in 1973 and 1979; and there was a fiscal deficit and a slow growth rate (Massey, 1995). So New Zealand faced a crisis, and many actors thought that it was time to leave the historical path. But not much happened in the years after Muldoon came into power as prime minister for the National Party in 1975.

So what happened in the shadow of the crisis, and what can be seen as potential blind spots, i.e. the roads so far not taken? The main answer was that economic actors in the treasury and the business community, claiming support from international organizations, worked for years on only one alternative solution: a broad programme of market liberalization and macro-economic disinflation, inspired by the New Right, as an alternative to Keynes, used by the social democrats (Goldfinch, 1997). The problem for this coalition was that they had had for some years a solution but no main political actor connecting it to the central problem of economic crisis (cf. Cohen, March, & Olsen, 1972). This was changed by Roger Douglas, the incoming minister of finance from the Labour Party, who rather surprisingly opened the window to reform after the snap election in 1984, implementing a radical NPM reform agenda (Aberbach & Christensen, 2001). The window was open for a short period of time, and the radical reforms enacted later led to a referendum ending in a new election system, having as a result a more fragmented party system.

So what is the core story of blind spots here, using our three main perspectives? First, the path dependency of the political-administrative system in New Zealand seemed to be very strong up to 1984, leaving a lot of possible alternative paths (blind spots) unused. This was paradoxical under a conservative prime minister and accumulated a lot of potential for change. Second, this potential for change was unleashed by Roger Douglas, with many symbols and a great deal of rhetorical overselling, which used a ready-made economic solution to crash through the window of opportunity that had been opened by a snap election in 1984. The solution chosen was very radical, rather unlikely, and left a lot of alternatives (blind spots) behind. It was made possible by the elective dictatorship system in Anglo-Saxon countries, i.e. the winner takes all. Third, after the radical reforms had been implemented, the empire was striking back, meaning that the actors, interests, and alternative economical solutions left behind (blind spots) managed to get implemented a new election system making such radical reforms less likely in the future because of modifications to the party system and resulting in coalition governments more often (Aberbach & Christensen, 2001).

CONCLUSION

This chapter primarily used three organization theory perspectives to systematically show how blind spots can be connected to general attention biases and their outcomes, but it has also touched upon them as mechanisms (cf. Christensen et al., 2007). As is seen in Table 3.1, according to an instrumental perspective, based on Simon's (1957) bounded rationality,

Table 3.1 Blind spots and organization theory perspectives: arguments and examples

	Arguments	*Examples*
Instrumental perspective	• Organization is the mobilization of bias • Structural design creates attention biases (both intra- and inter-organizational)—both degree and type of specialization • Both structural fragmentation and coordination leave biases • Structural hybridity creates biases • Non-decisions sustain attention biases	Allison (1971) on the Cuban missile crisis: geographical biases resulting from attention biases
Cultural perspective	• Biases related to mutual cultural adaptation • Path dependency leads to attention biases • Logic of appropriateness and matching; homogeneity creates biases • Efforts towards cultural compatibility create systematic biased attention	Westney (1987) on imitation of the West in the Meiji period: lack of cultural sensitivity when imitating and adapting leaves blind spots
Neo-institutional perspective	• Systematic symbolic attention bias and exaggerations create blind spots • Reputation profiles focus some internal aspects and some external stakeholders, which create biases • The balance of different types of reputation symbols leads to attention biases	Feldman and March (1981) on information as sign and symbols: biases related to lack of attention to information already gathered and the complexity of that information when the dominant norm is to ask for more information

blind spots are related to organizational design, both inside and between public organizations, which influences the attention structures of the actors and results in blind spots. As Schattschneider (1960) says, 'organization is the mobilization of bias' (p. 71) because some actors, problems, and solutions are organized in and some are organized out, the latter creating blind spots. Active and conscious design leads to blind spots but also to so-called non-decisions (Bachrach & Baratz, 1970), i.e. conscious efforts preventing actors, definition of problems, and solutions from being connected at all to choice opportunities, keeping them latent (Cohen et al., 1972). Gulick (1937) specifies some of the principles of formal design with his types of specialization and coordination, and these principles and their combination may be seen as mechanisms for creating blind spots. This is further exaggerated in hybrid public structures (Christensen & Lægreid, 2011).

According to a cultural perspective, path dependency means that of the original cultural context in the founding years of an institution, some cultural norms and values are carried further, while others—blind spots—are left behind (Krasner, 1988). The process creating cultural identity, the institutionalization process, is characterized by a mechanism called mutual adjustment, which is not that easy to grasp (Selznick, 1957). It is quite easy to imagine that such a mechanism leaves behind blind spots related to internal informal norms and values and certain cultural norms in the task environment. Another mechanism is the matching of situations, identities, and decision rule that March (1994) emphasizes. But matching implies potential blind spots, because the overall thought is that there is only one right and homogeneous set of these elements, while there are very likely other possible combinations or matches, which fill the function of blind spots (Christensen & Røvik, 1999). A third mechanism, the window-of-opportunity reasoning of Kingdon (1984), may result in questions such as why some windows are open and not the others, or why some actors, problems, and solutions jump through the window but not the others, all of which may be related to potential blind spots.

Lastly, myths and symbols may lead to a systematic bias in the attention of certain public actors, leading to blind spots (cf. Meyer & Rowan, 1977). The emerging reputation management literature is a good example of this (Wæraas & Maor, 2015). A reputation profile in a public organization may be broad and integrative but is also often very selective in what aspects are focused on, leaving many performative, professional, moral, and procedural reputation elements behind, which may function as blind spots.

Finally, in what ways might the structural and institutional biases and blind spots we have discussed be sustained or modified? First, they may be connected to laws and rules that have to be changed. Second, they are related to a power and influence structures, negotiations, and alliances between political and administrative actors, leading to a frozen structure, but these alliances could be renegotiated, which will potentially change the biases and blind spots. Third, leadership could systematically use an incentive system to keep a structure in place but also to change it. Fourth, external conditions, for example, crises or strong pressure, could change, which may have effects on internal structures and external collaboration but also cultural compatibility or reputation profiles. Fifth, history may be redefined, leading to different opinions on path dependency, identity, and matching, which again change dominant informal norms and values. Sixth, reputation profiles could be rebalanced and changed, creating new dynamics related to internal structure and cultures and to stakeholder relations in the environment.

References

Aberbach, J. D., & Christensen, T. (2001). Radical reform in New Zealand: Crisis, windows of opportunities, and rational actors. *Public Administration, 79*(2), 404–422.

Allison, G. T. (1971). *Essence of decision.* Boston: Little, Brown.

Bachrach, P., & Baratz, M. S. (1970). *Power and poverty: Theory and practice.* New York: Oxford University Press.

Berger, P. L., & Luckman, T. (1967). *The social construction of reality.* New York: Doubleday.

Brunsson, N. (1989). *Organization of hypocrisy: Talk, decisions and actions in organizations.* Chichester: Wiley.

Brunsson, N., & Olsen, J. P. (1993). *The reforming organization.* London: Routledge.

Carpenter, D. P. (2010). *Reputation and power: Organizational image and pharmaceutical regulation at the FDA.* Princeton: Princeton University Press.

Carpenter, D. P., & Krause, G. A. (2012). Reputation and public administration. *Public Administration Review, 72*(1), 26–32.

Chapleo, C., Durán, M. V. C., & Díaz, A. C. (2011). Do UK universities communicate their brands effectively through their websites? *Journal of Marketing for Higher Education, 21*(1), 25–46.

Christensen, T., & Gornitzka, Å. (2017). Reputation management in complex environments: A comparative study of university organizations. *Higher Education Policy, 30*(1), 123–140.

Christensen, T., & Lægreid, P. (2001). *New public management: The transformation of ideas and practice.* Farnham: Ashgate.

Christensen, T., & Lægreid, P. (2007). The whole-of-government approach to public sector reform. *Public Administration Review, 67*(6), 1059–1066.

Christensen, T., & Lægreid, P. (2011). Complexity and hybrid public administration: Theoretical and empirical challenges. *Public Organization Review, 11*(4), 407–423.

Christensen, T., Lægreid, P., Roness, P. G., & Røvik, K. A. (2007). *Organization theory and the public sector: Instrument, culture and myth*. London: Routledge.

Christensen, T., & Lodge, M. (2016). Accountability, transparency and societal security. In T. Christensen & P. Lægreid (Eds.), *The Routledge handbook to accountability and welfare state reforms in Europe* (pp. 165–179). London: Routledge.

Christensen, T., & Røvik, K. A. (1999). The ambiguity of appropriateness. In M. Egeberg & P. Lægreid (Eds.), *Organizing political institutions* (pp. 159–180). Oslo: Scandinavian University Press.

Cohen, M. D., March, J. G., & Olsen, J. P. (1972). A garbage can model of organizational choice. *Administrative Science Quarterly, 17*(1), 1–25.

Cyert, R. M., & March, J. G. (1963). *A behavioral theory of the firm*. Englewood Cliffs: Prentice-Hall.

Easton, D. (1965). *A systems analysis of political life*. New York: Wiley.

Egeberg, M. (2012). How bureaucratic structure matters: An organizational perspective. In B. G. Peters & J. Pierre (Eds.), *SAGE handbook of public administration* (pp. 157–167). London: Sage.

Feldman, M. S., & March, J. G. (1981). Information in organizations as signal and symbol. *Administrative Science Quarterly, 26*(2), 171–186.

Goffman, E. (1990). *The presentation of self in everyday life* (Rev. ed.). New York: Doubleday.

Goldfinch, S. (1997). Treasury and public policy formation. In C. Rudd & B. Roper (Eds.), *The political economy of New Zealand*. Auckland: Oxford University Press.

Gulick, L. (1937). Notes on the theory of organization: With special reference to government in the United States. In L. Gulick & L. Urwin (Eds.), *Papers on the science of administration* (pp. 2–45). New York: A. M. Kelley.

Kingdon, J. (1984). *Agendas, alternatives, and public policies*. Boston: Little, Brown.

Krasner, S. D. (1988). Sovereignty: An institutional perspective. *Comparative Political Studies, 21*(1), 66–94.

Lægreid, P., Sarapuu, K., Rykkja, L. H., & Randma-Liiv, T. (2015). New coordination challenges in the welfare state. *Public Management Review, 17*(7), 927–939.

Lasswell, H. D. (1936). *Politics: Who gets what, when, how*. New York: McGraw-Hill.

March, J. G. (1981). Decisions in organizations and theories of choice. In A. H. Van de Ven & W. F. Joyce (Eds.), *Perspectives on organization design and behavior* (pp. 205–244). New York: Wiley.

March, J. G. (1994). *A primer in decision making.* New York: Free Press.

March, J. G., & Simon, H. A. (1958). *Organizations.* New York: Wiley.

Massey, P. (1995). *New Zealand: Market liberalization in a developed economy.* New York: St. Martin's Press.

Meyer, J. W., & Rowan, B. (1977). Institutionalized organizations: Formal structure as myth and ceremony. *American Journal of Sociology, 83*(2), 340–363.

Pollitt, C., & Bouckaert, G. (2017). *Public management reform: A comparative analysis* (4th ed.). Oxford: Oxford University Press.

Røvik, K. A. (2002). The secrets of the winners: Management ideas that flow. In K. Sahlin-Andersson & L. Engwall (Eds.), *The expansion of management knowledge: Carriers, flows and sources* (pp. 113–144). Stanford: Stanford University Press.

Scharpf, F. W. (1999). *Governing in Europe: Effective and democratic?* Oxford: Oxford University Press.

Schattschneider, E. E. (1960). *The semisovereign people.* New York: Holt, Rinehart and Winston.

Scott, W. R., & Davis, G. F. (2007). *Organizations and organizing: Rationale, natural and open systems perspectives* (6th ed.). Upper Saddle River: Pearson Prentice Hall.

Selznick, P. (1949). *TVA and the grass roots.* Berkeley: University of California Press.

Selznick, P. (1957). *Leadership in administration.* New York: Harper & Row.

Simon, H. A. (1957). *Administrative behavior.* New York: Macmillan.

Streeck, W., & Thelen, K. (2005). Institutional change in advanced political economies. In W. Streeck & K. Thelen (Eds.), *Beyond continuity: Institutional change in advanced political economies* (pp. 1–39). Oxford: Oxford University Press.

Thompson, J. (1967). *Organizations in action.* New York: McGraw-Hill.

Van Riel, C. B. M., & Fombrun, C. (2007). *Essentials of corporate communication.* London: Routledge.

Wæraas, A., & Byrkjeflot, H. (2012). Public sector organizations and reputation management: Five problems. *International Public Management Journal, 15*(2), 186–206.

Wæraas, A., & Maor, M. (2015). *Organizational reputation in the public sector.* London: Routledge.

Waeraas, A., & Solbaak, M. N. (2009). Defining the essence of a university: Lessons from higher education branding. *Higher Education, 57*(4), 449–462.

Westney, D. E. (1987). *Imitation and innovation.* Cambridge, MA: Harvard University Press.

PART II

Blind Spots and Attention Bias

Professional Integrity and Leadership in Public Administration

Wolfgang Seibel

An Erroneous Taken-for-Grantedness: Professional Integrity in Public Administration

Citizens and scholars in rule-of-law-based constitutional states—roughly, the OECD world—take professional integrity of civil servants for granted, and rightly so. After all, the backbone of public administration in democracies is well-trained and non-corrupt personnel. It is here that, according to conventional wisdom, Max Weber's principles of pure bureaucracy are still valid and robust. We believe that it is useless to bribe a civil servant in Germany, the United States, Denmark, or France in an attempt to speed up the issuance of one's passport or to have one's son or daughter admitted to a higher education institution. We also, quite realistically, anticipate to be punished for such blunt assaults on a civil servant's integrity.

Yet bribery is by far not the only challenge to professional integrity in public administration. The real life of everyday public administration is characterized by circumstances that require pragmatic rather than strictly

W. Seibel (✉)
Department of Political and Administrative Sciences, University of Konstanz, Konstanz, Germany
e-mail: wolfgang.seibel@uni-konstanz.de

© The Author(s) 2019
T. Bach, K. Wegrich (eds.), *The Blind Spots of Public Bureaucracy and the Politics of Non-Coordination*, Executive Politics and Governance, https://doi.org/10.1007/978-3-319-76672-0_4

71

rule-bound decision-making, regardless of whether the rules are legal or professional in nature (cf. Alford & Hughes, 2008; Hildebrand, 2005, 2008; Miller, 2004; Shields, 2003, 2008; West & Davis, 2011). An entire school of thought in public administration theory is based on the notion of a 'logic of appropriateness' (cf. Olsen, 2008; March & Olsen, 1989, pp. 21–38) shaping the decision-making behaviour of civil servants in a way that highlights pragmatism as a strategy of securing both organizational effectiveness and individual survival in complex organizations, including the various bodies of public administration. However, the very blind spot of both traditional Weberian theory of bureaucracy and post-Weberian theorizing in public administration (cf. Seibel, 2010) is the under-researched problem of distinction. What is the difference between pragmatism for the sake of appropriate flexibility of, for example, 'street-level bureaucrats' (Lipsky, 2010 [1980]) and unacceptable rule bending in terms of neglected or even violated professional and legal standards?

It is not that the problem itself has been entirely ignored in the public administration literature. Two classics by Philip Selznick (1949, 1957) are eye openers whose argumentative thrust is mutually reinforcing. In his seminal book *TVA and the Grassroots* of 1949, Selznick analysed the adaptive behaviour of a huge federal bureaucracy, the Tennessee Valley Authority (TVA), one of the giant new deal institutions exposed to ferocious social and political hostility. In an attempt to mitigate that hostility and to enhance the general acceptance of the authority, TVA leadership decided to co-opt representatives of challenging societal groups such as influential local elites of rural areas. As a result, however, the main purpose of the TVA, which was the industrialization of the Tennessee Valley and the mitigation of racial discrimination, was blunted as well.

Selznick thus revealed an example of counterproductive mechanisms of adaptive behaviour at the expense of the actual purpose of public authorities. What was meant to be a democratic way to reconcile a federal agency with civil society turned out to be a classic case of agency capture by powerful pressure groups, which formed the background of his book on *Leadership in Administration* of 1957. Here, Selznick (1957, see especially pp. 119–133) strongly emphasized the role of leadership when it comes to the protection of professional integrity. Leadership, according to Selznick, requires not just commitment to organizational goals but a deeper understanding of mission, values, and the necessity to defend the integrity of an institution. 'Responsible leadership', Selznick (1957) wrote, 'is a blend of commitment, understanding and determination' (pp. 142–143). Yet, he added another lucid remark: 'The responsible leader recognizes the need for stable relations for the community of which his organization is a part, although he must test the environment to see how real that requirement is' (ibid., p. 147). In other words, stable and productive embeddedness of an administration in its societal and political environment must not affect its original purpose. Herbert Kaufman (1960), in yet another public administration classic (*The Forest Ranger*), analysed the countermechanisms that keep a public agency robust and non-corrupt despite considerable economic and social incentives to deviate from the right path, for example, clear and stable recruitment patterns and a culture of professional pride.

Selznick's (1949, 1957) twofold message was exactly this: public authorities have to mobilize the support of their societal, political, and institutional environment while protecting their professional integrity. This primarily hinges on responsible leadership. Capable leadership in public administration entails the ability to distinguish adaptability from opportunism and to make sure that responsiveness to outside requirements does not undermine professional integrity. As Paul 't Hart (2014) emphasizes, leadership, among other things, is about trustworthiness. Public administration in democratic systems should justify, on a daily basis, their clientele's trust in the unfettered willingness of civil servants to perform their task to the best of their professional ability. It is ultimately through individual civil servants' commitment that the professional standards of a relevant agency and the public interest actually converge (cf. Moore, 1995, pp. 52–56).

Bringing professional integrity to bear thus requires judgement, prioritization, and resolve. Whatever the nature of the actual challenges, responsible leadership for the sake of safeguarding professional integrity requires the leader to recognize challenges in the first place. Recognizing means that a leader is able and willing to make the required factual and value-based judgements (cf. Berlin, 1997). The factual judgement refers to the necessity to recognize the particular nature of a given situation, while value-based judgement requires one to acknowledge that safeguarding professional integrity is actually at stake. The judgement therefore has to entail an intellectual ability of prioritization. After all, professional integrity may compete with pragmatic requirements of the given circumstances. Accordingly, it might be indispensable to prioritize the values on which the very professional integrity is based over secondary values such as demands of the immediate societal, political, and institutional environment of a given authority. This is the point of reference of more recent debates on public values (Bryson, Crosby, & Bloomberg, 2014; Denhardt & Denhardt, 2011; Moore, 2014; Stoker, 2006; West & Davis, 2011; Williams & Shearer, 2011), although the very question of ranks and priority order of values is rather neglected in that strand of literature (cf. Seibel, 2016).

Finally, there is the necessity of resolve and courage. Value-based judgement and prioritization of values for the sake of professional integrity is a necessary but not a sufficient condition of responsible leadership (cf. Bruttel & Fischbacher, 2013). Leaders may know that they should act but do not act anyway. There may be good reasons for inaction. Time and again leaders face the question of whether it is worth the effort depending on the relative importance of an issue, the relative resistance against preferred solutions, and the amount of energy required for the 'right' decision. Moreover, many decisions in public administration are the result of cooperation and negotiation (cf. Benz, 1994). This often implies a logic of package deals in the sense that concessions to a more pragmatic solution at the expense of a principled decision in area A may be made in the hope to achieve a more principled decision in area B. The question remains, however, whether or not leaders in public administration are intellectually capable and psychologically determined enough to identify a critical situation in which the defence of professional integrity is at stake and where resolute and principled action instead of pragmatism is indispensable.

Professional Integrity Between Goal Attainment and System Maintenance

Professional activity takes place in a given institutional environment. However, that environment and the requirements of institutional stability are relatively independent from professional performance, since the requirements of performance and the actual institutional design in which performance takes place usually emerge along different trajectories. The overall institutional design of public administration in a given country emerges in the course of long-term historical developments, many times shaped by compromises between societal groups or organizational traditions, which are largely independent from present-day functional necessities and organizational effectiveness.

Hence there is a latent tension between goal attainment and system maintenance (cf. Deutsch, 1963, pp. 182–199, based on Parsons', 1951, distinction of adaptation, goal attainment, integration, and latency/pattern maintenance). The stability of the institutional environment and related system maintenance and goal attainment in a specific area of civil service are never entirely compatible with each other and, consequently, have to be harmonized by either additional regulation or ad hoc decisions. For example, centralized or decentralized assignments of tasks may turn out to be dysfunctional under particular circumstances. For instance, legal stipulation may allow for an appropriate adjustment of decentralization or, conversely, centralization of administrative competences. Alternatively, the degree of centralization or decentralization may be subject to individual discretion of functional elites or decision-making bodies. Either way, balancing out task-related goal attainment and system maintenance in a given institutional setting requires a sense of professional integrity. Task-related goal attainment is based on performance according to professional standards.

Those standards take various shapes in the broad spectrum of the tasks of public administration. In some areas, they are based on the observance of legal prescription when it comes to strictly rule-of-law-based decision-making. In other areas, however, task-related goal attainment is subject to considerable discretionary leeway and linked to what Bovens (1998, pp. 32–38) termed 'active responsibility': consideration for consequences, responsible use of autonomy, conduct based on a verifiable and consistent code, and commitment to role obligations. Typical examples are physicians in the public health system, forest rangers in the forest administration, construction engineers supervising the construction and maintenance of public infrastructure, chemists in food control agencies, physicists in authorities in charge of nuclear energy safety control, veterinarians in public abattoirs, and pharmacists tasked with licencing of drugs. All these various kinds of civil servants work on the basis of professional standards, to which they are committed and whose integrity they need to defend.

Most of the above-mentioned areas of professional activity in public administration, however, are exposed to frictions between goal attainment and system maintenance, potentially at the detriment of professional integrity. Physicians in the public health service may be urged to speed up the physical examination of their clientele for the sake of saving time and money but at the expense of professional diligence and accuracy. Forest rangers may act under pressure to sell timber to the benefit of the public

Table 4.1   Institutional requirements and logics of action

	Institutional requirements	
	Goal attainment	System maintenance
Logic of action	Performance based on professional integrity	Balancing performance and internal and external support

treasury but to the detriment of woodland sustainability. Similarly, construction engineers in a municipal administration may act under political pressure to neglect costly fire protection requirements. Threats to professional integrity in public administration are ubiquitous. And the above examples illustrate that they may, indeed, result from the requirements of system maintenance. Municipalities need to keep the budget under control, public officials do not like complaints about time-consuming administrative procedures, and hierarchical control may be a necessary complement to professional autonomy anyway. So the guardians of system maintenance and the guardians of goal attainment are acting under different and potentially divergent logics of action (see Table 4.1; cf. Thornton, Ocasio, & Lounsbury, 2012, pp. 128–147, for an overview of the 'institutional logic' perspective and its consequences for 'dynamics and organizational practices and identities'). Reconciling these two logics is the natural task of leadership in public administration.

A typical setting in which the reconciliation of professional integrity and system maintenance has to be managed on a routine basis is multi-level governance (cf. Enderlein, Wälti, & Zürn, 2010). Administrative federalism is a typical case in point. As Benz (2000) pointed out compellingly, joint tasks of administrative layers in a federalist system require smooth cooperation based on deliberation and negotiation—hence the risk of making professional integrity negotiable, one way or the other. Keeping that risk under control is a matter of judgement about the specificity of situational circumstances in terms of professional requirements and potential system stress. System stress may originate from ineffective performance in a specific area of tasks independent from system characteristics or from the quest for better performance requiring system adjustments. In a federalist system, decentralized jurisdiction in a certain area of tasks may cause system stress once it causes visible underperformance. It may also cause stress, however, once the agents of task-specific professionalism ask for system-related adjustments whose implementation requires energy and the mobilization of political capital.

In what follows, a conflict between professional integrity and related adjustments of a task-specific multi-level governance structure in German federalism and its mishandling at the expense of professional performance will be analysed. In terms of case study design and related case selection, it is a 'least likely case' in the sense that smooth adjustment in support of professional performance should have been a matter of routine given the risks and responsibilities at stake. The fact of the matter was literally a question of life and death, and, according to the judgement of those immediately involved, the multi-level governance structure of federalism was clearly an obstacle to effective performance of public administration. Moreover, the system stress caused by low performance should have been easy to anticipate, while system stress caused by the incompatibility of professional requirements and the existing governance structure was easy to avoid as well, since legal provisions for system adjustments were in place. Those provisions should and could have been used according to the standards of professional integrity. What is more, using them was precisely what the professionals were asking for. The fact that despite these favourable circumstances, system adjustment did *not* take place and persistent underperformance was tolerated sheds significant light on basic mechanisms that weaken effective leadership in public administration at the expense of professional integrity in general.

'SYSTEM MAINTENANCE' AT THE EXPENSE OF PROFESSIONAL INTEGRITY: SERIAL KILLINGS OF IMMIGRANTS IN GERMANY AND ABORTIVE ADJUSTMENTS OF FEDERALIST GOVERNANCE

In a period of seven years, between 2000 and 2007, German law enforcement authorities investigated serial killings of immigrant shopkeepers that ultimately turned out to be committed by a right-wing extremist group known as the National Socialist Underground (Nationalsozialistischer Untergrund). When the very root cause of the murders was revealed by mere coincidence in autumn 2011, security agencies were accused of not having performed their investigations with the required diligence and intensity due to their own myopia and xenophobic leanings. While the underperformance as such is undeniable, in-depth analysis of the case reveals (cf. Seibel, 2014) that no such myopia or neglect took place at the operational level of the investigating police authorities. On the contrary, the main criminal investigation unit in the state of Bavaria realized after the first series of five murders that their working hypothesis was disputable and that a more comprehensive and, thus, centralized organization of the criminal investigation was indispensable. These efforts on the part of the local detectives, however, were stifled by their own superiors, who were not willing to put stress on the cooperative relationship with the Federal Criminal Police Office (Bundeskriminalamt, BKA), whose representatives were allegedly not enthusiastic about the idea of assuming responsibility for a criminal investigation that primarily fell under the jurisdiction of police authorities at the state level—quite a typical pattern of the frictions and the necessities of cooperation within a multi-level governance system.

The transfer of competences from the state level to the federal level in German federalism is regulated by law. The relevant legal provision as far as jurisdiction and competences of law enforcement agencies are concerned is the Bundeskriminalamtgesetz (BKAG). Paragraph 4 of BKAG enables both state-level and federal authorities to transfer jurisdiction in individual cases of criminal investigation from the lower (state) level to the upper (federal) level under the condition that 'profound reasons' ('*schwerwiegende Gründe*') make such action advisable. This is a typical example of built-in flexibility within a multi-level system of governance that basically delegates jurisdiction and responsibility to the sub-central level: centralization is possible, but it remains the exception. Deciding whether or not to make use of the exception is a matter of executive judgement. It has to take into account the potential trade-off between performance based on professional integrity versus system maintenance that guarantees separated competences between the central and the sub-central level. The quest for unfettered professional performance may collide with existing institutional arrangements, but the maintenance of those arrangements is what ultimately makes performance possible.

It comes with the nature of federalism as a variant of multi-level governance that the discretionary leeway in use, as far as the rare exception of re-centralization of competences is concerned, is subject to pragmatic reasoning. A crucial and indispensable component of that reasoning is the specific fact of the matter that may require selective centralization. Obviously, criminal investigation into serial killings is a serious matter per se. Yet a diligent assessment of the advantages and disadvantages of a transfer of jurisdiction from the state level to the federal level remains indispensable. In general, lower levels of law enforcement will be inclined to keep the investigation in their own hands, since it is they who are familiar with the intricacies of the case. Upper levels will be reluctant to initiate formal steps of centralization for a double reason: transferring jurisdiction in a criminal investigation to federal authorities may have a frustrating effect on local criminal investigation units, while initiating the unusual step of centralization may be a decision of political significance that, at any rate, requires a decision of the state minister in charge. Accordingly, it is also about using and depleting political capital, which is a scarce resource anyway. Accomplished leaders in public administration are required to soberly calculate whether or not to make use of it in accordance with the stakes involved. Using up political capital for unimportant purposes is as much amateurish as lack of initiative when mobilizing political capital is indispensable for professional purposes.

By early 2004, the series of killings of immigrants in Germany had claimed the lives of five people. Three out of the five murders targeting Turkish immigrants, all of them small shopkeepers, had been committed in Bavaria, with two more committed in the city state of Hamburg and the state of Mecklenburg-Vorpommern. All three state-level police agencies were working on the hypothesis that the murders were connected to a network of organized crime, probably involving failed extortion and related blackmail attempts. All killings had been performed with one and the same weapon, according to the ballistic analyses.

After the fifth murder—of Mehmet Turgut in the city of Rostock on 25 February 2004—the investigating criminal detectives at the regional police authority of Mittelfranken (Polizeipräsidium) in Nürnberg came to the conclusion that, due to the cross-regional scope of the crime series and, accordingly, the necessary human and financial resources as well as technical infrastructure needed for further investigation, the BKA was supposed to assume overall responsibility. This view and the professional assessment on which it was based were shared by the relevant criminal investigation units in Rostock and Hamburg. Based on what became a largely shared conviction, according to which law enforcement authorities had allegedly pursued the criminal investigation with only limited efforts, the relevant police authorities asked for a more effective organization of the investigation, and they did so out of professional ethos.

The transfer of investigation competences to the federal level would not necessarily have prevented the five subsequent murders from happening, but it undoubtedly would have made the investigation efforts more effective. Not only would it have overcome the gap between a single and coherent, and according to all likelihood ongoing, murder series and a fragmented organizational structure of the criminal investigation, but it would also have widened the mental screens of the investigators whose working hypothesis as far as the nature of the serial killings was concerned had so far been focussed on transnational organized crime. According to the usual professional standards, the concentration of the investigation under the auspices of the BKA was indispensable. However, the necessary transfer of competences from the state level to the federal level required measures at the upper ranks of the police apparatus, especially in Bavaria, where the initiative to transfer the investigation competences to the federal level had originated. Moreover, rank-and-file police officers at the BKA, in the course of preparatory discussions with their colleagues from Nürnberg, Hamburg, and Rostock, were not overly enthusiastic about the idea of being burdened with additional workload.[1]

The key figure in the subsequent course of decision-making was the state police commissioner of Bavaria. It was his task to convince the Bavarian interior minister of the necessity of a formal move vis-à-vis the Federal Ministry of the Interior to transfer the competence for the criminal investigation in question from the state level to the federal level and, thus, to the BKA. He was informed by the head of the relevant investigation unit in Nürnberg that BKA officials, at the meeting with their counterparts from Bavaria, Mecklenburg-Vorpommern, and Hamburg, had been reluctant to assume jurisdiction. This implied that the state police commissioner was facing the delicate question of whether or not to move ahead and convince his own superior, the state interior minister in Bavaria, to take the initiative vis-à-vis his federal counterpart, the federal minister of the interior, with the intention to force the BKA to assume responsibility for the criminal investigation in the murder series—against the will of the very BKA officials who were to be made in charge of the investigation itself. This was clearly a matter of both collegiality and political sensitivity. Smooth cooperation based on a common *ésprit de corps* and related considerateness, as well as an appropriate understanding of the limited amount of political capital available for pushing through exceptional decisions within the multi-level governance structure of the federalist system, were presumably part and parcel of the state commissioner's pondering. Inevitably, encouraging the professional integrity of his own law enforcement officials and safeguarding the system of cooperative federalism were at odds with each other.

Sincere and sober minded though the state commissioner of police in Bavaria was, he nonetheless took the wrong decision. He refrained from initiating a formal motion to the federal minister of the interior to transfer jurisdiction over the criminal investigation into the serial killings of immigrants from the state level to the federal level in the form of the BKA. He did so, according to all likelihood, in an attempt to not put strain on Bavaria's relationship with the federal police authorities, in particular the BKA, whose representatives, according to what had been reported to him, were reluctant to assume responsibility for what in their own perception and definition remained a matter of state-level jurisdiction. The commissioner, in his own testimony before the parliamentary investigation committee of the Bundestag, was honest enough to admit that, in retrospect, he had made a mistake (Deutscher Bundestag, 2013, p. 512).

The irony of this sequence of events is that, according to further testimonies before the parliamentary investigation committee of the Bundestag, the commissioner's considerateness was misguided, not only from a professional point of view but also because the perceived reluctance of the BKA to assume the jurisdiction was virtually non-existent. As the then vice president of the BKA affirmed before the investigation committee, the entire initiative of the transfer of jurisdiction had never reached the desk of the actually responsible officials within the BKA. The information forwarded to the state police commissioner of Bavaria had just referred to informal talks between police detectives at the operational level on both sides. And the former vice president of the BKA, when asked by members of the parliamentary investigation committee of the Bundestag, asserted that the BKA would have definitely given its consent to the transfer of jurisdiction under its own auspices if only the upper ranks of the agency had been concerned with the matter (Deutscher Bundestag, 2013, p. 513).

The question remains, however, why the state commissioner of police in Bavaria took the assumed resistance within the BKA against the very transfer of jurisdiction—the implementation of which, in retrospect, the former vice president of the BKA characterized as a matter of course—seriously enough that it made him neglect what was ultimately at stake, namely the lives of future victims of an ongoing murder series. After all, this was the crucial point clearly articulated by his own subordinates. It is here that the misleading interpretation, according to which 'structural racism' was influential in shaping the mindset of law enforcement officials (Deutscher Bundestag, 2013, pp. 988–994), nonetheless reveals some truth, even if not in the original sense. Five more killings were in the offing when the state police commissioner in Bavaria made the decision not to follow the initiative of the investigation unit in Nürnberg to streamline the entire investigation and to make it more effective. There is no evidence at all that the police commissioner was driven by xenophobia or racist feelings. Rather, one may assume that his decision was based on a much more sober political calculation in terms of potential gains and losses. If it would not have been a clearly defined and tiny minority that was likely to fall prey to an ongoing murder series but, instead, a group of future victims whose scale and composition was unpredictable, it would have been almost unthinkable not to mobilize all available energy for making the criminal investigation as effective as possible. That scenario not only would have increased the readiness of an individual state police commissioner to use his own discretionary leeway and limited political capital for a transfer of jurisdiction to the relevant federal agency. It also would have eliminated any reluctance of federal agents to assume responsibility for the investigation into a murder series threatening the lives of future victims of indistinct social or ethnic affiliation.

This implies that the state police commissioner's self-admitted mistake was a matter of mistaken prioritization. His priority was evidently system maintenance in the sense of keeping the operative relationship with the federal counterpart in the form of the BKA smooth and stable. That intention outweighed the necessity to safeguard the professional integrity of his own subordinates in the Bavarian police apparatus. But the case also demonstrates that prioritization of either system maintenance or professional integrity is co-determined by the requirements of political support and legitimacy. This, however, does not alter the fact that the necessity to ascertain whether this kind of co-determination is acceptable or not is a matter of judgement as well. When professional integrity affects the protection of life and limb, its principles are not negotiable. It is here that the police commissioner misjudged what was actually at stake.

LIMITS OF PRAGMATISM: THE RELATIVITY OF PROFESSIONAL INTEGRITY AND ITS NON-NEGOTIABLE CORE

Frictions between professional integrity and system maintenance in public administration are common, and so are the behavioural patterns to deal with them. Leading staff in public administration are usually capable of striking an acceptable balance between professional requirements and the necessity of keeping the system running. For instance, over-performing nerds whose professional integrity is beyond any doubt may put considerable strain on team climate and social cohesion in a sub-unit of any private or public agency. But capable managers will be able to make use of their talents without endangering the stability of a division, let alone an entire firm or agency. Conversely, university presidents may be eager to enhance the resource basis of their institution through expanded international cooperation, but they will not do so at the expenses of academic standards. Federalist systems like the ones in Canada, the United States, Switzerland, Belgium, and Germany maintain strong emphasis on full-fledged autonomy of their respective sub-central territorial units—provinces, states, cantons, regions, and so on—but they leave sufficient discretionary leeway when the professional ethos and standards of, for example, fire fighters or law enforcement officials require selective re-centralization.

Failure to strike the right balance between professional integrity and system maintenance is a failure of leadership. What the above-reported case reveals, however, is that failure of leadership at the expense of professional integrity is not a matter of amateurism as opposed to professionalism, but rather a matter of counterincentives that work to the detriment of just and appropriate pragmatism as far as professional standards and integrity are concerned. The nature of those counterincentives may be subject to further research, but initial hypotheses are possible anyway. For instance, poor leadership in favour of system maintenance but to the detriment of professional integrity is favoured by institutional mechanisms or arrangements that diffuse rather than concentrate responsibility (cf. Hood, 2011). Moreover, counterincentives to the detriment of professional integrity may originate from imbalances between externalization pressures on the part of public administration and externalization resistance on the part of those affected by the action or inaction of public administration professionals as guardians of the specific task at hand. For instance, orphans or seniors in day care institutions or members of ethnic and religious minorities are more vulnerable than the average adult population but less articulate and thus more dependent on state protection. By the same token, however, public authorities are exposed to the moral hazard to neglect protection due to the anticipated weakness of those in need, thus making the affected groups even more vulnerable.

By way of illustration, in the above example, the relevant institutional arrangements were clearly characterized by fragmentation and a diffusion of responsibility in the first place. There was discretionary leeway to mitigate the resulting risk of underperformance against the relevant professional standards. However, the leeway remained unused. The reason was an anticipated conflict between two layers of a federalist system. Avoiding conflict among partners of cooperation in a multi-layer or multi-level governance system is a matter of pragmatism for the sake of system maintenance. But the limits of pragmatism are reached as soon as the quest for system maintenance and stability leads to the suspension of professional integrity, even when non-negotiable values are at stake. And failure to recognize the limits of pragmatism marks a blind spot not only in public administration itself but also in public administration as a scholarly discipline.

NOTES

1. The factual information given here and in the subsequent paragraphs of this chapter is based on Deutscher Bundestag (2013).

REFERENCES

Alford, J., & Hughes, O. (2008). Public value pragmatism as the next phase of public management. *The American Review of Public Administration, 38*(2), 130–148.

Benz, A. (1994). *Kooperative Verwaltung: Funktionen, Voraussetzungen und Folgen.* Baden-Baden: Nomos.

Benz, A. (2000). Two types of multi-level governance: Intergovernmental relations in German and EU regional policy. *Regional & Federal Studies, 10*(3), 21–44.

Berlin, I. (1997). Political judgement. In H. Hardy (Ed.), *The sense of reality: Studies in ideas and their history* (pp. 40–53). New York: Farrar, Straus and Giroux.

Bovens, M. (1998). *The quest for responsibility: Accountability and citizenship in complex organisations.* Cambridge: Cambridge University Press.

Bruttel, L., & Fischbacher, U. (2013). Taking the initiative: What characterizes leaders? *European Economic Review, 64,* 147–168.

Bryson, J. M., Crosby, B. C., & Bloomberg, L. (2014). Public value governance: Moving beyond traditional public administration and the New Public Management. *Public Administration Review, 74*(4), 445–456.

Denhardt, J. V., & Denhardt, R. B. (2011). *The new public service: Serving, not steering* (3rd ed.). Armonk: M. E. Sharpe.

Deutsch, K. W. (1963). *The nerves of government: Models of political communication and control.* New York: The Free Press.

Deutscher Bundestag. (2013). *17. Wahlperiode, Beschlussempfehlung und Bericht des 2. Untersuchungsausschusses nach Artikel 44 des Grundgesetztes* (Drucksache 17/14600, August 22, 2013). Berlin: Deutscher Bundestag.

Enderlein, H., Wälti, S., & Zürn, M. (Eds.). (2010). *Handbook on multi-level governance*. Cheltenham: Edward Elgar.

't Hart, P. (2014). *Understanding public leadership*. Basingstoke: Palgrave Macmillan.

Hildebrand, D. L. (2005). Pragmatism, neopragmatism, and public administration. *Administration & Society, 37*(3), 345–359.

Hildebrand, D. L. (2008). Public administration as pragmatic, democratic, and objective. *Public Administration Review, 68*(2), 222–229.

Hood, C. (2011). *The blame game: Spin, bureaucracy, and self-preservation in government*. Princeton: Princeton University Press.

Kaufman, H. (1960). *The forest ranger: A study in administrative behavior*. Hopkins: Baltimore.

Lipsky, M. (2010 [1980]). *Street-level bureaucracy: Dilemmas of the individual in public services* (30th anniversary expanded ed.). New York: Russell Sage Foundation.

March, J. G., & Olsen, J. P. (1989). *Rediscovering institutions: The organizational basis of politics*. New York: The Free Press.

Miller, H. T. (2004). Why old pragmatism needs an upgrade. *Administration & Society, 36*(2), 243–249.

Moore, M. H. (1995). *Creating public value: Strategic management in government*. Cambridge, MA: Harvard University Press.

Moore, M. H. (2014). Public value accounting: Establishing the philosophical basis. *Public Administration Review, 74*(4), 465–477.

Olsen, J. P. (2008). The logic of appropriateness. In R. E. Goodin, M. Moran, & M. Ren (Eds.), *Oxford handbook of public policy* (pp. 690–704). Oxford: Oxford University Press.

Parsons, T. (1951). *The social system*. New York: The Free Press.

Seibel, W. (2010). Beyond bureaucracy: Public administration as political integrator and non-Weberian thought in Germany. *Public Administration Review, 70*(5), 719–730.

Seibel, W. (2014). Kausale Mechanismen des Behördenversagens: Eine Prozessanalyse des Fahndungsfehlschlags bei der Aufklärung der NSU-Morde. *der moderne staat*, (2014/02), 375–413.

Seibel, W. (2016). Hybridity and responsible leadership in public administration. In G. Abels (Ed.), *Vorsicht Sicherheit! Legitimationsprobleme der Ordnung von Freiheit* (pp. 311–333). Baden-Baden: Nomos.

Selznick, P. (1949). *TVA and the grass roots*. Berkeley: University of California Press.

Selznick, P. (1957). *Leadership in administration*. New York: Harper & Row.

Shields, P. M. (2003). The community of inquiry: Classical pragmatism and public administration. *Administration & Society, 35*(5), 510–538.

Shields, P. M. (2008). Rediscovering the Taproot: Is classical pragmatism the route to renew public administration? *Public Administration Review, 68*(2), 205–221.

Stoker, G. (2006). Public value management: A new narrative for networked governance? *American Review of Public Administration, 36*(1), 41–57.

Thornton, P. H., Ocasio, W., & Lounsbury, M. (2012). *The institutional logics perspective: A new approach to culture, structure and process.* Oxford: Oxford University Press.

West, K., & Davis, P. (2011). What is the public value of government action? Towards a (new) pragmatic approach to values questions in public endeavours. *Public Administration, 89*(2), 226–241.

Williams, I., & Shearer, H. (2011). Appraising public value: Past, present and futures. *Public Administration, 89*(4), 1367–1384.

CHAPTER 5

The Alarms That Were Sent, but Never Received: Attention Bias in a Novel Setting

Helge Renå

Introduction[1]

On 22 July 2011, Norway suffered two disruptive terror attacks (hereafter called '22/7'). At 3:25 pm, a bomb exploded in the government complex in Oslo. Two hours later, a shooting massacre unfolded on the island of Utøya, 40 kilometres northwest of Oslo. In total, 77 people were killed. At approximately 6:36 pm, one perpetrator was arrested at Utøya. We now know he acted alone, but, at the time of arrest, the uncertainty was pervasive: Was he part of a larger operation? Were there other perpetrators on the run or possibly preparing a third attack?

Between 4:43 pm (roughly 80 minutes after the explosion) and 6:50 pm, the police sent three messages via their internal alarm system to Norway's 27 local police districts. All three messages contained information of utmost importance at the time. The first alert included information about a possible getaway car. The second alert reported that border control at the inner Schengen borders had been reintroduced to potentially

H. Renå (✉)
Department of Administration and Organization Theory, University of Bergen, Bergen, Norway
e-mail: helge.rena@uib.no

T. Bach, K. Wegrich (eds.), *The Blind Spots of Public Bureaucracy and the Politics of Non-Coordination*, Executive Politics and Governance, https://doi.org/10.1007/978-3-319-76672-0_5

stop accomplices from fleeing the country. The third alert reported that one perpetrator had been arrested at Utøya. Furthermore, it stated that the perpetrator, upon arrest, had explained there were two more cells in Norway, which had yet to strike. Only six of the 27 police districts registered any of the three alarms during the evening of 22/7 (Norges offentlig utredning [NOU], 2012, pp. 152–153; Politidirektoratet, 2012, p. 13).[2] Why did so few police districts register these alarms?

In brief, the police's alarm system was an email-based system to be used when 'the respective organizational units have information that should be distributed to other organizational units without delay' (internal document, 11 March 2010, Politidirektoratet).[3] Each police district had one freestanding personal computer (PC) with one single purpose only: to receive national alarms. The national alarms would be sent via email by the national special police agency, Kripos, upon request from the National Police Directorate (Politidirektoratet, POD) or one of the police districts.

Around midnight, two police districts contacted Kripos because they had thus far received no national alarm. Kripos sent a test alarm at 12:51 am on 23 July using a different set of email addresses. Fifteen of the total 27 police districts registered the test alarm. Thus, 12 police districts had still not registered any national alarm. The country had been subject to two terrorist attacks of unprecedented scale, the deadliest incident in Norway in the post-war era. Why did only two police districts actively question why they had not received any national alarms?

The aforementioned empirical puzzles form the starting point of this chapter's empirical analysis, which examines the following research question: *Why did the police's internal alarm system not work on 22/7?*

The basic argument is that the alarm system—and more broadly, swift crisis coordination on a national level in the police de facto—was a blind spot until 22/7. The police did not see the importance of a well-functioning alarm system because (i) crisis coordination in the police was traditionally a one-to-one interaction at the local level, (ii) there was no disruptive incident that put swift crisis coordination on the political agenda, and (iii) the political steering of the police was characterized by detailed and biased performance management—biased towards other issues than crisis preparedness. In this context, the decision to have an email-based alarm system was a result of locally rational behaviours (Cyert & March, 1992). The implementation of the alarm system failed due to a passive enactment of a novel and unclear organizational routine in a highly institutionalized setting. In the aftermath of 22/7, the alarm system was subject to more comprehensive scrutiny, and a changed political context resulted in a political request for a new and more advanced alarm system.

This chapter is a case study of a blind spot in a public organization, the police. The study has implications both for the crisis management literature and for practitioners. The study shows the importance of examining crisis responses in their broader social and historical settings. What may, at first glance, seem like operative errors often have more deeply rooted causes. For the practical implications, I discuss some strategies to handle the challenges policy makers face when implementing technical systems and routines for incidents that rarely occur.

Informed by an initial review of existing research on 22/7, I made a timeline outlining the process of developing a national alarm system for Norway from 2004 until 2011. This outline is supplemented by my examination of relevant internal documents and by my interviews with six persons (see Appendix to this chapter) who all had central roles in the process.

The remainder of the chapter is divided in four sections. First, I outline the theories I apply. I follow this outline with a description of the relevant characteristics of the Norwegian police. Then, I map and analyse the process of developing the alarm system, from detecting a need for such a system to finding a technical solution and subsequently implementing it. Finally, I discuss the findings and offer my conclusions.

Stability and Change, Agenda Shifts, and Local Rationalities

Questions of organizational stability and change have been a recurring theme for decades in organizational research (Cohen, March, & Olsen, 1972; Greenwood & Hinings, 1996; Hannan & Freeman, 1983; Kuipers et al., 2014; Lindblom, 1959). This section defines what I, in this chapter, mean by organizational change and outlines under what conditions organizational changes are likely to occur. I focus on attempts to invoke change in public agencies, that is, organizational bodies subject to political control, due to changes in their environments. Moreover, the focus is on stability and change in organizational routines understood as 'repetitive, recognizable patterns of interdependent actions, carried out by multiple actors' (Feldman & Pentland, 2003, p. 95). Thus, the simple introduction of new standard operating procedures, guidelines, or technical systems in an organization is not sufficient to qualify as a change in the organizational routines. The change in the formal structure or technical systems must also manifest itself in new practices. Thus, organizational routines are maintained and changed via the interactions of the organizational members, who interact and communicate in recognizable ways.

The impetus for change in organizational routines can have various origins. Change can, for example, be triggered by external shocks or via initiatives from actors inside or outside the organization (Thelen & Mahoney, 2010).[4] External shocks are of particular importance for this chapter and are related to the notion of risk. The extant crisis management literature has described what researchers see as the 'normalization of risk' problem (LaPorte, 2007; Perrow, 1999; Vaughan, 1996). Organizations tend to see deviations and novelty through the lens of their respective status quo, which in itself is a barrier to change (Lægreid, Christensen, & Rykkja, 2016, p. 25). Furthermore, many attempts to initiate organizational change have little or no significant effect due to barriers within the organization and/or its environment. In the following discussion, I highlight three such barriers, drawing on the literature on organizations as institutions and institutional change, organizational agenda-setting, and decision-making in organizations, respectively.

Organizations may gradually turn into institutions, that is, the formal structures set up by the organization may be infused with values beyond its technical requirements (Selznick, 1957, pp. 16–17). For example, differentiated organizational units develop vested interests and become centres of power 'by creating administrative rituals, symbols and ideologies' (Selznick, 1992, cited in Scott, 2013, p. 146). Over time, and through repeated practices, these interests and values become embedded in the organizational structure. Whether attempts to initiate organizational change are likely to succeed hinges on 'the mobilization of bias' (Schattschneider, 1960, p. 71), the dominant values and myths, and the established political procedures and rules of the game (Bachrach & Baratz, 1962, p. 952).

Thelen and colleagues (Streeck & Thelen, 2005; Thelen & Mahoney, 2010) put emphasis on the characteristics of the organization that are subject to change and its political context, respectively. What is central within the organization is the level of discretion the organization has, to enforce and interpret new routines. A high level of discretion yields more room for enforcing new routines, while the inverse reduces the likelihood of organizational changes. In a political context, the question is what veto possibilities political actors have, that is, to what extent they have the ability to block change (Thelen & Mahoney, 2010, pp. 18–19). Thus, if the political actors have many veto possibilities, they have many opportunities to stop any change initiatives in conflict with their interests and goals.

Paraphrasing the agenda-setting literature, the argument is that change in organizational routines is difficult because it hinges on three independent 'streams' coinciding in a 'window of opportunity': heightened attention to the problem (problem stream), an available and feasible solution (policy stream), and the motive to select a solution (politics stream) (Kingdon, 2003). An important point is that attention is a limited resource (Cohen et al., 1972), and decision-makers are affected by the dynamics of 'attention shifting' (Baumgartner & Jones, 1993). This is especially evident in politics. External shocks like crises heighten attention to specific problems but do not always result in actual changes in policies and practices (Kettl, 2007). If change in a public agency hinges on approval from its superior political body, the public agency has to provide a feasible solution before the attention of the politicians has shifted to other issues.

The structural characteristics of organizations can be a barrier to organizational change because they result in boundedly rational decision-making processes, akin to how cognitive characteristics constrain individual decision-making (cf. also introductory chapter by Bach and Wegrich in this volume). Moreover, the division of work in sub-units can result in biased searches and sub-optimal behaviour (Cyert & March, 1992). Most organizations, including the police, solve complex, interrelated problems by delegation and specialization. The complex problems are divided into sub-problems, which are delegated to specialized sub-units. These sub-units develop their own distinct sub-goals, which result in local rationalities. Their problem searches and attention will be biased towards issues enabling them to achieve their sub-goals most efficiently (Cyert & March, 1992, pp. 164–176).

These theoretical perspectives are used to analyse and explain why the alarm system remained a blind spot until 22/7. Research on organizations as institutions and the agenda-setting literature form important foundations for the next section on the characteristics of the police and their environment. The notion of 'local rationalities' helps explain the subsequent section, where I analyse the process of developing and implementing a new alarm system. In the discussion, I explain how the institutional characteristics and agenda shifts functioned as barriers for change and how the overall process, despite its tragic outcome on 22/7, can be seen as a result of decisions that were locally rational.

THE POLICE ORGANIZATION AND ITS ENVIRONMENT

In the following section, I outline the characteristics of the police organization as an institution and the environment in which the police operates. These factors are relevant because they can enable or can work as barriers for change.

Structural Stability

The vertical specialization of the Norwegian police is characterized by *continuity*. Since 1936 and throughout the twentieth century, the Ministry of Justice (MoJ) has governed at the national level. The local level was organized into 54 police districts until 2002, when that number was reduced to 27. Local commissioners govern in the police districts. The creation of the POD in 2001 marked a major shift in the vertical specialization of the police. The overarching aim was to strengthen the central governing capacity of the police. The white paper outlining the goals of the new POD summarized its primary tasks in 14 points. Recurring themes were strategic steering, governing, and coordination. One of the 14 points pertained to crisis management-related tasks: 'POD shall further develop the police operative crisis management apparatus at the central level' (Ministry of Justice, 1999, pp. 83–84). Thus, the POD was expected to take a lead role in developing the operative crisis management apparatus further, but this was only one of many tasks the POD was expected to take on.

Decentralized Police

There has been bipartisan consensus that the police should be decentralized, aim for union and uniformity (not be split up into many specialized organizations), have a civilian approach, and focus on prevention and community policing (NOU, 1981, pp. 73–86). The parliament has, on several occasions, explicitly and unanimously stated that these principles are still considered basic principles, most recently in 2015 (e.g. Standing Committee on Justice, 2006, 2015).

The emphasis on decentralization has institutionalized the Norwegian police as characterized by highly autonomous police districts where the commissioner has the final say in most police matters. All interviewees I talked to emphasized this point; the norm is that commissioners govern 'within their own turf'. Thus, the specialization within the police has historically been based on a geographic principle (Gulick, 1937), that is, a unitary police organization, organized in many local police districts, each capable of handling all police matters within their own police district (NOU, 1981; Standing Committee on Justice, 2005). An advantage of horizontal specialization based on geography, in countries with a heterogeneous topography like Norway, is that it enables the organization to adapt to local and regional differences. At the same time, there is the risk of too much local adaptation resulting in a fragmented police organization, which struggles to collaborate across police district borders. Local adaptation bias may also hinder the establishment of uniform codes of conduct and communication on relevant issues—for example, dissemination of salient information in a state of emergency. These are 'inherent weaknesses' of geographical specialization, as outlined in Bach and Wegrich's introductory chapter to this volume.

Peaceful Environment

In general, Norway has historically been subject to few terror incidents. Between 1970 and 22/7, the Global Terrorism Database registered only 15 incidents in Norway that could be classified as terrorist attacks (including ambiguous cases). Only 7 out of the 15 incidents resulted in casualties, and only 2 resulted in more than one casualty. None of these incidents put police crisis preparedness capacity through a tough test. Consequently, none of these incidents can be classified as external shocks triggering increased attention amongst stakeholders on the issue of crisis preparedness capacity in the police. More generally, the Norwegian police rarely deal with crimes in which firearms are involved. To illustrate, from 2002 to 2013 there were 31 incidents in which the Norwegian police used firearms (Politidirektoratet, 2014). This yields an annual average of 2.6 incidents in which the police used firearms. Thus, historically, the preparedness of the police for response to major, violent action has rarely been put to the test. Despite relatively peaceful domestic relations, politically motivated terror attacks were a real concern in the 1970s and 1980s due to numerous incidents on the European continent. This resulted in the establishment of a national anti-terror police unit, the Delta force (*Beredskapstroppen*), in 1976, which enhanced the crisis preparedness capacity in the police at the local level. Despite being a national police unit, the establishment of the Delta force did not entail substantial changes in the vertical specialization of the police. This was because the Delta force was organized as a sub-unit in the Oslo police district. If a local police district needed assistance from the Delta force, they sent a request to the Oslo police district. Thus, collaboration during crisis remained largely on the local level.

Crisis Preparedness Not a Political Priority

The political context within which the police operate, and the role of the MoJ more specifically, is of importance because their political and budgetary decisions trickle down through the police, influencing their culture, structure, and priorities (Vaughan, 2005, pp. 65–66).

Performance management instruments in general and annual performance contracts (*Tildelingsbrev*) in particular gained prominence in the Norwegian public sector during the 1990s. With their annual performance contracts, ministries signal what tasks and activities subordinate agencies should prioritize and how the delegated finances should be spent. Askim, Bjurstrøm, and Kjærvik (2017, p. 9) describe this system as characterized by quasi-contracting operated on a vertical approach, based on a foundation of authority. Several case studies have demonstrated the high importance of annual performance contracts in steering relations between Norwegian ministries and agencies (Eltun, 2013; Fremstad, 2013; Helle, 2016; Kaasin, 2016). The annual performance contracts from the MoJ to the POD have been among the most detailed, in terms of number of performance goals, compared to other ministries (Askim et al., 2017). Issues that are not among the list of objectives are less likely to be prioritized (Wathne, 2015).

The detailed annual performance contracts from the MoJ to the POD in the 2000s were biased against crime prevention and the prosecution processes. The performance contracts in general consist of primary goals, sub-goals, and output and activity indicators. During 2004–11, the number of primary goals set by the MoJ varied between four and six (see Table 5.1).[5] Although included as one of six primary goals from 2006 onwards, societal safety represents on average only 6 per cent of the output and activity indicators in the time period 2006–11. Prior to 2006, societal safety was not among the primary goals.

Table 5.1 Distribution of output and activity indicators in annual performance contracts, 2004–11

Year	Total number of primary goals	... of which on societal safety	Total number of output/ activity indicators	... of which on societal safety
2004	4	0	86	0
2005	4	0	63	0
2006	6	1	71	10
2007	6	1	81	3
2008	6	1	82	3
2009	6	1	84	4
2010	6	1	77	0
2011	5	1	61	8

A reasonable interpretation is that societal safety was not high on the agenda in the MoJ. In 2014, three years after 22/7, an audit of the MoJ criticized the structure of the annual performance contract and articulated fears that a possible effect was that work related to crisis preparedness and crisis capacity would be given low priority (Helsetilsynet, 2014).

According to the former national police commissioner (2001–11), the POD was given much professional leeway by the MoJ at the outset in 2001. This changed from 2003 onwards. The actual delegation diminished due to active political steering and control 'from the side' (Njåstad, 2017), reducing the discretion and independence of the police director. This curtailed discretion included prioritizing between different measures and disposal of their budgetary resources (Killengren, 2012, p. 12). An evaluation in 2004 concluded, inter alia, that the MoJ should strive 'to give the POD more leeway and better coordinate its own requests to the POD' and for 'less detailed steering of the police organization within the police professional area' (Bakli & Botheim, 2004, p. 7). An economic analysis reiterated in a newspaper article in 2016 showed that the majority of financial resources in the police organization are, in practice, not disposable for the POD or the commissioners in the police districts, because many of the finances are fixed on specific issues the government wants to prioritize (Inderhaug & Trædal, 2016). The police organization was subject to detailed and biased political steering and operated in a peaceful environment, and the police districts have traditionally been largely autonomous on police matters within their own districts.

An Internal Alarm System: From Identified Need to Viable Solution

In the following, I give a descriptive analysis of the police's internal alarm system, from the first identified need up until 22/7. First, I describe the characteristics of crisis coordination in the early 2000s. Second, I map the origin of the idea for establishing an internal alarm system; then, the process of selecting an appropriate solution; and, finally, the implementation of the selected option.

Crisis Coordination in the Police in the Early 2000s

The expectation that the local police districts handle all police matters, including extraordinary incidents, was still the norm in the early 2000s (Politidirektoratet, 2007, p. 11). Crisis coordination has traditionally taken the form of a one-to-one interaction at the local level. Any affected police district called adjacent police districts when it needed more police officers and called the Oslo police district, where the national anti-terror police are located, when it needed more specialized competence. The national level was, thus, rarely involved in actual crisis coordination, that is, coordinating resources involved in ongoing police operations on the ground.

At the same time, the police's general guidelines from 2007 listed a number of tasks for the POD in extraordinary incidents: give general orders to the local level, assist local commissioners, ensure that personnel and material resources are available, collect information from the local level, coordinate with national directorates from other sectors, write status reports to the MoJ, coordinate between affected commissioners, and, when needed, appoint one commissioner to be responsible for coordination at the local level (Politidirektoratet, 2007, p. 16).

In the case of an extraordinary incident, the affected police district was expected to alert the POD via its hotline, which was operated 24 hours a day. However, after office hours, incoming calls on the hotline were forwarded to the cell phone of one police officer in the POD, who was allotted a two-hour response time. This meant, in case of emergency, the officer on duty had to be at the headquarters of the POD within two hours after receiving the alert. In practice, this meant the POD did not have the capacity to play a central role in the initial phase of a crisis.

Moreover, there had been a low frequency of crisis incidents in general, and especially of incidents that pushed the capacity of existing crisis coordination practices to its outer limits. Thus, real-life incidents gave the police few opportunities to practise and develop their crisis coordination practices across police districts. Neither did practice exercises, because they were organized within the respective police districts. What was exercised instead was coordination inside police districts. In 2007, the POD started organizing an annual crisis exercise, which included the local, regional, and national levels. However, this annual exercise also took place in one police district. Thus, vertical coordination was exercised, but not horizontal coordination across police districts.

A Need for a Swift Alarm System

In April 2004, a NOKAS cash depot in Norway's third largest metropolitan area was robbed by a group of gunmen armed with bulletproof vests, helmets, and automatic weapons. The gunmen undertook extensive means to delay a police response, including blocking the car exit at the police local headquarters with a burning lorry, placing smoke bombs in front of the building, and spreading spikes across the road to burst the tires of police vehicles. When police arrived at the NOKAS cash depot, shots were exchanged, and one police officer was shot dead. The brutality of the bank robbers was unprecedented in the Norwegian context.

In the police's own evaluation report of the incident, the evaluators argued that, when larger incidents occur, the police 'need a swift and secure way to alert other police districts, as well as other collaborating actors nationally and internationally' (evaluation report of the NOKAS incident, cited in Sønderland, 2012, p. 11). Thus, the NOKAS robbery led to the first call for an alarm system in the police. To what extent police leaders and officers shared the assessment of the evaluators is unsure. Although the NOKAS robbery shocked the nation, it was one isolated incident.

In Search of an Appropriate Technical Solution

In the process of finding and selecting a technical solution for a national alarm system, three different police agencies were central: the POD, the Police ICT Services (*Politiets IKT-tjenester*, PIT), and Kripos. The primary task of PIT is development and maintenance of the ICT (information and communications technology)-based information systems in the police, and PIT has functioned as the technical experts for ICT-related issues. Kripos is a national, specialized police agency with international police collaboration (Europol, Interpol, etc.), including receiving and distributing international alarms, as one of its primary tasks. The POD led the process, while PIT and Kripos had designated tasks. Within the POD, the task of leading the process was delegated to the Crisis Management Unit (Politiberedskap). The Crisis Management Unit was on the lowest level in the organizational hierarchy. It was one of five administrative units subordinated within the Department of Police Operations (Avdeling for politifag), which was one of the five departments subordinated under the national police commissioner (Bakli & Botheim, 2004, p. 11).

The POD followed up the evaluation report from the NOKAS robbery by ordering PIT to, in collaboration with Kripos, develop a suggestion of 'how an efficient electronic alarm system can be developed *within current technological structure* in the police ... by June 1, 2005' (Politidirektoratet, 2012, p. 11, author's emphasis). One year overdue, PIT submitted their suggestion of a technical solution to the POD (Sønderland, 2012, p. 42).[6] PIT's solution would have cost several million Norwegian kroner (interviewee 3, 13 June 2017) and thus conflicted with the criterion 'within current technological structure', as set by the POD. The Crisis Management Unit in the POD informed the top management about the cost of the suggested solution; the reply was clear—the POD had no money available to invest in an alarm system (interviewee 2, 4 October 2016; interviewee 3, 13 June 2017). The reason was twofold, according to top management. The POD had, in practice, little economic leeway, due to the general goals and conditions set by the MoJ in its annual performance contracts to the POD. Moreover, what resources the POD had at its own disposal had already been spent on upgrading the general ICT infrastructure (interviewee 1, December 2016; see also Killengren, 2012).

In March 2008, nearly two years after PIT had submitted its suggested solution, a new meeting on the issue was held. The POD did not take an active lead role in the process this time (interviewee 6, 2 November 2017). The temporary pause of nearly two years is itself a clear indication that the issue was not a top priority in the POD. In the meeting, the POD asked PIT to come up with an updated alternative (NOU, 2012, p. 148). PIT developed a new alternative by August 2009 based on the existing police operative log system. Interviewees working in the POD at the time allude to uncertainties regarding cost and regarding how safe and solid the system was, as well as constraints on its functionality (interviewee 3, 13 June 2017; interviewee 4, 8 June 2017). The POD chose instead to develop a solution based on its Microsoft Outlook email system. This solution also had limited functionality and was not considered a safe and solid system by the experts in PIT (see below). The interviewees from the POD say this solution was chosen because the expenses were modest, and it was important to find a system that could be quickly implemented (interviewee 2, 4 October 2016; interviewee 3, 13 June 2017; interviewee 4, 8 June 2017). Thus, their reasoning was not based on functionality and quality but on cost- and time-efficiency. The latter is a paradox, considering they pondered the suggested solution for such a long time.

In November of that same year, PIT coincidentally became aware that the POD had chosen the 'Outlook alternative'; this happened without any formal involvement of PIT (interviewee 6, 2 November 2017). Upon becoming aware of this, PIT wrote a letter to the POD saying it would implement the system because it had been ordered to do so by the POD. However, PIT also wrote that it discouraged the POD's decision because the solution lacked redundancy, there was no guarantee messages would reach recipient(s) within an appropriate time, and the solution did not force the users to give the received alarm attention or confirm that they had received it (Sønderland, 2012, p. 42; interviewee 6, 2 November 2017).[7]

Implementing the Chosen Solution

Once the POD had decided on a plan, it was time to implement the system. In March 2010, the POD sent out a circular (*rundskriv*) to the police districts with guidelines on how the alarm system worked (internal document, 11 March 2010, Politidirektoratet). Circulars are supposed to be followed by the police districts but, in this case, the substance of the guidelines was vague on several points. The guidelines prescribed some information on what an alarm message should contain but were less clear on what recipients should do when receiving an alarm message. Moreover, the circular said nothing about who was responsible for the testing, controlling, and maintenance of the system—and nothing about the role and responsibility of the POD. These shortfalls could leave the impression that the POD did not have an explicit strategy on what role it would take.

In a subsequent letter sent in July, the POD ordered the police districts and national special agencies, 'to write a local guideline on operating the system, outlining, inter alia...procedures on testing the system'; furthermore, the POD emphasized that all police districts were expected to have installed PCs dedicated to the alarm system by 15 September 2010 (internal document, 6 July 2010, Politidirektoratet).

Thus, it seems that the POD addressed what tasks and roles the respective organizational entities in the police should have in various settings but left a void regarding its own role and responsibilities. The POD was not an integral part of either operating or maintaining the alarm system. Kripos was given the responsibility to test the system, while PIT dealt with technical issues. What role the POD had was less clear. An interviewee from Kripos said they missed an explicit, overall strategy on the alarm system (interviewee 5, 26 June 2017). The POD's own internal evaluation of 22/7 found that their interviewees' '...overview of the technical status of the alarm system was limited'; they had 'different views on whether the guidelines for alarm messages were sufficiently elaborate'; and they differed on whether 'the POD's lack of a role and responsibilities in relation to the execution of alarms are appropriate' (Politidirektoratet, 2012, p. 13). This leaves an impression of a disintegrated POD with no clear idea on what role it had regarding the maintenance of the alarm system and whether it would have an operative role in the case of a national alarm.

Although the POD ordered the police districts to have implemented the alarm system locally by mid-September 2010, this did not happen. As I will elaborate in the next section, the experiences with the alarm system in the subsequent months indicate that the police districts were slow to follow the orders given by the POD.

Limited Follow-up by the Police Districts

Upon a post office robbery on 23 December 2010, the Oslo police district issued a request to Kripos to send an alarm to relevant police districts. Kripos distributed an alarm via the email-based alarm system to 18 police districts and national special agencies. The email requested that the recipient(s) confirm they had received it. Six out of the 18 police districts and special agencies never confirmed they had received the email. Among those who confirmed, the response time varied from 5 minutes to 24 hours (Kripos, 2011).

In January 2010, a Kripos employee informed the POD about the incident via an email sent to an employee at the POD. The Kripos employee wrote that he sent the email to this employee 'because I do not know who in the POD is dealing with issues related to the electronic alarm system' (internal email, 6 January 2011). Kripos never received any response from the POD to this email (Kripos, 2011, p. 14). This could be construed as another indication the alarm system was not a top priority in the POD. Neither did Kripos make any efforts to follow up the initial email.

Due to the experienced limitations with the alarm system, Kripos ran a test of the system on 9 June 2011. The results were far from satisfactory. Among those police districts that responded,[8] the response time varied between one minute and three months. Moreover, very few responded in a way that enabled Kripos to identify on behalf of which police district they were responding. In many instances, several police officers responded from the same police district (Kripos, 2011, p. 14). The only back-up system Kripos had available was to send group messages via telefax (Sønderland, 2012, p. 45).

The few documented experiences with the alarm system, after it was established in 2010, clearly indicate that the pre-existing patterns of horizontal coordination between the police districts remained largely unchanged up until 22/7. Few responded swiftly when national alarms were sent, and even fewer responded in a way that was identifiable to Kripos. The implementation of the alarm system had, thus far, not manifested itself in a new organizational routine. This pattern persisted despite the fact that the POD had already, in June 2010, ordered the police districts to set up alarm PCs. However, the POD did not follow up its written order actively. According to one of the interviewees at the POD, the issue was raised orally on several occasions in the regular meetings between the leaders of the POD and the police districts, respectively, in fall/winter 2010 and spring 2011 (interviewee 3, 13 June 2017). Another interviewee from the POD, who visited several police districts and their operation centres in this time period, said that the police districts showed little interest in this issue. Sometimes, he even found the PCs designated for the alarm system stored away in drawers and cupboards (interviewee 4, 8 June 2017; see also Helsingeng, 2011).

LOCAL RATIONALITIES, AGENDA SHIFTS, AND BIASED ATTENTION

The NOKAS bank robbery in 2004 was an external shock triggering a call for a swift and secure way to alert the police districts and other collaborating actors. Although the problem was put on the agenda, it did not lead to a 'window of opportunity' (Kingdon, 2003). Firstly, the problem came onto the agenda primarily *inside* the police, not on the *political* agenda. While the police initiated an internal evaluation, there were no public inquiries or external analyses initiated by the government or the parliament. Secondly, there was no ready solution available, thus the solution stream was absent. Four years passed before the POD decided on a technical solution. In the meantime, no external shocks with a magnitude akin to the NOKAS incident occurred. Thus, awareness of the risks and vulnerabilities made apparent by the NOKAS incident gradually faded, and attention shifted to other issues considered more present and urgent.

The decision to have an internal alarm system based on email came as a result of locally rational decisions (Cyert & March, 1992). While the total cost of the system was a key concern for the POD, a well-functioning system was the primary concern for PIT. The POD leadership delegated the project management to its Crisis Management Unit, an administrative unit positioned on the lowest hierarchical level in the POD. Moreover, this unit had few employees in the early 2000s. One interviewee working in the unit at the time points to a discrepancy between the staffing (2 to 3 employees, of a total of 120 POD employees) and a growing task portfolio (interviewee 3, 13 June 2017). Thus, the task to lead the alarm system project came amidst a number of other pressing tasks. This may explain the lack of active steering from the POD and why the process of finding a solution took time. In the first phase, PIT spent one year longer than the initial deadline set by the POD to suggest a technical solution. Subsequently, almost two years passed before the POD followed up on the process, indicating that the issue was not a top priority to them. The POD had overall economic responsibility for the police organization and were the ones who would be held accountable by the MoJ if it exceeded its budget. Thus, the POD's focus on low costs was rational. Moreover, the chosen system did work upon the introduction of a more comprehensive test regime after 22/7 (see below). PIT, on the other hand, had maintaining and developing well-functioning ICT systems as its primary goal; thus, it was rational for PIT to give primacy to functionality rather than cost-efficiency.

There is also reason to believe the problem of finding an appropriate technical solution was related to a more general problem for the police: modernizing their ICT infrastructure. In 2010, two evaluations expressed harsh critiques of both the POD and PIT and their efforts to modernize the police's ICT infrastructure in the preceding years. The evaluations claimed that the POD and PIT lacked control and overview, that the governing of the projects was poor, and that the POD lacked the requisite competence on the subject matter to function as an effective project leader (Helsingeng & Sæther, 2010).

Implementing the alarm system was evidently not a prioritized issue in the police districts, while the POD was reluctant to use coercive power towards the police districts. Prior to 22/7, the police districts had never experienced a strong need for such an alarm system, perhaps with the exception of the NOKAS bank robbery. Such a need remained a blind spot until 22/7. Thus, when the POD distributed guidelines and information about the new alarm system, the police districts had scant experiences to draw from which could function as 'historical analogies' (Brändström, Bynander, & 't Hart, 2004). The lack of follow-up by the police districts can also be perceived as an illustration of the power balance between the POD and the local police districts and how the POD exerted its role. The POD ordered the police districts to implement the alarm system but never controlled whether the alarm system was actually tested (Bergsaker & Melgård, 2011). In this sense, the implementation was characterized by weak enforcement. This lack of enforcement must be seen in relation to how the POD generally functioned. A decentralized police organization with autonomous police districts was a value institutionalized over years as part of the police's organizational structure, and this system had unanimous bipartisan support. Two evaluations of the POD, conducted in 2005 and 2013, concluded that the POD struggled to find its role in the hierarchy, that it had few steering instruments, and that it was reluctant to use the ones it had (Bakli & Botheim, 2004; Direktoratet for forvaltning og IKT, 2013).

After 22/7, the alarm system in the police was instantly subject to much attention. First, the external inquiry commission appointed by the government, the 22 July Commission, revealed that the perpetrator could possibly have been stopped on his way to Utøya *if* the police had had a more well-functioning internal alarm system (NOU, 2012). Thus, the need for a well-functioning alarm system was no longer unclear. Second, the increased attention made the existing alarm system subject to comprehensive scrutiny. Kripos conducted monthly tests of the alarm system, and the results were reported to the POD. Soon after, all police districts responded within a few minutes during the tests (interviewee 3, 13 June 2017; interviewee 5, 26 June 2017). This demonstrates that the email-based alarm system the police had chosen could have worked better *if* the police districts had been better at following-up on the orders they were given, *if* the POD and Kripos had taken the initial warning signals more seriously, and *if* the POD had been more persistent towards the police districts. Third, crisis preparedness was now the primary concern of 'everyone': the media, the parliament, the government and the MoJ, and the police. Only months after 22/7, a parliamentary inquiry committee asked the minister of justice what she had done to ensure that the alarm system would work more efficiently in the event of a new terrorist attack (Politidirektoratet, 2011). From being an internal issue in the police, the alarm system had now transformed into being a politically prioritized issue. Political pressure on the issue persisted. In 2012, the minister of justice decided a new alarm system was needed, and a new alarm system was implemented by POD in 2013.

CONCLUSION

In retrospect, the police's choice of an internal alarm system based on email seems baffling, as does the fact that it took four years to come to implement even this limited solution. Furthermore, the implementation process was characterized by an unclear role structure, and active steering was absent. The consequence was that pre-existing patterns of horizontal coordination between the police districts remained largely unchanged until 22/7 in 2011. Swift alerts and communication to all police districts via an alarm system existed in theory, not in practice—it was a blind spot. I have argued that the decision to have an alarm system based on email was a result of decisions that were locally rational. The call for an alarm system, triggered by a brutal bank robbery in 2004, gradually lost attention. New disruptive incidents did not occur, and the detailed steering exerted by the MoJ was targeted at issues other than crisis preparedness.

This analysis illustrates the challenge of implementing technical systems and organizational routines designed for incidents which rarely occur. One practical implication, which can be drawn from the analysis, is the importance of clarifying to all future users of a new routine (or system) why it is relevant and important and, subsequently, of implementing it in a way that ensures frequent testing and practising. Finally, the analysis illustrates the importance of examining crisis responses in their broader social, and historical, settings. What may, at first glance, seem like operative errors often have more deeply rooted causes. The police districts' failures to register the national alarms distributed on 22/7 were not primarily a result of operative or technical error. Rather, and more fundamentally, they were a

result of a flawed implementation process. If we as researchers and evaluators are unable to detect the underlying causes of flawed crisis responses, it
is just a matter of time before the detected 'operative errors' will reappear
(Vaughan, 2006).

Appendix

List of Interviewees

1. Ingelin Killengreen, former national police commissioner, POD
   (2000–11). Correspondence with author (email and telephone) in
   December 2016.
2. Vidar Refvik, assistant director, POD (2005–17). Interviewed by
   the author on 4 October 2016.
3. Oddbjørn Mjølhus, commissioner, later chief inspector; leader of
   the Crisis Management Unit in the POD (2001–12). Retired in
   2015. Interviewed by the author on 13 June 2017.
4. Martin Strand, senior police officer, POD (2010–11). Had implementing the alarm system as one of his main tasks. Interviewed by
   the author on 8 June 2017.
5. Hans-Peder Torgersen, police inspector, employed with Kripos
   since 1992. Worked from 1996 to 2005 in the department operating the alarm system. Interviewed by the author on 26 June 2017.
6. Mats Berg, senior advisor, working in PIT since 2002. From 2005
   onwards, was involved in the processes related to developing new
   technical solutions for an alarm system. Interviewed by the author
   on 2 November 2017.

Notes

1. For comments on earlier drafts, I am grateful to Per Lægreid, the editors,
   the participants at a workshop for this edited volume, and at a seminar at
   the Norwegian Institute for Social Research respectively.
2. An Official Norwegian Report (Norsk offentlig utredning, NOU) is a report
   written by an ad hoc advisory commission appointed by the national government or one of the ministries. The 22 July Commission report was written by an independent commission appointed by the government to
   investigate 22/7 (see NOU, 2012).

3. All citations from references in Norwegian have been translated to English by the author.
4. Subtle change is outside the scope of this chapter and is thus not further discussed (see Feldman & Pentland, 2003, for an elaboration).
5. The performance contracts for the period 2001–03 are excluded because their format is less elaborate. The operationalization draws on Askim and colleagues' large-N studies of annual performance contracts (Askim, 2015; Askim et al., 2017). The numbers have also been validated by cross-checking with an existing study on political control and steering in police (Fremstad, 2013). I thank Askim, Bjurstrøm, and Fremstad for giving me access to their data.
6. In the aftermath of 22/7, the national police commissioner set up an internal committee to evaluate the police response, called the Sønderland committee after the name of the leader of the committee (see Sønderland, 2012). In addition, the respective police districts, agencies, and the POD conducted their own internal evaluations of their own response. When referring to these reports, I use the name of the police agency (e.g. Kripos, 2011).
7. There are some parallels between PIT's response, which signal both professional autonomy and loyalty, and the chapter in this volume by Wolfgang Seibel on the tension between the 'logic of professional integrity' and the 'logic of system maintenance'.
8. The data source does not say anything about the total number of police districts that did and did not respond respectively.

References

Askim, J. (2015). The role of performance management in the steering of executive agencies: Layered, imbedded, or disjointed? *Public Performance & Management Review, 38*(3), 365–394.

Askim, J., Bjurstrøm, K. H., & Kjærvik, J. (2017). *Quasi-contractual ministerial steering of state agencies: Its intensity, modes and association with agency characteristics* (Working paper, March 2017). Department of Political Science, University of Oslo, Oslo.

Bachrach, P., & Baratz, M. S. (1962). Two faces of power. *American Political Science Review, 56*(4), 947–952.

Bakli, O., & Botheim, I. (2004). *Nytt direktorat – Nye roller* (Rapport 2004:3). Oslo: Statskonsult.

Baumgartner, F., & Jones, B. D. (1993). *Agendas and instability in American politics.* Chicago: University of Chicago Press.

Bergsaker, T., & Melgård, M. (2011, December 28). Riksalarm ble aldri testet før 22. juli. *Dagbladet.* Retrieved from http://www.dagbladet.no/a/63457437

Brändström, A., Bynander, F., & 't Hart, P. (2004). Governing by looking back: Historical analogies and crisis management. *Public Administration, 82*(1), 191–210.

Cohen, M. D., March, J. G., & Olsen, J. P. (1972). A garbage can model of organizational choice. *Administrative Science Quarterly, 17*(1), 1–25.

Cyert, R. M., & March, J. G. (1992). *A behavioral theory of the firm* (2nd ed.). Malden, MA: Blackwell.

Direktoratet for forvaltning og IKT. (2013). *Evaluering av Politidirektoratet* (Rapport 2013:3). Oslo: Direktoratet for forvaltning og IKT.

Eltun, R. (2013). *Mål- og resultatstyring av Norges forskningsråd 2004–2012.* Master's thesis, University of Oslo, Oslo.

Feldman, M. S., & Pentland, B. T. (2003). Reconceptualizing organizational routines as a source of flexibility and change. *Administrative Science Quarterly, 48*(1), 94–118.

Fremstad, E. H. (2013). *En målstyrt etat i en regelstyrt verden? En studie av styringspraksisen i politi- og lensmannsetaten.* Master's thesis, University of Oslo, Oslo.

Greenwood, R., & Hinings, C. R. (1996). Understanding radical organizational change: Bringing together the old and the new institutionalism. *Academy of Management Review, 21*(4), 1022–1054.

Gulick, L. (1937). Notes on the theory of organization: With special reference to government in the United States. In L. Gulick & L. Urwin (Eds.), *Papers on the science of administration* (pp. 2–45). New York: A. M. Kelley.

Hannan, M. T., & Freeman, J. (1983). Structural inertia and organizational change. *American Sociological Review, 49*(2), 149–164.

Helle, P. K. N. (2016). *Etatsstyring med flere prinsipaler: En studie av styringen av fylkesmannen.* Master's thesis, University of Oslo, Oslo.

Helsetilsynet. (2014). *Rapport fra tilsyn med samfunnssikkerhets- og beredskapsarbeidet i Justis- og beredskapsdepartementet.* Oslo: Statens Helsetilsyn.

Helsingeng, T. (2011, November 17). Flere politidistrikt mottok aldri Riksalarmen. *Verdens Gang.* Retrieved from http://www.vg.no/nyheter/innenriks/22-juli/artikkel.php?artid=10031521

Helsingeng, T., & Sæther, A. S. (2010, October 12). Mangler kontroll: Her er den hemmelige rapporten. *Verdens Gang,* p. 4.

Inderhaug, E., & Trædal, T. (2016, August 16). Derfor har politidistriktene dårlig råd. *Politiforum.* Retrieved from http://www.politiforum.no/no/nyheter/2016/august/Derfor+har+politidistriktene+d%C3%A5rlig+r%C3%85d.d25-T2JDU38.ips

Kaasin, H. (2016). *Etatsstyringen av Innovasjon Norge 2011–2015: Omlegging til koordinert styring mot alle odss?* Master's thesis, University of Oslo, Oslo.

Kettl, D. F. (2007). *System under stress: Homeland security and American politics* (2nd ed.). Washington, DC: CQ.

Killengren, I. (2012, May 30). Interview given to the 22 July Commission. Oslo: National Archives of Norway.

Kingdon, J. W. (2003). *Agendas, alternatives, and public policies* (2nd ed.). New York: Longman.

Kripos. (2011). *Kripos' evaluering 22. juli 2011.* Retrieved from https://www.politiet.no/aktuelt-tall-og-fakta/tall-og-fakta/22.-juli-evalueringsrapport/

Kuipers, B. S., Higgs, M., Kickert, W., Tummers, L., Grandia, J., & Van Der Voet, J. (2014). The management of change in public organizations: A literature review. *Public Administration, 92*(1), 1–20.

Lægreid, P., Christensen, T., & Rykkja, L. H. (2016). Ambiguities of accountability and attention: Analyzing the failure of a preventive security project. *Scandinavian Journal of Public Administration, 20*(1), 21–44.

LaPorte, T. R. (2007). Critical infrastructure in the face of a predatory future: Preparing for untoward surprise. *Journal of Contingencies and Crisis Management, 15*(1), 60–64.

Lindblom, C. E. (1959). The science of 'muddling through'. *Public Administration Review, 19*(2), 79–88.

Ministry of Justice. (1999). *Ot.prp. nr. 7 (1999–2000): Om lov om endringer i politiloven.* Oslo: Ministry of Justice.

Njåstad, M. (2017). *Mål- og resultatstyring av politiet. En studie av Justis- og beredskapsdepartementet sin mål- og resultatstyring av Politidirektoratet i perioden 2004–2016.* Master's thesis, University of Oslo, Oslo.

Norges offentlig utredning (NOU). (1981). *Politiets rolle i samfunnet. Delutredning I* (No. 1981:35). Oslo: Justis- og politidepartementet.

Norges offentlig utredning (NOU). (2012). *Rapport fra 22. juli-kommisjonen* (No. 2012:14). Oslo: Departementenes servicesenter.

Perrow, C. (1999). *Normal accidents: Living with high-risk technologies.* Princeton: Princeton University Press.

Politidirektoratet. (2007). *PBS I: Politiets Beredskapssystem Del I, Retningslinjer for politiets beredskap* (Politidirektoratet 2007/04). Oslo: Politidirektoratet.

Politidirektoratet. (2011). *Vedrørende spørsmål fra Stortingets 22. juli komité.* Oslo: Politidirektoratet.

Politidirektoratet. (2012). *Evaluering av Politidirektoratets håndtering av hendelsene 22. juli.* Retrieved from https://www.politiet.no/aktuelt-tall-og-fakta/tall-og-fakta/22.-juli-evalueringsrapport/

Politidirektoratet. (2014). *Politiets trussel om bruk av skytevåpen eller bruk av skytevåpen 2002–2014.* Oslo: Politidirektoratet.

Schattschneider, E. E. (1960). *The semisovereign people: A realist's view of democracy in America.* New York: Holt, Rinehart and Winston.

Scott, W. R. (2013). *Institutions and organizations: Ideas, interests, and identities* (4th ed.). Thousand Oaks: Sage.

Selznick, P. (1957). *Leadership in administration: A sociological interpretation.* New York: Harper & Row.

Sønderland, O. (2012). *22. juli 2011: Evaluering av politiets innsats* (POD-publikasjon 2012/03). Oslo: Politidirektoratet.

Standing Committee on Justice. (2006). *Innstilling fra justiskomiteen om politiets rolle og oppgaver* (Innst. S. nr. 145 (2005–2006)). Oslo: Standing Committee on Justice.

Standing Committee on Justice. (2015). *Innstilling fra justiskomiteen om endringer I politiloven* (Innst. 306 S (2014–2015)). Oslo: Standing Committee on Justice.

Streeck, W., & Thelen, K. A. (Eds.). (2005). *Beyond continuity: Institutional change in advanced political economies.* Oxford: Oxford University Press.

Thelen, K. A., & Mahoney, J. (2010). *Explaining institutional change: Ambiguity, agency, and power.* Cambridge: Cambridge University Press.

Vaughan, D. (1996). *The Challenger launch decision: Risky technology, culture, and deviance at NASA.* Chicago: University of Chicago Press.

Vaughan, D. (2005). Organizational rituals of risk and error. In B. Hutter & M. Power (Eds.), *Organizational encounters with risk* (pp. 33–66). Cambridge: Cambridge University Press.

Vaughan, D. (2006). The social shaping of commission reports. *Sociological Forum, 21*(2), 291–307.

Wathne, C. T. (2015). *Som å bli fremmed i eget hus: Politiets opplevelse av mening og motivasjon i nye styringssystemer.* Doctoral thesis, University of Oslo, Department of Criminology and Sociology of Law, Oslo.

PART III

Bureaucratic Politics: Reputation, Blame, and Turf

Why Cooperation Between Agencies is (Sometimes) Possible: Turf Protection as Enabler of Regulatory Cooperation in the European Union

Eva Heims

INTRODUCTION

Cooperation and coordination between organizations is usually regarded as one of the core problems in bureaucracies. It has been described as one of the central limits of administration (Hood, 1976) and one of the most persistent problems public administrations face (Peters, 2015; Wilson, 2000 [1989]). In many ways, it is hardly surprising that cooperation in bureaucracies is prone to failure. After all, bureaucratic organizations usually have other work to get on with, and cooperation is unlikely to be at the top of their to-do lists. Like any organization, bureaucratic organizations have limited resources, not only in financial terms. They have limited time, staff, and expertise, as a result of which they need to take decisions about which part of their work to prioritize and which problems to pay

E. Heims (✉)
Department of Politics, University of York, York, UK
e-mail: eva.heims@york.ac.uk

© The Author(s) 2019
T. Bach, K. Wegrich (eds.), *The Blind Spots of Public Bureaucracy and the Politics of Non-Coordination*, Executive Politics and Governance, https://doi.org/10.1007/978-3-319-76672-0_6

most attention to. In short, any organization focuses its attention selectively. In this context, bureaucratic organizations can be expected to focus their attention on their core mission and key tasks (Wilson, 2000 [1989]). Cooperation activities compete with activities directed at fulfilling an organization's core mission (Bardach, 1998, p. 168). Failures to cooperate productively are hence often a result of deliberative selective attention that is focused on an organization's core mission at the expense of peripheral tasks.

This insight has two crucial implications that are too often overlooked in public administration scholarship and that this chapter highlights. First, the relationship between mission focus, selective attention, and cooperation implies that organizations are usually not good at cooperating because they think this would distract them from carrying out their missions to the best of their abilities. Usually, we want organizations to be focused on their missions, so blaming them for being zealous, selfish turf protectors if they fail to cooperate with other agencies is often misplaced. In other words, cooperation is indeed often flawed in bureaucracies, but for good reason. Second, the inherent mission focus and selective attention of bureaucratic organizations have a logical flip side that is too often ignored by scholars of bureaucracy: if organizations are not good at cooperating because cooperation is often a peripheral task, they should be more enthusiastic about cooperation if it helps them in carrying out their core mission. Put differently, the turf protection behaviour of agencies renders non-cooperation into a ubiquitous but not an inevitable weak spot of bureaucracies.

This chapter sheds light on these two overlooked dynamics by developing a typology of the four different cooperation outcomes resulting from the turf-driven bureaucratic behaviour. Whether we can expect productive cooperation between bureaucratic actors or not depends on the degree of mission overlap between them and the extent to which cooperation provides each of the participating organizations with additional resources that are useful in fulfilling their core mission ('mission-related resource complementarity'). This typology also highlights that there are latent opportunities for cooperation where organizations have mission-related resource complementarity without being aware of this due to low mission overlap. The chapter hence contributes to our knowledge about the variety of cooperation outcomes of intentional organizational behaviour that is driven by agencies' tendency to chiefly focus in their core mission.

To demonstrate the value of this theoretical construct, the chapter applies the two most crucial dynamics (destructive turf protection and productive cooperation) to bureaucratic agencies in the multi-level framework of the European Union (EU). This is a particularly interesting area for application because agencies in the EU and in its member states often have particularly high levels of mission overlap, which, in theory, should increase the likelihood of turf fights between them. The chapter presents two such cases, maritime safety and food control agencies, in order to demonstrate that mission overlap is only half of the story: the respective absence and presence of mission-related resource complementarity in the two cases help us to understand why turf protection dynamics occur among maritime safety authorities but not between food control authorities.

Overall, the chapter emphasizes that non-coordination and cooperation are too easily blamed on a simple lack of willingness to cooperate and even maliciousness on part of bureaucratic organizations. The perspective advanced here highlights that organizations have perfectly good reasons to focus on their core mission, and in many ways, they do exactly what is expected of them by doing so. In other words, non-cooperation can be an effect of rational organizational behaviour, as already highlighted in the introductory chapter by Bach and Wegrich. At the same time, rational organizational behaviour can also result in productive cooperation. This means that turf-driven behaviour results in a politics of (non-)cooperation with a variety of different cooperation outcomes, ranging from turf fights to latent opportunities for productive cooperation.

Coordination and Cooperation as Peripheral Task

For any public agency that is formally or informally required to cooperate with other agencies, cooperation is a peripheral task. Their core tasks focus on solving particular problems, providing particular expertise, or providing particular services. Organizational theory and scholarship on bureaucracies give us good reason to believe that organizations focus their energies on performing their core task to the best of their abilities (Wilson, 2000 [1989]). Doing so allows them to be recognized at being good at their jobs, which gives them a certain level of wriggle from political interference (Carpenter, 2001, 2010). It also helps them to ensure their organizational survival in the long run. Their core mission is hence fundamentally linked to their distinctive identity and their 'distinctive competence' (Selznick, 1957).

Often, cooperation with other agencies will not contribute to fulfilment of a public organization's core mission. As a result, a given public agency does not pay attention to cooperation activities, not because of 'malicious' turf protection but because doing its job well means focusing on its core mission. At the same time, a focus on its core mission helps the agency to guard its turf by building a reputation of doing its job well. Turf in this regard is usually regarded as a particular 'domain of problems, opportunities, and actions over which an agency exercises legitimate authority' (Bardach, 1998, p. 164). This type of dynamic is often seen as typical bureaucratic behaviour, as if obstruction to cooperation is an innate trait of bureaucracies. This means that an agency's focus on its mission is often equated with obstructive behaviour and selfish turf protection. Turf-driven behaviour that focuses an organization's behaviour on particular aspects of its work at the expense of others is hence usually interpreted as motivated by the malicious intentions of bureaucratic organizations.

I argue instead that a lack of cooperation due to the rational institutional interest to focus on an organization's core mission needs to be recognized as normal, and even desirable, behaviour. If public agencies were not focused on the fulfilment of their core missions and on maintaining their reputation in order to have autonomy to do so, they would usually not be able to fulfil the public objectives they have been entrusted with. While some students of bureaucracy have clearly recognized that turf protection can have beneficial social consequences (Bardach, 1998, p. 194), the selfish dimension of turf protection weighs more heavily in the public imagination of bureaucracies. However, if public agencies were enthusiastic about engaging in activities that do not directly support them in their core functions, they would not be doing their job at all. Organizations may protect their turf in order to protect their agencies' missions precisely because of wanting to act in the public interest (Bardach, 1998, p. 165; Peters, 2015, p. 10). They are also likely to think that they are the only organization that is able to protect the public interest in their specific field of action. While this may be a very skewed and partial vision of how to safeguard the public interest, focusing on a core mission can hardly be regarded as selfish organizational behaviour, per se. In this context, various motivations are likely to blend into and reinforce each other, and organizations are likely to regard the protection of the public interest as being dependent on their organization's survival. In other words, yes, the politics of non-coordination and non-cooperation is an inherent element of public bureaucracies, but this is not the case because they are innately prone to obstruct cooperation. Rather, this is the case because they are innately prone to want to fulfil their public mission, and they may fear that cooperation with other organizations will undermine these efforts (Bardach, 1998, p. 167). Cooperation and coordination are also liable to upset established routines, which can be costly and is hence avoided if possible (cf. Pierson, 2000).

Even less recognized than the potentially virtuous rationale for turf protection is the flip side of this argument: if everything that bureaucratic authorities do is determined by what they regard to be their core missions, they should want to engage in cooperation with other organizations if this is helpful in this respect. In such cases, then, we may expect agencies to engage in cooperation with partner authorities with much greater enthusiasm. This means that even in a mission-centred view of organizations, non-cooperation is not an inherent outcome of bureaucratic behaviour. This flip side of destructive turf protection dynamics is too often overlooked. In this scenario, organizations do not engage in cooperation in order to absorb other organizations in 'imperialist' fashion (cf. Bardach, 1998, p. 34), but cooperation is used to maintain and expand turf through better performance of an organization's core mission as a result of the additional resources gained by cooperating.

This means that it is crucial to be able to identify whether cooperation activities help an organization in carrying out its core mission or not. The chapter suggests that whether or not cooperation helps a public agency to perform its core mission depends on two crucial dimensions: the degree of overlap between the organizations' core missions and the degree of mission-related resource complementarity for carrying out this task between Organization A and Organization B (the conceptualization of these two dimensions is further elaborated). On the one hand, this shows that deliberate forms of selective attention relating to turf protection can foster as well as impede cooperation. It also shows that cooperation in some areas could be mutually useful for organizations, which, however, will not recognize this if their core tasks do not clearly relate to each other (see Fig. 6.1).

Mission Overlap

In order to conceptualize whether cooperation helps an agency to achieve its core mission, we need to identify whether there is a high or low degree of mission overlap between agencies. In other words, we need to know to

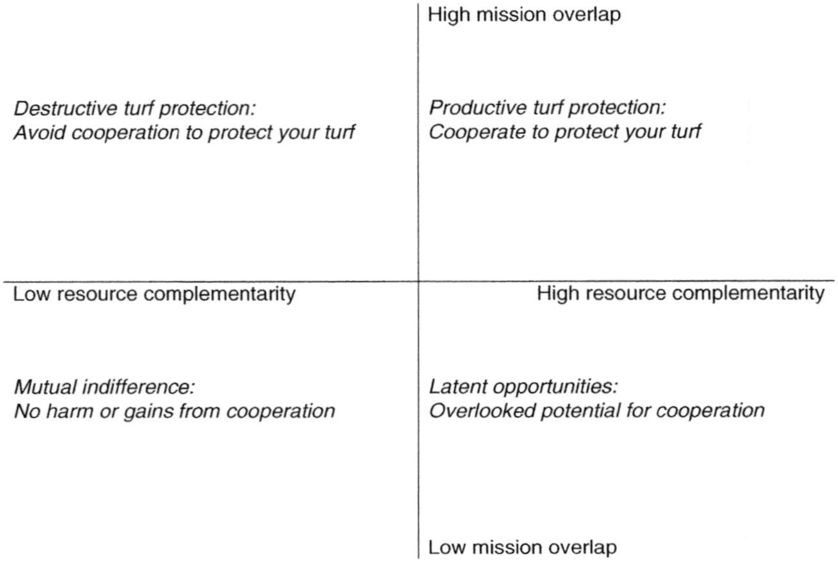

High mission overlap

Destructive turf protection: *Avoid cooperation to protect your turf*	*Productive turf protection:* *Cooperate to protect your turf*

Low resource complementarity   High resource complementarity

Mutual indifference: *No harm or gains from cooperation*	*Latent opportunities:* *Overlooked potential for cooperation*

Low mission overlap

Fig. 6.1 Four cooperation outcomes of the politics of (non-)cooperation

what extent two (or more) agencies carry out similar types of work and have similar interpretations of their core missions (Lerner, 1986). For example, agencies in different countries or at different levels of government with the task to authorize medicinal products to the market have a high degree of task overlap and are likely to have a similar conception of their core mission. So do agencies that issue trademarks or scientific risk assessments in a specific field. Overlaps as conceptualized here also exist where tasks are not identical but highly related. For example, in the multi-level context of the EU, national agencies are usually in charge of inspecting regulated businesses. EU bodies, in turn, are in charge of inspecting the national inspectors. Tasks clearly overlap in relation to using inspections as a regulatory tool to approximate regulated businesses' and national regulators' practices.

Bureaucratic politics scholarship has been prone to see task overlap as a trigger of destructive turf protection dynamics (Bardach, 1996, 1998; Peters, 2015, p. 17; Wilson, 2000 [1989], p. 188ff.): there is no clearer sign that another organization is infringing on your turf than if that organization is effectively doing the same thing as you. Mission overlap has all the hallmarks of turning a potential partner organization into a rival that needs to be fought in order to ensure one's own organizational maintenance and survival. This chapter posits that mission overlap is not the whole story when it comes to turf protection dynamics and the politics of (non-)cooperation. The chapter puts forward that two (or more) organizations are likely to recognize the potential of productive cooperation if their tasks overlap and if they are able to give each other something that they value in relation to carrying out their mission: mission-related resource complementarity.

Mission-Related Resource Complementarity

The theoretical underpinning of this chapter puts forward that organizations mainly care about fulfilling their core mission. A key factor determining their ability to do so is the resources they possess. Resources include financial income but crucially also relate to other key factors that enable organizations to fulfil their missions. I argue here that they also include boots on the ground, expertise, information and data, de facto authority, and reputation. While some of these factors are clearly 'hard' resources, 'softer' factors (such as reputation) are also key organizational resources that are cultivated as a means to carry out core missions (Busuioc, 2016; Carpenter, 2001; Etienne, 2015; Maor, 2010). What is key for our purposes here is that the resources in question are directly relevant for carrying out an organization's core mission. If they are not, organizations are much less likely to value to them. For example, a regulator with a core mission of keeping consumers of medicines safe and a core task of scientific risk assessments may value expertise and specific forms of data but may not value a large number of staff trained for on-site inspections in pharmaceutical companies as much. This captures Wilson's (2000 [1989]) core idea that organizations do not try to grow at any cost and will try to avoid taking on new tasks that distract them from their core mission.

Elements of this notion are captured in theories of inter-organizational cooperation grounded in resource dependence theory (see also Fink and Ruffing in this volume). This perspective highlights that agencies are willing to cooperate if their resource bases depend on each other (Alexander, 1995; Oliver, 1990). The perspective also highlights that cooperation in this regard may bring resources other than money, such as social legitimacy. However, the perspective advanced here argues that the focus on resource dependence alone is too narrow: complementary resources need to be directly relevant to the organization's core mission, and overlap of core missions across organizations is also crucial in order to understand cooperation dynamics.

Combining mission overlap with the resource complementarity dimension provides us with four possible cooperation dynamics. A high degree of mission overlap combined with a lack of mission-related resource complementarity results in destructive turf protection dynamics. Mission overlap combined with a presence of mission-enhancing resources, however, offers potential for productive cooperation. Absence of mission overlap and resource complementarity results neither in turf fights nor in cooperation. Instead Organization A and Organization B are likely to be mutually indifferent to one another. The combination of a lack of mission overlap and a presence of mission-related resource complementarity provides potential for fruitful cooperation between agencies, which, however, is unlikely to materialize if Organizations A and B are unaware or uninterested in one another due to a lack of mission overlap. These four conceptualizations of cooperation dynamics are further elaborated upon below.

Destructive Turf Protection Dynamics

'Turf protection' relates to the guarding of relatively undisputed jurisdiction over specific tasks and ways of carrying them out (Wilson, 2000 [1989], p. 183). In other words, trying to protect your bureaucratic turf is about protecting your mandates and your autonomy to fulfil these mandates (ibid.). This dynamic is arguably the archetype (as well as stereotype) of 'obstructive' organizational behaviour that prevents effective cooperation between agencies. Often turf fights are seen as direct consequence of mission overlap, which result in an organization's tendency to 'fight' (or at least to obstruct cooperation with) organizations sharing an organizational mission with them. The conceptualization of mission overlap presented here, however, is sensitive to the extent to which organizations have overlapping missions *and* mission-related resource complementarity. Turf fights are much more likely in cases in which organizations have overlapping core missions and cannot gain resources they value from cooperating with organizations with the same (or very similar) tasks. Only in these cases do organizations have a clear rationale not to cooperate: a partner organization with very similar (or identical) tasks but no promising resources has nothing to offer its counterpart by way of achieving its organizational missions. This means this organization has the potential to replace the other organization or at least to undermine its resources, reputation, and hence organizational maintenance. As a result, organizations are likely to obstruct cooperation and to undermine each other where possible. This is a consequence of rational, normal—and largely welcome—organizational behaviour. It is thus important to recognize those destructive cooperation dynamics as one possible outcome of the politics of non-cooperation in order to provide incentives for effective cooperation (further discussed in the last section of this chapter). This is bound to be a far more fruitful avenue than declaring bureaucracies to be inherently obstructive for pursuing the mission that was given to them.

Productive Turf Protection Dynamics

The theoretical framework advanced in this chapter highlights that mission overlap does not necessarily result in turf protection dynamics and a lack of cooperation. Rather, as highlighted earlier in the text, we need to be sensitive to the combination of mission overlap and mission-related resource complementarity. If agencies have identical or similar tasks but cooperation provides them with access to resources that are helpful in pursuing the organization's core mission, we can expect to observe productive cooperation. If cooperation with Organization B will give Organization A access to, for example, types of data Organization A cannot otherwise get a hold of, Organization A has a clear incentive to cooperate with Organization B, even if this organization has a similar mission. This is the case because cooperation will enhance the ability of Organization A to pursue its mission successfully, which is a form of turf protection in itself. To follow this theoretical thinking, we need to go back to the theory of organizational behaviour that focuses on mission: in this thinking, safeguarding and pursuing your mission is the clearest form of turf protection. This means effective cooperation is not impossible even in cases of mission overlap. Too often the risk of turf protection dynamics in case of mission overlap is overstated in scholarship and public discourse. Some scholars of bureaucratic cooperation explicitly recognize this possibility (Busuioc, 2016; Peters, 2015, p. 34). However, there is a dearth of empirical examples of this, and existing scholarship does not highlight the relationship between mission overlap and resource complementarity. This chapter remedies this theoretical shortfall and provides empirical examples for such instances of mission overlap and cooperation (see next section).

Latent Opportunities: Overlooked Potential for Effective Cooperation

There are two further dynamics resulting from different combinations of mission overlap and mission-related resource complementarity. One of these is situations in which Organizations A and B do not have similar tasks but where cooperation could provide both organizations with resources that they need to pursue their core missions. In these instances, the selective organizational attention paid to core missions is likely to result in a lack of cooperation if neither organization recognizes this potential. In short, Organizations A and B may not cooperate even though this could be beneficial to them (and to the public interest) because neither of them is aware of the resources they can offer each other. Once again, this needs to be seen as a by-product of rational, and, ultimately quite sensible, organizational behaviour: time and other resources are limited, as a result of which neither organization can afford to scan the horizon for such latent opportunities. The identification of deliberate organizational attention biases alerts us to the need to identify latent opportunities.

Mutual Indifference

The final of the four cooperation dynamics highlights scenarios in which Organization A and Organization B do not have similar missions and do not have resources to share that help the respective agencies in fulfilling their core missions. In this scenario, the two organizations lack a meaningful, let alone cooperative, relationship with each other. Bottom-up cooperation is not expected to emerge in this scenario. Mandated cooperation can be expected to fail due to lack of interest and motivation to invest time into cooperative efforts. In contrast to destructive turf protection dynamics, organizations in this scenario do not invest time and resources in order to discredit the other organization. Rather, cooperation does not work because neither shared tasks nor resource complementarity give an incentive to do so.

*   *   *

To conclude the discussion of this framework, it is crucial to emphasize that it is based on the assumption that organizational behaviour is rational, but that an interpretive lens of what rationality implies for individual organizations is necessary. In line with this thinking, focusing on a core mission to safeguard autonomy, reputation, and organizational maintenance is rational on the part of organizations. However, what an organization *perceives* to be its core mission is far from simple to detect from a superficial reading of its mandate. I propose an interpretative lens on rational organizational behaviour in the sense that we need to understand an organization's perception of its core mission from within. Ultimately, it is this internal interpretation of an organization's mission that attention is biased towards. Rational budget- and bureau-shaping views (Niskanen, 1994 [1971]; Dunleavy, 1991) are well-known for being too restrictive in their view of rationality in this regard. Organizations' own interpretations of their core mission are unlikely to be determined by budget- or bureau-shaping views alone, as, for example, the increasing literature on organizational reputation aptly demonstrates (Busuioc & Lodge, 2016; Carpenter, 2010; Gilad, Maor, & Ben-Nun Bloom, 2015; Maor, Gilad, & Ben-Nun Bloom, 2013; see also Boon et al. in this volume). Even a rationally acting organization is embedded in a highly complex web of actors and complex environments that will shape organizations' interpretations of their core mission, which then get institutionalized over time.

THE POLITICS OF (NON-)COOPERATION IN ACTION: REGULATORY COOPERATION IN THE EU

This volume aims to highlight the importance of blind spots and other perennial weak points of bureaucracies not because their existence is an unrecognized or a new phenomenon, but because in a world with more complex policy problems the effects of these flaws are becoming more obvious. In relation to cooperation, this is very clearly demonstrated by the example of cooperation between regulatory agencies in the EU. The EU has created a regulatory system based on centralized standard setting but administrative fragmentation when it comes to putting these shared rules into practice. In other words, the system is characterized by a fundamental mismatch between standard-setting authority and overall regulatory capacity (Heidbreder, 2014; Majone, 2000). Cooperation between regulators in the forum of EU agencies has been designed to combat this shortfall in regulatory capacity. The integration of markets and the ensuing need to level the playing field as well as to manage cross-border risks have vastly increased the importance of this type of regulatory cooperation in the EU. This is also true in relation to the integration of global markets and the increasing importance of international regulatory cooperation. While coordination and cooperation in government has always been a key challenge (6, 2004), the identification of different cooperation outcomes associated with the politics of (non-)cooperation is more crucial than ever in a rapidly globalizing world. The politics of (non-)cooperation framework put forward here also offers a fresh perspective in relation to previous accounts of regulatory cooperation in the EU. Some of the EU governance literature implicitly sees mission overlap between agencies as a facilitator of regulatory cooperation, since agencies with similar tasks are seen to be underpinned by the professional norms of epistemic communities (e.g. Dehousse, 1997; Eberlein & Grande, 2005). The bureaucratic politics perspective of this chapter highlights that cooperation is not inevitably forthcoming due to the presence of shared professional norms, since mission overlap can trigger destructive turf protection dynamics. At the same time, cooperation is not necessarily obstructed due to mission overlap, as conventional bureaucratic politics perspectives tend to assume.

Destructive Turf Protection Dynamics: Maritime Safety Authorities

In previous research, I have highlighted a key example of destructive turf protection dynamics in a multi-level regulatory context (Heims, 2016, pp. 888f., 2017). A focus on UK and German maritime safety authorities revealed that they perceive the European Commission and the European Maritime Safety Agency (EMSA) to be 'on their turf'. This has resulted in dynamics in which German and UK authorities (and other national agencies) are not willing to contribute openly in shared sessions of EMSA, which are aimed at coordinating practices and fostering cooperation. National authorities have also resisted the push to coordinate an EU-wide position ahead of International Maritime Organization (IMO) meetings by the European Commission. Moreover, they have fought the European Commission's aim to become a full member of the IMO. This is largely the case because national authorities do not think that the European Commission and EMSA are helpful in pursuing their mission. To the contrary, German and British authorities regard their mission as making the maritime industry as safe as possible in order to prevent adverse effects on the environment and people (including seafarers). In their view, this mission is best pursued through international cooperation in the IMO, in which they have been major players for many decades. While they are eager to cooperate internationally, they have not enthusiastically embraced European cooperation. This shows that these agencies are not obstructive in relation to cooperation, per se, but that they choose to cooperate actively in areas and with bodies that help them to pursue their core mission. Their own perception of their core mission is firmly rooted in the highly international and highly mobile nature of the maritime industry. Many national maritime authorities perceive European efforts in this field to undermine the goodwill of international partners on which they are reliant in order to effectively regulate a global industry that has no barriers to entry.

Our analytical framework helps us to make sense of this. The regulatory missions of EMSA, the European Commission, and national agencies overlap to a significant degree: national authorities inspect foreign-flagged vessels in their ports (so-called port state control inspections), and EMSA's task is to inspect national inspectorates' work. However, EMSA and the European Commission only provide mission-related resource complementarity to a very limited degree. EMSA provides operational support to national agencies by running a satellite observation services for the detection of oil spills and by operating emergency rescue vessels. While this is valuable to national authorities, it is much less so for high-capacity authorities (e.g. the German and British agencies) than for low-capacity authorities. More crucially, these EMSA services provide operational support in emergency situations to national authorities, which does not add value to the core mission of national authorities, which is focused on preventing these type of emergencies (such as oil spills) in the first place. In this regard, EMSA and the European Commission merely provide reassurance to all national authorities that their sister authorities in other countries are undergoing the same quality control inspection regime as them. While German and British authorities value this, it does not provide them with tangible resources that help them to achieve their core mission. The degree of overlap of core mission and lack of meaningful resource complementarity trigger damaging turf protection dynamics.

Productive Turf Protection Dynamics: Food Control Authorities

In many ways, the example of maritime safety authorities seems to match the well-known stereotype of bureaucratic behaviour: cooperation is hampered by agencies trying to protect their turf from another agency that works in their field. Too often, we assume that such dynamics are inevitable if bureaucratic agencies' missions overlap. However, research in a different area of the EU multi-level bureaucratic system shows that this is not necessarily the case. Agencies tasked with food controls operate in a similar governance framework as the maritime safety authorities, but cooperation is embraced by the German and UK authorities in this field (Heims, 2014, pp. 139–153, 2017). Food control authorities are in charge of verifying whether food businesses adhere to all relevant food safety and food hygiene regulations through inspections. Due to the great number of food businesses of all sizes that are spread out geographically, food control inspections in Germany and the UK are carried out by local authorities that are overseen by a central government authority. It is a significant regulatory challenge for the central authorities in both countries to ensure that all local food inspectors carry out their work effectively. As a result, the German Bundesamt für Lebensmittelsicherheit und Verbraucherschutz (BVL) and the UK Food Standards Agency (FSA) both regard their core mission in food controls to be the effective supervision and steering of this highly decentralized network of local authorities.

The EU office in charge, the Food and Veterinary Office (FVO), has the core task to verify and ensure that EU food standards are adequately enforced by the administrations of the member states (please note that this office has recently been subsumed into the Directorate-General for Health and Food Safety). There is hence a high degree in mission overlap between these national authorities and their EU counterpart. Based on the relevance of mission alone, we hence expect destructive turf protection dynamics to develop. Instead, however, we can observe productive cooperation between the FVO and the BVL and the FSA, respectively. The German and British authorities embrace the role played by the FVO because it provides them with additional resources to fulfil their core mission: the steering of local level actors. FVO inspection of national food control systems provides the BVL and the FSA with additional authority to coax local authorities into appropriate action. As a result, the FVO is not seen as a rival authority by the BVL and the FSA. This point is powerfully demonstrated by the fact that, in contrast to the British and German authorities, the Dutch food control authority (the Netherlands Food and Consumer Product Safety Authority) at times contests the role of the FVO and is less enthusiastic about cooperation with the European authority (as becomes evident in its responses to FVO reports; for example, see Netherlands Food and Consumer Product Safety Authority, 2011, 2013).

The Dutch authority carries out food inspections in a centralized manner and hence does not face the conundrum of how to effectively steer a large number of local authorities. As a result, its core mission overlaps with the FVO, while the FVO does not provide it with additional means to carry out its core task: it possesses the centralized authority for food inspections itself, and the FVO enforcement mechanism does not provide the same value to it as it does to its German and British counterparts. This example of the Dutch authority provides evidence that shared mission-related resources may be more crucial than normative agreement about how to solve a particular policy problem (the latter is a factor that Bardach has stressed heavily his work on inter-agency collaboration; see Bardach, 1998).

The comparison between the maritime and food control cases demonstrates how seriously we need to consider the question of whether cooperation provides participating bureaucratic actors with additional means to carry out their core missions or not. Too often, scholarship is focused on mission overlap alone. Mission overlap, as such, does not automatically lead to damaging turf protection dynamics. While there is a recognition that turf protection dynamics have a flip side that may enhance, rather than undermine, cooperation (Peters, 2015), empirical examples of such a dynamic are few and far between in public administration scholarship. This chapter provides a clear empirical example in this respect. The nature of this example, however, raises the question of whether the specific combination of mission overlap and mission-related resource complementarity is most likely to appear in a multi-level governance context.

CONCLUSIONS

EU cooperation is often argued to work well because of being facilitated by underpinning norms of professional communities (Eberlein & Grande, 2005; Sabel & Zeitlin, 2010; Trondal, 2010, p. 22), but this perspective largely ignores the variation in how group norms operate in different professional communities (Heims, 2016) as well as the importance of organizational politics (Bach, De Francesco, Maggetti, & Ruffing, 2016; cf. Bardach, 1998, p. 26; Busuioc, 2016; Heims, 2017). That has often resulted in taking EU regulatory cooperation for granted as well as a general tendency to overstate the degree and effectiveness of cooperation. A bureaucratic politics perspective represents a corrector to this view, as it highlights organizational attention bias and turf protection dynamics. At the same time, this perspective has the potential pitfall of underestimating the extent of effective regulatory cooperation in the EU. Coming from a bureaucratic politics perspective, we may be surprised that EU regulatory cooperation works as well as it does, given that EU regulatory bodies and national regulators tend to have such a high degree of mission overlap. Mission overlap is usually seen as key trigger for turf fights that impede effective cooperation (Wilson, 2000 [1989], p. 181ff.). Indeed, as demonstrated in this chapter, such instances exist in EU regulatory cooperation. What the politics of (non-)coordination and (non-)cooperation framework of this chapter clearly adds is to show that mission overlap can infringe on as well as strengthen an agency's turf, depending on mission-related resource complementarity. This means that organizational attention bias towards fulfilling the organization's core mission can either hinder or facilitate cooperation. Deliberate attention biases of government agencies hence need to be taken very seriously, as they have the capacity to deter organizations from cooperating. While EU governance literature has not been very good at recognizing this, the bureaucratic politics literature tends to focus too much on the obstructive qualities of turf protection dynamics. This chapter highlights that turf protection dynamics can also enable proactive and productive cooperation, and analysts (as well as policy makers) need to be careful to distinguish between these two sets of dynamics.

The mention of policy makers sparks the question of which, if any, policy implications can be drawn from this chapter. Does it help us to design structures for more effective cooperation? Mission overlap and mission-related resource complementarity can, at least in theory, be taken into account when designing and reforming agencies' mandates and resources. However, most agencies are not designed for cooperation as a primary objective, and other rationales are likely to take precedence when establishing new agencies or reforming existing ones. This may result in a lack of incentives to cooperate, as payoffs may simply not be big enough (Peters, 2015, p. 46). Equally, this chapter highlights that it is crucial how agencies perceive and interpret their missions as well as how they perceive other agencies' missions. As highlighted in the theoretical framework in the introductory chapter by Bach and Wegrich, this means that missions have to be understood from inside an organization, since this is where perceptions of missions are established and institutionalized. Deliberate design is hence likely to run into trouble in trying to influence perceptions of missions a priori. This chapter's framework can be used, however, to analyse whether certain organizations are more or less likely to cooperative productively *before* basing the achievement of particular policy aims on the blind faith that cooperation will work. Equally, we may also want to encourage organizations to identify latent opportunities for cooperation with organizations that have different missions but may possess complementarity resource. Particularly fruitful in this regard are likely to be organizations with related missions that do not directly overlap. When EU agencies are concerned, this encouragement may indeed not be necessary: the European Chemicals Agency, the European Food Safety Authority, and the European Medicines Agency, for example, have established ad hoc working partnerships and memoranda of understanding with each other in order to harmonize scientific opinions, to share expertise and data, and even to exchange staff. Where mission-relevant resources complement each other and organizations appear on each other's radar (as is the case when EU agencies are concerned), government agencies can clearly be highly motivated to cooperate with each other.

REFERENCES

6, P. (2004). Joined-up government in the western world in comparative perspective: A preliminary literature review. *Journal of Public Administration Research and Theory, 14*(1), 103–138.

Alexander, E. R. (1995). *How organizations act together: Interorganizational coordination in theory and practice.* Luxembourg: Gordon and Breach.

Bach, T., De Francesco, F., Maggetti, M., & Ruffing, E. (2016). Transnational bureaucratic politics: An institutional rivalry perspective on EU network governance. *Public Administration, 94*(1), 9–24.

Bardach, E. (1996). Turf barriers to inter-agency collaboration. In D. F. Kettl & H. B. Milward (Eds.), *The state of public management* (pp. 168–192). Baltimore: Johns Hopkins University Press.

Bardach, E. (1998). *Getting agencies to work together: The practice and theory of managerial craftsmanship.* Washington, DC: Brookings Institute.

Busuioc, E. M. (2016). Friend or foe? Inter-agency cooperation, organizational reputation, and turf. *Public Administration, 94*(1), 40–56.

Busuioc, E. M., & Lodge, M. (2016). The reputational basis of public accountability. *Governance, 29*(2), 247–263.

Carpenter, D. P. (2001). *The forging of bureaucratic autonomy: Reputations, networks, and policy innovation in executive agencies, 1862–1928.* Princeton: Princeton University Press.

Carpenter, D. P. (2010). *Reputation and power: Organizational image and pharmaceutical regulation at the FDA*. Princeton: Princeton University Press.

Dehousse, R. (1997). Regulation by networks in the European Community: The role of European agencies. *Journal of European Public Policy, 4*(2), 246–261.

Dunleavy, P. (1991). *Democracy, bureaucracy and public choice: Economic explanations in political science*. London: Pearson Education.

Eberlein, B., & Grande, E. (2005). Beyond delegation: Transnational regulatory regimes and the EU regulatory state. *Journal of European Public Policy, 12*(1), 89–112.

Etienne, J. (2015). The politics of detection in business regulation. *Journal of Public Administration Research and Theory, 25*(1), 257–284.

Gilad, S., Maor, M., & Ben-Nun Bloom, P. (2015). Organizational reputation, the content of public allegations, and regulatory communication. *Journal of Public Administration Research and Theory, 25*(2), 451–478.

Heidbreder, E. G. (2014). Administrative capacities in the EU: Consequences of multi-level policy-making. In M. Lodge & K. Wegrich (Eds.), *The problem-solving capacity of the modern state: Governance challenges and administrative capacities* (pp. 218–237). Oxford: Oxford University Press.

Heims, E. M. (2014). *Managing European risks without a European state: Transnational coordination between regulators in the European Union*. Doctoral thesis, London School of Economics and Political Science, London.

Heims, E. M. (2016). Explaining coordination between national regulators in EU agencies: The role of formal and informal organization. *Public Administration, 94*(4), 881–896.

Heims, E. M. (2017). Regulatory coordination in the EU: A cross-sector comparison. *Journal of European Public Policy, 24*(8), 1116–1134.

Hood, C. (1976). *The limits of administration*. London: Wiley.

Lerner, A. W. (1986). There is more than one way to be redundant: A comparison of alternatives for the design and use of redundancy in organizations. *Administration and Society, 18*(3), 334–359.

Majone, G. (2000). The credibility crisis of community regulation. *Journal of Common Market Studies, 38*(2), 273–302.

Maor, M. (2010). Organizational reputation and jurisdictional claims: The case of the US Food and Drug Administration. *Governance, 23*(1), 133–159.

Maor, M., Gilad, S., & Ben-Nun Bloom, P. (2013). Organizational reputation, regulatory talk and strategic silence. *Journal of Public Administration Research and Theory, 23*(3), 581–603.

Netherlands Food and Consumer Product Safety Authority. (2011). *Response of the Competent Authorities of the Netherlands to the recommendations of Report ref. DG(SANCO)/2011-6019-MR of an audit carried out from 12 to 23 September 2011. European Commission Health and Consumers Directorate-General, Directorate F—Food and Veterinary Office*. Retrieved from http://ec.europa.eu/food/audits-analysis/act_getPDFannx.cfm?ANX_ID=6562

Netherlands Food and Consumer Product Safety Authority. (2013). *Response of the Competent Authorities of the Netherlands to the recommendations of Report ref. DG(SANCO)/2012-6312-MR of an audit carried out from 19 to 23 November 2012. European Commission Health and Consumers Directorate-General, Directorate F—Food and Veterinary Office*. Retrieved from http://ec.europa.eu/food/audits-analysis/act_getPDFannx.cfm?ANX_ID=7214

Niskanen, W. A. (1994 [1971]). *Bureaucracy and public economics*. Brookfield: Elgar Publishing.

Oliver, C. (1990). Determinants of interorganizational relationships: Integration and future directions. *The Academy of Management Review, 15*(2), 241–265.

Peters, B. G. (2015). *Pursuing horizontal management: The politics of public sector coordination*. Lawrence, KS: University Press of Kansas.

Pierson, P. (2000). Increasing returns, path dependence and the study of politics. *American Political Science Review, 94*(2), 251–267.

Sabel, C. F., & Zeitlin, J. (2010). *Experimentalist governance in the European Union: Towards a new architecture*. Oxford: Oxford University Press.

Selznick, P. (1957). *Leadership in administration: A sociological interpretation*. New York: Harper & Row.

Trondal, J. (2010). *An emergent European executive order*. Oxford: Oxford University Press.

Wilson, J. ([1989] 2000). *Bureaucracy: What government agencies do and why they do it*. New York: Basic Books.

CHAPTER 7

Blame, Reputation, and Organizational Responses to a Politicized Climate

Markus Hinterleitner and Fritz Sager

INTRODUCTION

When it comes to exploring the interplay of various political phenomena and public service delivery, scholars of politics and public administration often sit 'at separate tables' (Almond, 1988). Scholars studying Western politics strive to keep track of the newest political developments, such as polarization or populism, but often employ an overly narrow understanding of 'policy' (Hacker & Pierson, 2014). Concurrently, scholars that study public service delivery in Western democracies are well aware of political pressures but often struggle to incorporate current political developments, such as the marketization of public services and their impacts on public service delivery, in their research (Thomann, Hupe, & Sager, 2017). We suggest that both strands of research can profit from occasionally reaching across tables. To contribute to this discussion, this chapter explores how public sector organizations (PSOs) react to elite polarization, which is an increasingly common phenomenon in many Western

M. Hinterleitner (✉) • F. Sager
KPM Center for Public Management, University of Bern, Bern, Switzerland
e-mail: markus.hinterleitner@kpm.unibe.ch; fritz.sager@kpm.unibe.ch

© The Author(s) 2019
T. Bach, K. Wegrich (eds.), *The Blind Spots of Public Bureaucracy and the Politics of Non-Coordination*, Executive Politics and Governance, https://doi.org/10.1007/978-3-319-76672-0_7

democracies. For this purpose, this chapter conceptualizes a mechanism that depicts the path leading from elite polarization to PSOs' prioritization of tasks.

Elite Polarization and Public Service Delivery

Many Western democracies are experiencing increased levels of elite polarization (Hetherington, 2009; Kriesi et al., 2012). Elite polarization is a political situation that is marked by a growing ideological divide between political opponents, more extreme policy positions, and, accordingly, fewer opportunities for compromise (Hetherington, 2009; Layman, Carsey, & Horowitz, 2006). In a polarized political system, political elites increasingly engage in generating blame, negative messaging, or scandalizing (Flinders, 2014; Layman et al., 2006; Nai & Walter, 2016; Weaver, 2013). The adoption of such strategies represents a rational response to a change in contextual conditions, since they appear more credible and thus promise higher electoral payoff in light of a gridlocked political system (Parsons, 2007; Weaver, 2013).

The research examining the implications of elite polarization for public service delivery is extensive but limited in its scope. The existing studies mostly focus on the political arena in which political conflicts over policy unfold, new policies are crafted, and existing policies are changed (Barber & McCarty, 2015; Layman et al., 2006). Unfortunately, this research direction means that changes to public service delivery that transcend or bypass formal policy change remain unstudied. This is problematic, since policies can change in a myriad of often gradual and piecemeal ways—even in the absence of 'big legislative changes' (Hacker & Pierson, 2014, p. 644; Mahoney & Thelen, 2010).

In this chapter, we discuss a particular implication of elite polarization for public service delivery. PSOs, such as regulatory agencies, local government units, and executive departments and ministries, are tasked with the application of policies and regulations in concrete cases. While they must fulfil their formal mandates, many of these organizations enjoy considerable discretion and autonomy in their daily operations (Bækkeskov, 2017). Based on this insight, we aim to show how elite polarization influences the daily actions of PSOs and can thus have an effect on public service delivery that is independent of formal policy change.

For this purpose, we conceptualize a mechanism that leads from elite polarization to PSOs' prioritization of tasks (see Fig. 7.1). The multiple

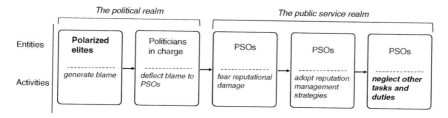

Fig. 7.1 The causal mechanism between elite polarization and public service delivery

steps that connect elite polarization to task prioritization can be conceptualized as entities engaging in activities, where the activities are causal forces that lead from one step to the next (Beach & Pedersen, 2013). The mechanism begins in the political realm, where polarized political elites generate increased levels of blame. The politicians in charge shift a significant share of this blame 'downwards' to PSOs operating within their sphere of responsibility. Since this blame represents a threat to their reputations, PSOs react by adopting various reputation management strategies to protect their reputations. By necessity, PSOs that are increasingly concerned with reputation management have less time and fewer resources at their disposal to focus on other tasks. In the remainder of this chapter, we describe and illustrate this mechanism in detail.

Why Elite Polarization Matters for PSOs

PSOs should be affected by increased elite polarization and receive some of the 'excess' blame generated in the political realm for at least two interrelated reasons. For politicians bearing political responsibility for public service delivery, blame holds reputation-damaging potential (Busuioc & Lodge, 2016; Weaver, 1986). Therefore, they try to eliminate this blame. This is especially true in controversial cases of policy failure where politicians frequently try to deflect blame to other actors or entities that are somehow involved in the policy failure (Hinterleitner & Sager, 2015). PSOs operating in the sphere of responsibility of incumbent politicians are primary blame-deflection targets. Although the nature of policy failures is frequently contested and 'failure' is not just related to the primary PSO task (i.e. the application of a policy), it is most often the latter which triggers blame (McConnell, 2010). While PSOs may not be responsible for a failure, they are usually the ones that get caught with their pants down. Therefore, PSOs represent ideal 'lightning rods' for office holders during crisis situations (Bach & Wegrich, 2016), which polarized elites are eager to exploit as 'blaming opportunities' (Hinterleitner, 2017a).

In lockstep with greater blame from politicians, we can expect that PSOs also receive more blame from the media and the public. Administrative reform trends in most Western countries have led to the break-up of monolithic bureaucracies and their frequent replacement with fuzzy governance structures, consisting of a multiplicity of public, semi-public, or private actors operating in a policy field (Bache, Bartle, Flinders, & Marsden, 2015; Mortensen, 2016; Verhoest, Van Thiel, Bouckaert, & Lægreid, 2012). These reforms, frequently summarized under the term 'agencification', have pushed public service delivery within arm's length of politicians' direct control. For politicians in charge, this has the welcome effect of appearing *less involved* in the application of policies as 'architects', 'managers', or 'decision makers'. The less involved they appear, the less 'likely that they are to be held liable for poor performance' (Weaver, 1986, p. 390). At the same time, many reforms inspired by New Public Management, such as agencification, have made the activities of PSOs *more visible* and have exposed them to greater public scrutiny and criticism (Mortensen, 2016).

THE REPUTATION MANAGEMENT OF PSOs

An increase in the number and intensity of blame attacks from politicians, the media, and the public represents a threat to the reputations of PSOs. Research has shown that PSOs are concerned about their reputation and, consequently, react to reputational threats (Busuioc, 2016; Carpenter, 2010a; Maor & Sulitzeanu-Kenan, 2013). How PSOs build and protect favourable reputations and how they respond to reputational threats are some of the key questions involved in research on organizational reputation in a public sector context (Busuioc & Lodge, 2016; Wæraas & Maor, 2015).

The literature on the determinants of bureaucratic behaviour is primarily concerned with explaining the gap between the behaviour of bureaucracies (or PSOs more generally) as prescribed in legal policy mandates and their actual behaviour (Bækkeskov, 2017; Niskanen, 1971; Pressman & Wildavsky, 1984; Wilson, 1989). In recent years, reputation-seeking has emerged as an important explanatory factor of PSO behaviour

(Carpenter, 2010b; Carpenter & Krause, 2012; Maor, 2011; Maor, Gilad, & Ben-Nun Bloom, 2013). The reputation of a PSO can be defined as 'a set of symbolic beliefs about the unique or separable capacities, roles, and obligations of an organization, where these beliefs are embedded in audience networks' (Carpenter, 2010b, p. 45).

Especially in situations where PSOs are under pressure, they seek to actively manage their reputation vis-à-vis the general public, their policy targets, or politicians (Alon-Barkat & Gilad, 2016). This may involve attempts to preserve a good reputation and measures to ameliorate a bad one. It is important to note that picturing PSOs as reputation-sensitive entities does not merely constitute an attribution of 'individual' preferences to complex organizational entities for the sake of analytical parsimony, but rather it is based on intra-organizational observations (Bækkeskov, 2017).

PSOs, which in organizational reputation research are generally considered to be rational and politically conscious entities (Wæraas & Maor, 2015), are interested in a good reputation because it helps them to achieve and conserve regulatory power (Carpenter, 2010b). A PSO with a good reputation enjoys increased autonomy and political support and can attract and keep valued employees (Alon-Barkat & Gilad, 2016; Busuioc & Lodge, 2016; Carpenter, 2002). On the contrary, a PSO with a bad reputation must fear interventions and attacks from political principals, since for the latter, a PSO with a bad reputation presents a political liability. PSOs may become entangled in stricter regulations or suffer brain drains, and PSO managers may be forced to pack their bags and go if their political principals sacrifice them during a crisis situation.

A good reputation can thus be conceived as a 'blame shield' that protects PSOs in two ways. On one hand, a good reputation should decrease the likelihood that a PSO receives much of the excess blame created by polarized elites, because the latter risk blame reversion if they decide to attack a reputed PSO (Hood, 2011). If a reputed PSO reverses the blame, it is much more likely to receive support from the media and the public. On the other hand, and for the very same reasons, a good reputation can be used as an asset if politicians shift blame downwards. Hence, an inverse relationship should exist between a PSO's reputation and its lightning rod quality for political principals.

The literature reveals a considerable number of substantive and symbolic PSO responses to reputational threats (Alon-Barkat & Gilad, 2016; Busuioc & Lodge, 2016). With regard to *substantive responses*, scholars have examined the role of reputational threats for a PSO's prioritization of tasks (Carpenter, 2002; Gilad, 2012, 2015); for a PSO's decision to cooperate with other PSOs (Busuioc, 2016); for regulatory enforcement decisions, such as the willingness to detect noncompliant firm behaviour (Etienne, 2015), or the speed of enforcement decisions (Maor & Sulitzeanu-Kenan, 2013); for jurisdictional claim-making (Maor, 2010); and for a PSO's overall output performance (Maor & Sulitzeanu-Kenan, 2016). Concerning the *symbolic responses* of PSOs, studies have shown that reputational threats determine how PSOs react to external performance judgements (Maor et al., 2013) and that reputational threats influence the strength and type of PSOs' responses to public allegations (Gilad, Alon-Barkat, & Braverman, 2016; Gilad, Maor, & Ben-Nun Bloom, 2015).

While this literature has made great progress in explaining the role of reputational threats in PSO behaviour, we believe that differentiating between anticipatory and reactive forms of reputation management can conceptually enhance it. The benefits of this distinction for our understanding of the multi-faceted role of reputation in the public sector become obvious if we consider the previously described role of reputation as a blame shield. PSOs benefit from a good reputation when they are blamed; a good reputation also helps them to avoid becoming a blame target in the first place. Therefore, we can expect that PSOs engage in reputation management not only *after* they have been blamed but also *before* a potentially reputation-damaging situation emerges.

ANTICIPATORY REPUTATION MANAGEMENT

We suggest that the concept of *anticipatory blame avoidance* allows us to further explore and better categorize PSOs' actions in anticipation of reputational threats. Anticipatory blame avoidance aims to keep potentially blame-attracting events off the agenda and to prepare for blame-attracting events (Hinterleitner & Sager, 2017; Leong & Howlett, 2017; Sulitzeanu-Kenan & Hood, 2005). Existing research has mainly examined the use of anticipatory blame avoidance strategies by political elites (Arnold, 1990; Bache et al., 2015; Pierson, 1996; Vis, 2016; Weaver, 1988). However, the research on organizational responses to demands for transparency (Hood & Rothstein, 2001) and blame avoidance in public administrations (Hood, 2007, 2011) suggests that this concept can also be fruitfully applied to the behaviour of PSOs.

Differentiating between anticipatory and reactive forms of blame avoidance helps to account for the fact that the need to avoid blame does not only arise *after* a crisis or policy failure has occurred and provoked blame. Under particular circumstances, officeholders, as well as PSOs, can anticipate the reputation-damaging potential of an event and will thus try to prepare for it (Arnold, 1990; McGraw, 1991). When PSOs realize—for instance, through past experience or negative media coverage—that their future conduct may give rise to blame, they can attempt to make their role, capacities, and obligations appear less blameworthy (Carpenter, 2010b; Maor & Sulitzeanu-Kenan, 2013). We can even expect that for PSOs, anticipatory blame avoidance is comparatively more important than reactive reputation management. Unlike political elites, they only possess limited amounts of the resources which often tip the scale during a reactive blame game, such as privileged access to the media or the possibility of demonstrating commitment by launching inquiries or symbolic reforms (Hinterleitner & Sager, 2017). PSOs should thus put particular emphasis on avoiding reactive blame games in the first place.

A look at the research examining the responses to reputational threats adopted by PSOs reveals that scholars do not yet explicitly distinguish between anticipatory and reactive forms of reputation management. While the symbolic responses of PSOs studied thus far describe different *reactions* to public allegations and performance judgements (Gilad, Maor, et al., 2015; Gilad, Alon-Barkat, et al. 2016; Maor et al., 2013), most of the substantive responses examined in the previous work cover both anticipatory and reactive forms of reputation management. In practice, these responses are mostly analysed in a reactive context, but PSOs could theoretically also apply them in an anticipatory fashion. When it comes to cooperation with other PSOs, for instance, a PSO may stop cooperating during a crisis situation because cooperation depletes important reputational resources, or it may anticipate its reputation vulnerability without previously going through a blame-attracting situation (Busuioc, 2016).

To further illustrate the potential of explicitly considering *anticipatory* forms of reputation management, we describe and provide examples for three types of anticipatory strategies that PSOs apply to fortify their blame shield. Each of these strategies works towards protecting a PSO's reputation by decreasing the likelihood of it being blamed in the first place and by preparing for blame attacks. While this categorization is neither exhaustive nor mutually exclusive, it broadens our view of the various facets of reputation management and should facilitate future empirical work.

Redesigning Policy Measures

Many PSOs have significant discretion when applying policy mandates to concrete cases (Bækkeskov, 2017). This creates an opportunity to bring policy application in line with the beliefs and opinions of critical audiences. If PSOs have the chance to choose between particular measures, they can opt to no longer apply measures that are particularly blameworthy. If possible, PSOs can also seek to dispose of a blameworthy obligation altogether by delegating it or shifting it upwards or sideways. If PSOs cannot get rid of potentially blame-attracting obligations, they can at least attempt to redesign them. Manipulating a PSO's output in this way can signal preemptive obedience to audiences and thereby reduce the likelihood that the PSO's output could become a bone of contention.

An example of this strategy can be found in a study by Maor and Sulitzeanu-Kenan (2016), who show that Centrelink, the Australian government's main social policy delivery agency, uses its discretion to adapt its output performance in response to negative media coverage. While the authors examine output adaptation in reaction to negative media coverage, it is also likely that PSOs try to anticipate the effects of their output decisions on media coverage and blame. In other words, PSOs try to make their output levels appear less blame-attracting in the future. Hinterleitner (2017a), examining the sanctioning practices of Swiss youth crime agencies, provided an example of how PSOs redesign policy measures in the face of reputational threats. In recent years, several aggravated assaults committed by juveniles have triggered a public outcry in Switzerland. This represented a reputational threat to cantonal crime agencies, which traditionally enjoy considerable leeway in sanctioning juvenile offenders. If a cantonal crime agency opted for an educational measure instead of a severe sanction, it risked being publicly blamed in cases where the treatment of the juvenile offender did not pay off and the latter then committed another crime. Cantonal crime agencies responded by changing their sanctioning practices. Sanctions that were widely considered to not be punitive enough were applied in fewer cases to signal a tougher stance on youth crime. This reduced the likelihood that a crime agency would be blamed for a soft, leftish legal practice in cases where youth offenders were to recidivate. Youth advocates later indicated that the more critical public assessments of their decisions and the resulting fear of negative reactions from the media have increasingly influenced the sanctioning practices of their agencies (Mez, 2015).

Image Cultivation

PSOs can not only redesign or change their output to avoid future blame generation, but they can also make their overall role in public service delivery appear less blameworthy. A PSO with a positive image reduces the likelihood of future blame attacks and prepares the PSO for situations in which it becomes the object of blame attacks. One way this can be done is by rebranding the PSO. Research by Marland, Lewis, and Flanagan (2017) showed that political elites are increasingly concerned with spinning government messages 'to coordinate a consistent, constant, and unified response [towards a] noisy, fragmented, pressure-filled media landscape' (p. 127). Importantly, pressures to trim government messages are not only felt by political elites, but they also trickle down to PSOs (Marland et al., 2017). A PSO that pre-emptively adopts the branding strategies promulgated by its political principal signals its willingness to fully operate in the interest of the latter. This reduces the likelihood of blame attacks and autonomy-curtailing interventions.

A telling example of a PSO's rebranding is the renaming of the UK's Department of Social Security to the Department for Work and Pensions in 2001. While this departmental reorganization was publicly justified due to its coordination advantages, a 'whiff of New Labour spin', as the Guardian aptly put it, could be detected as well: 'The Department for Social Security smacked of work-shy dependency. The Department for Work and Pensions, in contrast, conjured up an image of productivity and prudence' (Wylie, 2005). In an ideological context in which the unemployed are increasingly portrayed as a non-deserving policy target group, it is obvious that a branding strategy that suggests that the department is applying a carrot-and-stick approach attracts less blame from political elites.

Controlling Information

Next to image cultivation and the redesign of policy measures, PSOs can also engage in genuine information control to reduce the likelihood of political attacks and media allegations. As with the application of policy mandates to concrete cases, and despite far-reaching transparency requirements, PSOs often enjoy significant room to limit and control the information that is made available to the public. Since new information about problems in public service delivery is the basis on which blame can be created, scarcer (potentially blame triggering) information reduces the opportunities that political elites have to attack PSOs.

The research by Hood and Rothstein (2001) showed that PSOs involved in risk regulation only reluctantly respond to demands for transparency and openness. The authors explained this response as an indication of the desire for blame prevention. PSOs engage in 'institutional blame prevention engineering … because more transparency, participation, and accountability can increase the threat of blame and liability for failures' (Hood & Rothstein, 2001, p. 25). An example from the UK illustrates the application of this strategy and its effects. In 2000, the low visitor numbers of the Millennium Dome exhibition in Greenwich, London, attracted frequent criticism from political elites and the media. The Millennium Dome Commission, the organization responsible for the management of the exhibition, received a lot of the blame, which emerged every time it published its weekly visitor numbers. From June onwards, the commission stopped publishing weekly numbers, simply arguing that they were not representative of overall performance. Although the media quickly noted this action and expressed its indignation (e.g. King, 2000), subsequent negative coverage relating to low visitor numbers declined significantly. For the commission, controlling information represented an easy way to deprive the media and political elites of future occasions to generate blame.

Implications for the Study of (Anticipatory) Reputation Management

The strategies described earlier and their examples reveal several important implications for the future study of PSOs' reputation management. First, at an empirical level, it may often be difficult to identify whether the impulse for the application of a reputation management strategy comes from the PSO itself, is imposed by the political principal, or is a result of a combination of the two. The rebranding of the UK's Department of Social Security was certainly part of a more general framing strategy of the Labour government, but a PSO that eagerly adopts this framing will attract less blame from politicians. In reality, therefore, PSOs and their political principals may often act in concert when engaging in reputation management.

Second, and contrary to a widespread belief in the literature, the examples suggest that PSOs are not always interested in protecting and enhancing a *unique* reputation; that is, to cultivate their 'unique or separable capacities, roles, and obligations' (Carpenter, 2010b, p. 45). To the contrary, there may be reputation management strategies, such as image cultivation, which aim to manage a reputation that is firmly in line with the image of the government of the day. When it comes to reputation-damaging political attacks, it may constitute a disadvantage if PSOs stick their heads out too prominently.

Third, the previous examples also emphasize a difficulty inherent in the distinction between anticipatory and reactive forms of reputation management. What looks like the reaction to past allegations and blame from one perspective can be simultaneously interpreted as an anticipatory strategy to avoid *future* allegations and blame. Thus, one could argue, the distinction between anticipatory and reactive forms of reputation management is a mere question of perspectives; often, reputation management may constitute both. However, situating reputation management in time (Pierson, 2004) forces us to combine those perspectives, not blur them. Anticipatory forms of reputation management do not necessarily need a trigger in the form of materialized blame to make a PSO realize that its reputation is in danger. PSOs can equally survey their environment by considering events in the distant past that are unrelated to current events, by monitoring media coverage and the political treatment of related issues, or by observing what is going on in other jurisdictions. The implication is that anticipatory forms of reputation management may be far more widespread than the many studies examining reputation management in reactive contexts lead us to assume. Just like an iceberg is much bigger below the water's surface, it could be that reputation management is much more widespread if we consider all the cases in which PSOs apply them in the absence of a concrete blame trigger.

Repercussions for Public Service Delivery

A look at these strategies suggests that their more frequent application in response to increased blame generation in the political realm will not be without repercussions. Two specific types of consequences for public service delivery suggest that the mechanism at the heart of this chapter does not end here. While both consequences are slowly evolving as PSOs increasingly focus on reputation management, one is *unintended*, and the other is *purposeful* in nature (see chapter by Lodge in this volume).

First, we can assume that PSOs which prioritize reputation management have less time and resources at their disposal to focus on other tasks. Gilad (2012), for example, showed that PSOs that concentrate on reputation management become slower at adapting to new cues from their environment. PSOs that spend increasing resources on reputation management are thus more likely to experience surprises in their environment (Lodge in this volume): information that is potentially vital for effective public service delivery is neglected as PSOs predominantly scan their environment for reputational threats. This constitutes an unintended consequence of reputation management, since PSOs do not deliberately turn a blind eye to public service-relevant information; they are simply distracted by a concern for their reputation.

Second, a reputation-conscious type of service delivery can be in open conflict with predefined policy goals in some cases. The previously mentioned Swiss youth crime agencies, which increasingly apply more punitive measures to juvenile offenders to please critical publics and conservative politicians, are a case in point. The increased application of stricter measures runs contrary to the mandate of the Swiss juvenile justice policy, in which the primary goals are the protection, education, and (re)integration of young offenders into society (Hinterleitner, 2017a). The research overwhelmingly shows that these goals are best achieved through integrative measures, not by punishing juvenile offenders. The conclusions of this example are supported by the broader literature on blame avoidance and reputation management, which suggests that elites and PSOs deliberately prioritize to avoid blame and protect their reputations over other motivations when they feel threatened (Bækkeskov, 2017; Hinterleitner, 2017b; Weaver, 1986). The deliberate neglect of tasks and duties for the sake of intensified reputation management constitutes a purposeful change to public service delivery.

In sum, PSOs' greater focus on reputation management contributes to forms of task prioritization by PSOs which can be problematic from both a policy and a democratic perspective. Intensified reputation management by PSOs may decrease policy effectiveness. PSOs that prioritize crafting responses to reputational threats may (consciously or unconsciously) neglect tasks and duties that are potentially decisive for effective and problem-oriented public service delivery. Moreover, task prioritization in response to increased blame generation is also problematic from a democratic perspective. If a pressure group wants to change policy, it must usually go through majoritarian channels. If it does not find a majority, its request for policy change will be blocked. The mechanism posited in this chapter suggests that pressure groups can bypass democratic channels if they only shout loud enough.

Scope Conditions for the Mechanism's Operation

Whether the mechanism leading from elite polarization to PSOs' prioritization of tasks unfolds as described earlier depends on the presence of scope conditions. Relevant scope conditions are those aspects of a setting 'which allow the mechanism to produce the outcome' (Falleti & Lynch, 2009, p. 1152). In other words, scope conditions are a prerequisite for each entity to engage in the activity posited by the mechanism. For example, if a PSO does not fear reputational damage from political blame, it will hardly intensify (usually costly) reputation management efforts. In that case, the mechanism breaks down and does not lead to changes in task prioritization.

The literature on organizational reputation suggests a number of important conditions that must be present for elite polarization to have an effect on public service delivery. First, how much a PSO fears reputational damage from blame deflection by elites depends on whether this blame relates to the unique reputation(s) of a PSO. Reputation uniqueness 'refers to the demonstration by agencies that they can create solutions and provide services found nowhere else in the polity' (Gilad et al., 2015, pp. 453–454). Blame that threatens to erode unique reputation(s) is much more dangerous for PSOs than blame that is related to more peripheral tasks and duties.

Second, as already mentioned, whether a PSO can respond to reputational threats depends on the presence and extent of its discretion to apply policy mandates to concrete cases (Bækkeskov, 2017). A PSO that has its hands tied (i.e. it cannot adopt reputation management strategies to respond to reputational threats) will not—at least in the way described—contribute to changes in public service delivery, even though it may well be aware of the reputation-damaging potential of blame attacks.

Third, whether a PSO increasingly engaging in reputation management unwittingly neglects other tasks and duties also depends on the availability of resources. Since reputation management is costly and occupies attention, resource availability should at least partially be responsible for whether PSOs can uphold public service delivery, even in high-blame environments. A concurrent political phenomenon—austerity—dampens optimism in this regard, as many Western public administrations suffer from increased resource constraints (Hinterleitner, Sager, & Thomann, 2016; Lodge & Hood, 2012; Sager & Hinterleitner, 2016). Finally, whether a PSO predominantly focusing on reputation management is willing to forgo other tasks and duties for this purpose depends on its organizational identity (Gilad, 2015). A PSO with an identity that prioritizes particular goals and tasks should be less willing to subsume those tasks under the imperative of reputation management.

CONCLUSION

In this chapter, we attempt to connect the research on salient current political developments with the research on public service delivery by exploring and conceptualizing a link between elite polarization and task prioritization by PSOs. This entails two specific contributions to the literature. First, by connecting the political realm with the public service realm, we outline a way to keep track of the multiple policy implications of current political phenomena, such as elite polarization or populism. This approach allows the crafting of truly 'political' explanations for public service developments such as reputation-sensitive task prioritization. Our chapter further suggests that the links between the political realm and the public service realm may often be difficult to identify and conceptualize, as they involve several steps. Examining these steps may require zooming in on various actors and entities and carefully studying their motivations and behaviour.

Second, and with regard to the specific mechanism examined in this chapter, we show that research can profit from the improved conceptualizing of PSOs' responses to reputational threats. Looking at anticipatory forms of reputation management, although empirically challenging, should broaden our perspective on this important phenomenon and provide us a better understanding of its pervasiveness.

Finally, a limitation regarding pervasiveness is in order. As the section on scope conditions has already detailed, several conditions must come together for elite polarization to leave an imprint on public service delivery. Therefore, to conclude that in today's polarized political environment PSOs have little else to do other than manage their reputations towards critical audiences would be grossly overstated. Instead, it is necessary to consider the influence of reputation-seeking in conjunction with other motivations for PSO behaviour to get a grasp of the importance of this phenomenon.

REFERENCES

Almond, G. A. (1988). Separate tables: Schools and sects in political science. *PS: Political Science and Politics, 21*(4), 828–842.

Alon-Barkat, S., & Gilad, S. (2016). Political control or legitimacy deficit? Bureaucracies' symbolic responses to bottom-up public pressures. *Policy & Politics, 44*(1), 41–58.

Arnold, R. D. (1990). *The logic of congressional action*. New Haven: Yale University Press.

Bach, T., & Wegrich, K. (2016). Regulatory reform, accountability and blame in public service delivery: The public transport crisis in Berlin. In T. Christensen & P. Lægreid (Eds.), *Routledge handbook to accountability and welfare state reforms in Europe* (pp. 223–236). London: Routledge.

Bache, I., Bartle, I., Flinders, M., & Marsden, G. (2015). Blame games and climate change: Accountability, multi-level governance and carbon management. *British Journal of Politics and International Relations, 17*(1), 64–88.

Bækkeskov, E. (2017). Reputation-seeking by a government agency in Europe: Direct evidence from responses to the 2009 H1N1 'swine' influenza pandemic. *Administration & Society, 49*(2), 163–189.

Barber, M. J., & McCarty, N. (2015). Causes and consequences of polarization. In N. Persily (Ed.), *Solutions to political polarization in America* (pp. 15–58). Cambridge: Cambridge University Press.

Beach, D., & Pedersen, R. B. (2013). *Process-tracing methods: Foundations and guidelines*. Ann Arbor: University of Michigan Press.

Busuioc, E. M. (2016). Friend or foe? Inter-agency cooperation, organizational reputation, and turf. *Public Administration, 94*(1), 40–56.

Busuioc, E. M., & Lodge, M. (2016). The reputational basis of public accountability. *Governance, 29*(2), 247–263.

Carpenter, D. P. (2002). Groups, the media, agency waiting costs, and FDA drug approval. *American Journal of Political Science, 46*(3), 490–505.

Carpenter, D. P. (2010a). Institutional strangulation: Bureaucratic politics and financial reform in the Obama administration. *Perspectives on Politics, 8*(3), 825–846.

Carpenter, D. P. (2010b). *Reputation and power: Organizational image and pharmaceutical regulation at the FDA*. Princeton: Princeton University Press.

Carpenter, D. P., & Krause, G. A. (2012). Reputation and public administration. *Public Administration Review, 72*(1), 26–32.

Etienne, J. (2015). The politics of detection in business regulation. *Journal of Public Administration Research and Theory, 25*(1), 257–284.

Falleti, T. G., & Lynch, J. F. (2009). Context and causal mechanisms in political analysis. *Comparative Political Studies, 42*(9), 1143–1166.

Flinders, M. (2014). Explaining democratic disaffection: Closing the expectations gap. *Governance, 27*(1), 1–8.

Gilad, S. (2012). Attention and reputation: Linking regulators' internal and external worlds. In M. Lodge & K. Wegrich (Eds.), *Executive politics in times of crisis* (pp. 157–175). Basingstoke: Palgrave Macmillan.

Gilad, S. (2015). Political pressures, organizational identity, and attention to tasks: Illustrations from pre-crisis financial regulation. *Public Administration, 93*(3), 593–608.

Gilad, S., Alon-Barkat, S., & Braverman, A. (2016). Large-scale social protest: A business risk and a bureaucratic opportunity. *Governance, 29*(3), 371–392.

Gilad, S., Maor, M., & Ben-Nun Bloom, P. (2015). Organizational reputation, the content of public allegations, and regulatory communication. *Journal of Public Administration Research and Theory, 25*(2), 451–478.

Hacker, J. S., & Pierson, P. (2014). After the 'master theory': Downs, Schattschneider, and the rebirth of policy-focused analysis. *Perspectives on Politics, 12*(3), 643–662.

Hetherington, M. J. (2009). Review article: Putting polarization in perspective. *British Journal of Political Science, 39*(2), 413–448.

Hinterleitner, M. (2017a). Policy failures, blame games and changes to policy practice. *Journal of Public Policy.* https://doi.org/10.1017/S0143814X16000283

Hinterleitner, M. (2017b). Reconciling perspectives on blame avoidance behaviour. *Political Studies Review, 15*(2), 243–254.

Hinterleitner, M., & Sager, F. (2015). Avoiding blame: A comprehensive framework and the australian home insulation program fiasco. *Policy Studies Journal, 43*(1), 139–161.

Hinterleitner, M., & Sager, F. (2017). Anticipatory and reactive forms of blame avoidance: Of foxes and lions. *European Political Science Review, 9*(4), 587–606.

Hinterleitner, M., Sager, F., & Thomann, E. (2016). The politics of external approval: Explaining the IMF's evaluation of austerity programmes. *European Journal of Political Research, 55*(3), 549–567.

Hood, C. (2007). What happens when transparency meets blame-avoidance? *Public Management Review, 9*(2), 191–210.

Hood, C. (2011). *The blame game: Spin, bureaucracy, and self-preservation in government.* Princeton: Princeton University Press.

Hood, C., & Rothstein, H. (2001). Risk regulation under pressure: Problem solving or blame shifting? *Administration & Society, 33*(1), 21–53.

King, I. (2000, June 27). 10 weeks to dome's doom. *The Sun.*

Kriesi, H., Grande, E., Dolezal, M., Helbling, M., Höglinger, D., Hutter, S., & Wüest, B. (Eds.). (2012). *Political conflict in Western Europe.* Cambridge: Cambridge University Press.

Layman, G. C., Carsey, T. M., & Horowitz, J. M. (2006). Party polarization in American politics: Characteristics, causes, and consequences. *Annual Review of Political Science, 9*(1), 83–110.

Leong, C., & Howlett, M. (2017). On credit and blame: Disentangling the motivations of public policy decision-making behaviour. *Policy Sciences, 50*(4), 599–618.

Lodge, M., & Hood, C. (2012). Into an age of multiple austerities? Public management and public service bargains across OECD countries. *Governance, 25*(1), 79–101.

Mahoney, J., & Thelen, K. A. (2010). A theory of gradual institutional change. In J. Mahoney & K. A. Thelen (Eds.), *Explaining institutional change: Ambiguity, agency, and power* (pp. 1–37). Cambridge: Cambridge University Press.

Maor, M. (2010). Organizational reputation and jurisdictional claims: The case of the US Food and Drug Administration. *Governance, 23*(1), 133–159.

Maor, M. (2011). Organizational reputations and the observability of public warnings in 10 pharmaceutical markets. *Governance, 24*(3), 557–582.

Maor, M., Gilad, S., & Ben-Nun Bloom, P. (2013). Organizational reputation, regulatory talk, and strategic silence. *Journal of Public Administration Research and Theory, 23*(3), 581–608.

Maor, M., & Sulitzeanu-Kenan, R. (2013). The effect of salient reputational threats on the pace of FDA enforcement. *Governance, 26*(1), 31–61.

Maor, M., & Sulitzeanu-Kenan, R. (2016). Responsive change: Agency output response to reputational threats. *Journal of Public Administration Research and Theory, 26*(1), 31–44.

Marland, A., Lewis, J. P., & Flanagan, T. (2017). Governance in the age of digital media and branding. *Governance, 30*(1), 125–141.

McConnell, A. (2010). Policy success, policy failure and grey areas in-between. *Journal of Public Policy, 30*(3), 345–362.

McGraw, K. M. (1991). Managing blame: An experimental test of the effects of political accounts. *American Political Science Review, 85*(4), 1133–1157.

Mez, B. (2015). Alltag einer jugendanwältin. In F. Riklin (Ed.), *Schweizer jugendstrafrecht: Vorbildlich oder überholt?* (pp. 27–31). Bern: Stämpfli.

Mortensen, P. B. (2016). Agencification and blame shifting: Evaluating a neglected side of public sector reforms. *Public Administration, 94*(3), 630–646.

Nai, A., & Walter, A. (Eds.). (2016). *New perspectives on negative campaigning: Why attack politics matters.* Colchester: ECPR Press.

Niskanen, W. A. (1971). *Bureaucracy and representative government.* Chicago: Aldine, Atherton.

Parsons, C. (2007). *How to map arguments in political science.* Oxford: Oxford University Press.

Pierson, P. (1996). The new politics of the welfare state. *World Politics, 48*(2), 143–179.

Pierson, P. (2004). *Politics in time: History, institutions, and social analysis.* Princeton, NJ: Princeton University Press.

Pressman, J. L., & Wildavsky, A. B. (1984). *Implementation: How great expectations in Washington are dashed in Oakland*. Berkeley: University of California Press.

Sager, F., & Hinterleitner, M. (2016). How do credit rating agencies rate? An implementation perspective on the assessment of austerity programs during the European debt crisis. *Politics & Policy, 44*(4), 783–815.

Sulitzeanu-Kenan, R., & Hood, C. (2005). *Blame avoidance with adjectives? Motivation, opportunity, activity and outcome*. Paper prepared for ECPR Joint Sessions, Granada, Spain, April 14–20, 2005.

Thomann, E., Hupe, P., & Sager, F. (2017). Serving many masters: Public accountability in private policy implementation. *Governance*. https://doi.org/10.1111/gove.12297

Verhoest, K., Van Thiel, S., Bouckaert, G., & Lægreid, P. (Eds.). (2012). *Government agencies: Practices and lessons from 30 countries*. Basingstoke: Palgrave Macmillan.

Vis, B. (2016). Taking stock of the comparative literature on the role of blame avoidance strategies in social policy reform. *Journal of Comparative Policy Analysis: Research and Practice, 18*(2), 122–137.

Wæraas, A., & Maor, M. (Eds.). (2015). *Organizational reputation in the public sector*. London: Routledge.

Weaver, R. K. (1986). The politics of blame avoidance. *Journal of Public Policy, 6*(4), 371–398.

Weaver, R. K. (1988). *Automatic government: The politics of indexation*. Washington, DC: Brookings Institution.

Weaver, R. K. (2013). *Policy leadership and the blame trap: Seven strategies for avoiding policy stalemate* (Governance Studies at Brookings). Washington, DC: Brookings Institution.

Wilson, J. Q. (1989). *Bureaucracy: What government agencies do and why they do it*. New York: Basic Books.

Wylie, I. (2005, November 5). The job to mend all jobs. *The Guardian*. Retrieved from https://www.theguardian.com/money/2005/nov/05/careers.work3

CHAPTER 8

Passing the Buck? How Risk Behaviours Shape Collaborative Innovation

Krista Timeus

INTRODUCTION

Collaboration is nowadays widely considered a 'good practice' for public sector organizations attempting to improve their innovative capacity (Agger & Sørensen, 2014; Bommert, 2010). The most commonly cited benefits of collaborative innovation are that it allows public organizations to share ideas and knowledge with people from outside the public sector and that this diversity of disciplines and backgrounds encourages more creative solutions to particular problems (Ansell & Torfing, 2014; Bekkers, Edelenbos, & Steijn, 2011). Despite these benefits, collaborative innovation can be very challenging to achieve. One of the reasons, as this chapter will argue, is that public managers work with incentives to minimize the risks of innovation as much as possible. These risk attitudes are likely to impact their willingness and ability to participate in collaborative innovation networks, as these add complexity and costs to the already risky innovation process. Based on this reasoning, the aim of this chapter is to

K. Timeus (✉)
Center for Public Governance, ESADE Business and Law School,
Barcelona, Spain

© The Author(s) 2019
T. Bach, K. Wegrich (eds.), *The Blind Spots of Public Bureaucracy and the Politics of Non-Coordination*, Executive Politics and Governance, https://doi.org/10.1007/978-3-319-76672-0_8

explore how risk attitudes shape public managers' motivations to participate in collaborative innovation ventures.

As a starting point, this chapter argues that collaboration, which we know is costly for the actors involved (Huxham, Vangen, Huxham, & Eden, 2000), can compound the risks of innovation for public managers. Once we consider this, we begin to understand why achieving collaborative innovation is challenging in the public sector. If innovation is already risky, why would public managers take on the additional risk of collaboration? To answer this question, this chapter explores how public managers' risk perceptions about innovation affect their decisions to collaborate with other actors.

Collaborative networks can improve the likelihood that public organizations assess and negotiate innovation proposals with a wider community of stakeholders. This helps ensure that the resulting innovations provide real value. Sørensen and Torfing (2011) have argued that beyond encouraging the generation of new ideas, competition between different views and preferences can ensure that the best ideas will be selected and that they will actually be implemented, as all parties have joint ownership over the process. Collaboration can also offer opportunities to ensure that different risk perspectives are discussed and assessed (Boholm & Corvellec, 2011). Such discussions can lead to improvements in the innovation process and to strategies for the eventuality that those risks materialize. This requires public actors in the network to be willing to openly assess risks and negotiate with others about which risks can be accepted as necessary parts of the innovation process (e.g. the failure of the project and the loss of some funds). This is of course more challenging if the public mangers involved are more likely to try to minimize risk than to engage with it openly.

MOTIVATIONS FOR COLLABORATIVE INNOVATIONS: WHAT IS THE ROLE OF RISK?

Although there are competing definitions for the term, collaboration is understood here, as defined by Ansell and Gash (2008), as 'a governing arrangement where one or more public agencies directly engage state or non-state stakeholders in a collective decision-making process that is formal, consensus oriented, and deliberative and that aims to make or implement public policy or manage public programs or assets' (p. 544). In the case of this chapter, we analyse collaboration aimed at generating and implementing public innovations.

One example of collaborative innovation is a recent telemedicine programme for high-risk heart patients in rural areas of Spain, who are unable to regularly go to the hospital for check-ups (Ferrado, 2014). The programme was designed and executed jointly by telecommunications provider Telefonica, a publicly owned Barcelona hospital, and the Catalan Department of Health; it is considered very successful (ibid). It is considered innovative because it has completely changed how the hospital organizes its resources and activities to treat these patients.

The mechanisms proposed in the literature to explain how collaboration increases innovation capacity are quite straightforward: collaboration can facilitate innovation by enabling people from different organizations, disciplines, and backgrounds to share unique skills and knowledge with each other and thus to develop more creative solutions to particular problems (Ansell & Torfing, 2014; Bekkers et al., 2011). In the example earlier, Telefonica was able to contribute its expertise in data and telecommunications to the hospital's cardiology unit. The joint ownership fostered through collaboration on such programmes is also thought to enhance the dissemination and sustainability of innovation projects in the long term, as more diverse stakeholders are involved from the project's design to its implementation (Abrahamson & Rosenkopf, 1997; Rogers, 2010).

This view of how collaboration can facilitate innovation directly addresses some arguments in the public management literature about the organizational factors that arguably constrain innovation in public sector organizations (Lægreid, Roness, & Verhoest, 2011; Walker, 2014). The first argument is that years of New Public Management (NPM) reforms have led public professionals to become overly specialized in narrowly defined, technical policy fields that 'rarely cross departmental boundaries' (Radnor & Osborne, 2013, p. 273). The result has been a so-called silo mentality or selective perception among public managers, who tend to understand and approach problems according to their own narrowly specialized mind-set (see introductory chapter by Bach and Wegrich in this volume). This routine problem-solving approach can prevent new, creative ideas from entering the various organizational units (Hambleton & Howard, 2013; Mulgan, 2012). Similarly, strict hierarchies are thought to limit communication between management levels, which could also limit opportunities to exchange information and ideas (O'Toole, 1997).

Another argument is that the public sector has too many procedural safeguards and too much red tape, which discourage experimentation and risk-taking (Wynen, Verhoest, Ongaro, & Van Thiel, 2014). These public administration characteristics favour behaviours that enforce stability and predictability over experimentation and disruption (which innovation relies on).

Given the normative connotation of innovation already discussed, these characteristics of public organizations are often referred to in the innovation literature as 'barriers' to innovation, with a negative undertone (De Vries, Bekkers, & Tummers, 2016). These characteristics are also the reason why the public sector has traditionally been perceived as lacking the capacity to innovate, especially in comparison to the private sector. Again, collaboration is portrayed as a way to overcome these barriers by exposing individuals in the public administration to external ideas and by allowing them to harness external resources for innovation (Torfing & Triantafillou, 2016).

What the innovation literature does not discuss is that some of these so-called barriers to innovation have developed from the institutional logic of public sector organizations. Public organizations are expected to work with a high degree of professionalism, following strict procedural safeguards, applying rules consistently and systematically, and respecting hierarchies. These norms exist to ensure not only bureaucratic efficiency but also the uniform applications of rules to all society (Meyer, Egger-Peitler, Höllerer, & Hammerschmid, 2014). The resulting norms and values of this institutional logic create an organizational culture and individual behaviours that prioritize authority, rule following, and consistency and that contrast sharply with innovation, which inherently requires change and experimentation. As discussed in the introductory chapter to this volume, we must also consider that public organizations operate in a political context, even if they seek to be apolitical internally. Perhaps now more than ever before, the media and the public scrutinize and contest the decisions of the bureaucracy and its political leadership (see Hinterleitner and Sager in this volume). This exerts additional pressure on public managers to follow the status quo and avoid trying new approaches that might fail.

The organizational culture we see in the public sector and its political context also reinforce risk-averse behaviours among public managers, which in turn can also constrain innovation capacity (Osborne & Brown, 2011). Generally, innovation is perceived as being risky because it entails uncertainty about potential failure due to unforeseeable factors or whether it will have unintended consequences (Bysted & Jespersen, 2014).

Previous studies have shown that almost half of all innovations will not succeed or will exceed their planned budget (Osborne & Flemig, 2015; Tidd & Bessant, 2013). Such risks are usually considered necessary elements of the innovation process in the private sector, but they can be judged harshly within the public sector and in its broader political context.

For public managers, the risks of innovation are mainly personal. The most prominent concern is the risk of being personally blamed for innovation failures, even if these are understood internally as a necessary part of the innovation process. The media and public can be especially reactive if there is a perception that an organization has wasted public money when innovation projects do not have the desired outcomes. Politicians can also try to avoid public criticism by shifting blame for any project failure to public managers and the bureaucracy (see Hinterleitner and Sager in this volume). Public managers' reputations, chances of being promoted, current positions, or remuneration can be harmed if they get blamed for policy or programme failures (Hood, 2011; Moynihan, 2012).

Another personal risk that innovators face in public organizations is the risk of rejection and opposition from their colleagues and superiors. Innovation champions in the public sector are challenging established methods, relationships, norms, and expectations (Bysted & Jespersen, 2014). In public organizations, such changes are not always welcome. Such resistance is even more likely if employees believe that the term 'innovation' is being used as a euphemism for cutting costs in the public sector (Klein, Mahoney, McGahan, & Pitelis, 2010). Public managers also risk affecting the performance of their team. The disruption and uncertainty that inevitably accompany innovation can cause the staff stress or create conflicts (Bysted & Jespersen, 2014; Janssen, Van de Vliert, & West, 2004). Pushback from staff can be perceived as a failure for the public manager, especially if it halts the innovation process (Hartley, 2013).

Of course, we must acknowledge that public managers are certainly willing and able to deal with risk, as many of their decisions contain some degree of uncertainty (Brown, 2010; Harrow, 1997). Nonetheless, they still operate in an institutional context marked by a bureaucratic logic that reinforces stability, predictability, and procedural safeguards, and in a political environment where decisions are often scrutinized. This chapter argues that such a context encourages risk-minimizing behaviours and makes collaborative innovation more challenging for public managers than the literature might suggest.

Given the current enthusiasm around innovation, it is unlikely that it will be completely avoided despite these risks. In fact, there are many innovation processes currently underway in governments around the world and innovation units whose role is to pursue innovation (Puttick, Baeck, & Colligan, 2014). The existing literature encourages these managers to seek out collaboration to increase their organizations' innovation capacity. Once we consider the importance of minimizing risks in their political context, the question of collaborative innovation becomes puzzling, because collaboration is very likely to entail additional risks for the public organization.

To Collaborate or Not?

The Costs of Collaboration: Compounding Risks

Where innovation can entail risks for the individuals behind it, collaboration brings its own set of risks to the entire organization. From an individual's perspective, the organizational risks of collaboration can be thought of as compounding or intensifying the risks they already face during innovation processes. Collaboration makes the public organization dependent on the efforts of others to perform well. As argued by Wilson (1989), this can be a source of risk because sharing responsibility with other actors makes the public organization vulnerable to blame for 'the mistakes caused by the bad judgment of other ... members not controlled by [the main responsible organization]' (p. 190). Poor performance is reflected on the whole network, which means that collaboration can affect a public organization's reputation, even when a mistake is not its own (Klijn & Teisman, 2003; Koppenjan, 2008; see also Heims in this volume). Reputational damage can also threaten an organization's autonomy if mistakes in the innovation process provoke budget cuts or increased political scrutiny (Busuioc, 2016). Limiting its authority in the already risky innovation process might, therefore, not be in the organization's best interest.

Risks of conflict also exist when the collaboration brings together competing institutional logics and administrative cultures. In order to prevent this clash of organizational cultures from leading to conflicts or errors, the organization will need to spend resources on managing the collaboration (Vangen, Hayes, & Cornforth, 2015; Vangen & Winchester, 2014). This makes collaboration costly. If public organizations fail to do this and public mistakes or conflicts arise for which the public organization is ultimately blamed, it might provoke interference from their political leadership, who want to protect their public image and agenda (Carpenter, 2001; Wilson, 1989). The costs of managing collaboration can give public managers further reason to be wary of it. This can be especially true when collaboration is sought out for the purpose of developing innovations that might receive additional political and public attention.

A number of scholars have discussed these tensions between collaboration and management in public organizations and the importance of acknowledging them in public administration research (Huxham & Vangen, 2005; Vangen & Winchester, 2014; Willem & Lucidarme, 2014). Nonetheless, theoretical arguments about how collaboration can facilitate innovation have not considered how public organizations, which have motivations to protect their autonomy and turf, might perceive important risks in collaboration. This is surprising because the costs of collaboration are likely to be only exacerbated in the context of innovation, which, as argued earlier, already entails risks for public managers.

The question for public managers who are motivated to pursue innovation in their organizations is whether they should seek out collaborative networks for their potential benefits (e.g. exchange of ideas and expertise) or whether they should manage innovation processes internally. The latter would enable them to control the risks of innovation processes as much as possible. Given these risks of collaborative innovation and public managers' risk aversion, one can argue that an effective risk minimization strategy is actually to avoid collaboration. Based on this, one can hypothesize that:

H1: Public managers are motivated to avoid collaborative innovation by a desire to minimize risk as much as possible.

In this case, risk-minimizing behaviours, which are rational for public managers, have the effect of discouraging collaboration with other organizations.

THE BENEFITS OF COLLABORATION: DIFFUSING RISK

Of course, it is important to consider that organizations do sometimes collaborate when they stand to gain significant advantages from it. This is referred to as the 'collaborative advantage' that each party achieves by working with partners instead of alone (Huxham & Macdonald, 1992;

Huxham, 1996; see also Heims in this volume). As already mentioned, in the context of innovation, these advantages can include the exchange of ideas and resources.

One advantage of collaboration is that it can give public mangers opportunities to diffuse some of the risks of innovation among the collaboration network. This would also have the effect of minimizing risks for public managers and their organization. This benefit could possibly outweigh the costs of engaging in collaboration. Based on this reasoning, a second hypothesis for this study is that:

H2: Public managers pursue collaborative innovation when they can benefit from transferring the risks of innovation to other actors.

This argument is reflected in the rationale for public–private partnerships (PPPs), a particular type of collaboration. Part of the rationale for creating PPPs is, precisely, that they allow public sector organizations to transfer certain risks to private sector actors, especially operational and financial ones (Hodge & Greve, 2005). Edelenbos and Klijn (2009) even define PPPs as 'a co-operation between public and private actors in which actors develop mutual products and/or services and in which risk, costs and benefits are shared' (p. 311). Some scholars have focused on the innovation potential of PPPs, claiming that PPPs can foster innovation because they enable the partners to tap into each other's knowledge resources and combine them in new, creative ways (Brogaard, 2017; Parker & Hartley, 2003). Even so, these partnerships can also lead to increased costs and uncertainty in the process (Ysa, Esteve, & Longo, 2013), so their benefits must be significant in order to attract interest from public managers. The fact that risk is shared in these partnerships might also be a driver of innovation. However, an important difference is that PPPs are usually governed by contracts that specify conditions for risk sharing. In the case of collaboration, at least as the term is used in the innovation literature, the terms of the partnerships are less explicit. This might explain why risk sharing has not been as prominent in the collaboration literature. Nonetheless, similar mechanisms for risk sharing can operate in collaborative networks, even if these include more partners whose relations are organized horizontally.

In sum, risk-averse behaviours in the bureaucracy are likely to influence collaborative innovation processes more than the literature has assumed. This study hypothesizes that, on the one hand, risk-averse behaviours have the effect of discouraging collaborative innovation. On the other hand, risk aversion could motivate public mangers to pursue collaboration in order to transfer innovation risks to other actors.

The validity of these hypotheses is explored through a series of interviews with public managers working on innovation processes in Barcelona municipality. The next section presents some brief background information on Barcelona municipality's current innovation strategy and the empirical analysis.

Case Background: Innovation in Barcelona Municipality

Barcelona municipality was selected as a case of a municipality that is improving its innovation capacity and that has publicly announced an intention to collaborate with other actors (Viladecans-Marsal & Arauzo-Carod, 2012). Besides this political intention to develop collaborative networks, its innovation strategy included an organizational restructuring to improve the local administration's innovation capacity. In 2013, Barcelona won the European Capital of Innovation Award, which inspired further political and administrative commitment to innovation.

The innovation strategy has mostly focused on smart city applications aimed at developing new services for citizens and new economic sectors (Gavaldà & Ribera-Fumaz, 2012). Examples of innovative concepts pursued in the city are the smart city campus 22@, which is a project to transform an old industrial district of Barcelona that had suffered significant decay into a new urban space for the creative and knowledge economy to concentrate in (Viladecans-Marsal & Arauzo-Carod, 2012). Another project is the development of a City Protocol, which is an explicit commitment to pursue more collaboration with civil society, businesses, public organizations, and citizen groups to develop new public service and solutions to the city's challenges (Wise, Wegrich & Lodge, 2014).

This innovation strategy was accompanied by an organizational rearrangement in the Barcelona City Council to oversee these initiatives. In 2011, the city government, led by mayor Xavier Trias of the Democratic Convergence of Catalonia party (a liberal, regionalist Catalonian party), created innovation teams in each of the four main administrative departments of the city municipality: the Department of Urban Habitat; the Department for Quality of Life, Equality, and Sports; the Department for Economy, Business, and Employment; and the Office of Culture,

Knowledge, Creativity, and Innovation. Each of these teams was specifically tasked with creating and overseeing that department's innovation strategy and had a director and a dedicated staff. To complement this structure, in 2013 the City Council created a coordination group for innovation in which the directors of each municipal department's innovation team was represented, as well as representatives of the mayor's office. The existence of these teams offers a clear sample for a qualitative analysis of public managers' motivations to pursue collaborative innovation.

This approach to innovation in Barcelona makes it an interesting and relevant case for exploring the merits of this study's theoretical propositions. On the one hand, the creation of these innovation teams signals a commitment to develop innovation within the City Council. On the other hand, the local government has communicated a willingness to work collaboratively with external partners, as signalled in the City Protocol (Wise et al., 2014). This context allows us to explore when and why people charged with the innovation strategy in the City Council choose to actually pursue collaboration or not.

To explore the role of risk perceptions as possible disincentives to collaborate, a qualitative analysis using interview data was considered the most appropriate approach, as it allows for a close study of the proposed mechanisms while leaving room for interesting, unexpected findings (Yin, 2013). Qualitative data to analyse motivations to pursue or avoid collaborative innovation were gathered through 15 semi-structured interviews with public managers responsible for innovation. Interviewees were identified using the method of referral sampling, stopping once referrals became repetitive.

ANALYSIS: INNOVATION PROCESSES IN BARCELONA CITY COUNCIL

The interview data suggest that the main innovation risks that public managers perceived were (a) organizational risks (e.g. reputational damage to the organization from public blame for innovation failures and loss of political support, autonomy, and funding) and (b) personal risks (e.g. being individually blamed by the executive leadership for innovation failures and experiencing career setbacks if they were to lose support from their supervisors or from their political leadership).

The findings also show that public managers' risk perceptions limit their willingness to engage in collaborative innovation in the early phases of innovation. At this stage, they preferred to maintain as much control over the process as possible. Collaboration was only sought out in the implementation phase to finance innovation projects. At this stage, it becomes beneficial for public managers and their organizations to transfer financial and operational risks to private actors. This collaboration was formal and contractual, rather than open and dynamic. The findings are summarized in this section according to the main themes that emerged during the analysis of the interview data. The resulting codes and categories from the interview analysis are summarized in Table 8.1.

Main Themes from the Interview Data

Types of Risk Perceived During Innovation Processes

Regarding their perception of risk, most interviewees thought that innovation had a higher likelihood of failure than other traditional public sector projects and was therefore also riskier. This supports the theoretical

Table 8.1   Codes and categories from interview data

Codes	Categories
Organizational risk	Types of perceived risk
Personal risk	
Loss of funds	Perceived risk of innovation
Loss of support	
Public opinion backlash/criticism	
Pressure not to waste money	
Failure of not scaling up	
Discontinued pilot projects	
Public criticism	
PPP	Type of collaboration
Collaboration with private sector	
Collaboration with civil society organizations	
Blame deflection (failure to deflect all blame)	Blame avoidance
Collaboration seen as important	Motivations for collaboration
Financial risk transfer	
Lack of technical capacity	
Lack of financial capacity	
Risk containment (in innovation unit)	

expectation that innovation is seen as a risky activity in public organization. Several managers and administrative staff members said they felt the pressure of knowing that many of the projects they worked on entailed heavy risks, mainly because innovative projects have a much higher likelihood of never getting off the ground, due to loss of funding and support or due to limited technical capacity. This suggests that most of the risks perceived by the interviewees were organizational or personal risks. Under the organizational risks, there was general agreement that one of the main risks is a public opinion backlash against a particular innovation initiative. In such cases, the organization's reputation and authority suffers. Another type of risk that was mentioned often by the interviewees is the potential loss of public funds due to failed innovation projects. There were many pilot projects that did not survive past the first trial stage, which they said the media sometimes portrayed as wasteful. Several interviewees said that as a result, they are under pressure not to 'waste' taxpayers' money. They added that this is an essentially sensitive topic in the context of current austerity measures.

Regarding who faced these risks, there was general agreement that most of this risk is borne personally by the department heads and especially by the directors of the innovation units. In turn, directors of the innovation units said that they knew that some risk of blame was part of their job description but that they accepted it. Interviewees mentioned one specific example of an innovation project led by the mayor's office that was perceived as a failure by the public and caused significant public backlash. The project's overall goal was to redevelop a commercial zone in Barcelona by integrating information and communications technology into the infrastructure. The project was planned through a citizen participatory process, which granted it high visibility. The project's eventual failure was heavily scrutinized and eventually led to the dismissal of the mayor's second-in-command, who had overseen the innovation process. This shows that, indeed, innovative projects are riskier than traditional ones and that managers are the main targets of blame. This also shows that blame is both an organizational and a personal risk: when the public directs its blame to the organization as a whole, an individual manager can become a scapegoat to limit damage to the organization.

Type of Collaboration Pursued

The interviewees all said that collaboration was important for achieving their departments' innovation goals. However, in the initial stages of the innovation process, the interviews show that the process was mostly managed internally and with very little outreach to external organizations. Several interviewees mentioned that they feel pressure to show their organizations' leadership that innovation processes are 'under control'. The innovation managers have established an innovation strategy and only pursue innovative ideas that can be clearly aligned with it. The approach for evaluating and selecting ideas is very structured.

Collaboration arrangements were more common in the financing and implementation stages of innovation projects (especially large projects involving digitalization or construction). At least one expert said that it is precised because there is such a structured organizational strategy to manage the innovation process internally that collaboration is limited to the sharing of financial risk. The interviewees provided examples of collaborative innovation that were more akin to traditional PPPs. That is probably linked to the type of risks that were shared. The main partners that were approached for innovation were usually private firms and, to a lesser extent, civil society organizations. Several interviewees said that most large innovation projects were dependent on collaboration between private sector actors or civil society organizations and the municipality because the municipality by itself lacked the technical, financial, or personnel capacity to implement the projects it developed. Two examples of these are the construction of living labs, where start-up firms can construct prototypes and test them in the city with the municipality's support, and an e-government initiative that aims at gathering data from the city's smart infrastructure in real time.

Motivations for Collaboration

Regarding the motivations for pursing collaboration for the purpose of innovating, interviewees mentioned the benefits of knowledge and idea exchange in collaborative settings but also said that the main advantage was that collaboration enabled them to attract external financial resources to the projects. A third of the interviewees specifically said that the main advantage was that financial risk could be shared with external partners. One person said, 'This way, if the project fails, the citizen cannot say that we wasted public money'. This was especially the case for innovation projects coming from the Department of Urban Habitat, possibly because of the large investments they often entail. Several interviewees said that setting up partnerships with firms or civil society organizations that could take on the actual implementation of the projects was 'essential for successful innovation in the municipality' and that working with private actors 'definitely means that we can pursue more radical and far-reaching innovations because they can provide more financial resources'.

Blame Avoidance Opportunities
Despite having clearly stated that an advantage of collaboration with private sector firms was to transfer some of the financial and technical risks of innovation away from the public sector, the interviews also suggest that the municipality is not able to deflect all blame for implementation failures. Several interviewees mentioned that, ultimately, citizens will still blame the municipality—especially during elections—for failures in public service projects, regardless of whether they were built by a private third party. According to the interviewees, the benefit of collaboration in such cases is only to 'soften the blow', because the public organization can assure them that mostly private sector funds were at stake, but it cannot entirely shield the organization from public blame.

The next section discusses these findings according to the chapter's theoretical framework and the existing literature on the role of risk and collaboration in public sector innovation.

Do Risk Perceptions Limit Collaborative Innovation?

The findings from the empirical analysis support the first hypothesis: public managers' risk perceptions regarding innovation and collaboration actively discourage them from pursuing collaborative innovation in city councils. While collaboration was sought out by innovation managers to finance initiatives, it was actually avoided in the early stages of innovation, such as idea generation and selection, or when the innovation projects were small in scale. During this early phase, the interviewees developing the projects suggested that they preferred to maintain as much control over the process as possible. From their perspective, collaboration in the early stages of innovation actually intensified the risks by increasing the complexity of the process. Reflecting discussions in the collaborative innovation literature, the interview analysis showed that managers perceived that collaboration not only put more pressure on their organizations' already scarce financial and human resources but also made it more dependent on the efforts of others to perform well (Klijn & Teisman, 2003; Koppenjan, 2008; Wilson, 1989).

The interview data also supported the second hypothesis: in some cases of innovation, managers perceive that the risks of collaboration are compensated by the benefit of being able to transfer risk to other actors. In such cases, collaboration is beneficial, and managers decide to pursue it. The interview data showed that public managers saw the diffusion of financial risk as a significant benefit of collaborative innovation. Another significant advantage was the ability to harness the technical capacity of private sector actors, especially in the implementation of large-scale innovation projects, such as digitalization initiatives. In practice, this can be positive for the public administration's innovation capacity: private sector actors are often more experienced in assessing and managing financial and technical types of risk (Osborne & Flemig, 2015), so engaging them can allow the public sector to experiment with larger-scale innovation, especially in the area of urban development and technology, without risking taxpayers' money.

In sum, the findings show that the effects of risk behaviours on collaborative innovation are different in the design stage and in the implementation stage of innovative projects. In the design stage, the findings support the argument that, despite the potential benefits of collaboration, public managers generally want to minimize risks and thus avoid collaborative ventures. In the implementation stage, the benefits of transferring financial risk to third parties were significant enough to pursue collaboration.

In fact, even when collaboration was described in the interviews, it more closely resembled a traditional PPP than a dynamic, consensus-oriented deliberative process between state and non-state actors, as has been described in the collaborative innovation literature (Doberstein, 2016; Mandell, Keast, & Chamberlain, 2017). The reason for this similarity might be that the transfer of technical and financial risks usually requires formal contractual agreements. That makes the partnership more like a formal PPP than a dynamic collaboration. As Klijn and Teisman (2003) have argued, however, the rigidity of PPPs can limit innovation because it leads to a separation of responsibilities within the partnerships to avoid conflict and control risk, rather than to an open exchange of ideas. This suggests that, even when the interviewed managers were willing to pursue collaboration, the terms of the collaboration were shaped by motivations to minimize risks. The result is a more limited scope of collaboration.

In sum, the analysis shows that in the case of Barcelona's City Council, public managers' primary concern was to minimize the risks of innovation. This risk-averse behaviour limited the extent to which they sought out collaborative partnerships for innovation. Collaboration was an attractive idea but was perceived as costly, and it compounded the risks of innovation by introducing additional complexity to the process. The consequence of these risk attitudes is that they effectively discourage public managers from taking opportunities to collectively define, assess, and manage the risks of innovation with stakeholders outside the public administration. This is problematic because innovation projects that do not consider the risk perspectives of a range of different stakeholders tend to be less sustainable and less effective at solving problems (Brown & Osborne, 2013).

Conclusions

This chapter explored how public managers' risk perceptions shape their motivations whether to pursue collaborative innovation or not. Qualitative analysis of a series of semi-structured interviews with public managers working on innovation in Barcelona municipality showed that they applied a risk minimization strategy to collaborative innovation. In the design stage of innovation, they avoided collaboration in order to retain as much control over the innovation process as possible. In the implementation stage of innovation, they pursued collaboration to transfer financial and operational risks away from the public sector. At this stage, however, collaboration was more formal than open and dynamic.

This analysis shows that public managers' risk perceptions limit their willingness to collaborate precisely when collaboration can most benefit the innovation process: in the project or programme design stage. Collaboration can be especially advantageous in the design stage of an innovation process because this is when external ideas and perspectives can shape a policy or programme in a new, different way. The problem for public managers is that the design stage of innovation already entails high degree of uncertainty regarding outcomes, so giving up any control over the process to external actors would only increase the innovation risk. The organizational culture and norms of the public sector, as well as the political context in which public managers operate, encourage them to prioritize risk minimisation over collaboration.

To conclude, this chapter contributes to the study of executive politics in two ways: first, the discussion emphasizes the need to be more critical about public managers' ability to manage the risks of innovation—and, more fundamentally, their willingness to do so—in collaborative networks. Understanding this better can lay the groundwork for further research into the management of collaborative networks and how to correct the effects of behaviours that, while perfectly rational for the bureaucracy, effectively limit its opportunities to develop new approaches to complex problems. Second, the study argued that the collaborative innovation literature has ignored the effects of more traditional bureaucratic culture and norms that still shape public managers' risk behaviour, such as motivations, to protect their organizations' autonomy and reputation by avoiding or minimizing risks and avoiding costly joint ventures unless these offer significant benefits. One the one hand, it is important to acknowledge those motivations to understand the limits of collaboration in practice. On the other hand, it can also provide a different lens from which to investigate how managing risk perceptions in the bureaucracy can be the basis for improving collaboration in the public sector.

References

Abrahamson, E., & Rosenkopf, L. (1997). Social network effects on the extent of innovation diffusion: A computer simulation. *Organization Science, 8*(3), 289–309.

Agger, A., & Sørensen, E. (2014). Designing collaborative policy innovation: Lessons from a Danish municipality. In C. Ansell & J. Torfing (Eds.), *Public innovation through collaboration and design* (pp. 170–208). Abingdon: Routledge.

Ansell, C., & Gash, A. (2008). Collaborative governance in theory and practice. *Journal of Public Administration Research and Theory, 18*(4), 543–571.

Ansell, C., & Torfing, J. (Eds.). (2014). *Public innovation through collaboration and design.* Abingdon: Routledge.

Bekkers, V., Edelenbos, J., & Steijn, B. (2011). An innovative public sector? Embarking on the innovation journey. In V. Bekkers, J. Edelenbos, & B. Steijn (Eds.), *Innovation in the public sector: Linking capacity and leadership* (pp. 197–221). New York: Palgrave Macmillan.

Boholm, Å., & Corvellec, H. (2011). A relational theory of risk. *Journal of Risk Research, 14*(2), 175–190.

Bommert, B. (2010). Collaborative innovation in the public sector. *International Public Management Review, 11*(1), 15–33.

Brogaard, L. (2017). The impact of innovation training on successful outcomes in public–private partnerships. *Public Management Review, 19*(8), 1184–1205.

Brown, L. (2010). Balancing risk and innovation to improve social work practice. *British Journal of Social Work, 40*(4), 1211–1228.

Brown, L., & Osborne, S. P. (2013). Risk and innovation. *Public Management Review, 15*(2), 186–208.

Busuioc, E. M. (2016). Friend or foe? Inter-agency cooperation, organizational reputation, and turf. *Public Administration, 94*(1), 40–56.

Bysted, R., & Jespersen, K. R. (2014). Exploring managerial mechanisms that influence innovative work behaviour: Comparing private and public employees. *Public Management Review, 16*(2), 217–241.

Carpenter, D. P. (2001). *The forging of bureaucratic autonomy: Reputations, networks, and policy innovation in executive agencies, 1862–1928.* Princeton: Princeton University Press.

De Vries, H. A., Bekkers, V., & Tummers, L. G. (2016). Innovation in the public sector: A systematic review and future research agenda. *Public Administration, 94*(1), 146–166.

Doberstein, C. (2016). Designing collaborative governance decision-making in search of a 'collaborative advantage'. *Public Management Review, 18*(6), 819–841.

Edelenbos, J., & Klijn, E.-H. (2009). Project versus process management in public–private partnership: Relation between management style and outcomes. *International Public Management Journal, 12*(3), 310–331.

Ferrado, M. L. (2014). Doctor smart on the phone. *Barcelona Metròpolis, 91,* 20–21.

Gavaldà, J., & Ribera-Fumaz, R. (2012). *Barcelona 5.0: From knowledge to smartness* (Working Paper Series No. WP12–002). Barcelona: Universitat Oberta de Catalunya.

Hambleton, R., & Howard, J. (2013). Place-based leadership and public service innovation. *Local Government Studies, 39*(1), 47–70.

Harrow, J. (1997). Managing risk and delivering quality services: A case study perspective. *International Journal of Public Sector Management, 10*(5), 331–352.

Hartley, J. (2013). Public and private features of innovation. In S. P. Osborne & L. Brown (Eds.), *Handbook of innovation in public services* (pp. 44–59). Cheltenham: Edward Elgar.

Hodge, G. A., & Greve, C. (2005). *The challenge of public–private partnerships: Learning from international experience.* Cheltenham: Edward Elgar.

Hood, C. (2011). *The blame game: Spin, bureaucracy, and self-preservation in government.* Princeton: Princeton University Press.

Huxham, C. (1996). *Creating collaborative advantage.* London: Sage.

Huxham, C., & Macdonald, D. (1992). Introducing collaborative advantage: Achieving inter-organizational effectiveness through meta-strategy. *Management Decision, 30*(3), 50–56.

Huxham, C., & Vangen, S. (2005). *Managing to collaborate: The theory and practice of collaborative advantage.* Abingdon: Routledge.

Huxham, C., Vangen, S., Huxham, C., & Eden, C. (2000). The challenge of collaborative governance. *Public Management: An International Journal of Research and Theory, 2*(3), 337–358.

Janssen, O., Van de Vliert, E., & West, M. A. (2004). The bright and dark sides of individual and group innovation: A special issue introduction. *Journal of Organizational Behavior, 25*(2), 129–145.

Klein, P. G., Mahoney, J. T., McGahan, A. M., & Pitelis, C. N. (2010). Toward a theory of public entrepreneurship. *European Management Review, 7*(1), 1–15.

Klijn, E., & Teisman, G. R. (2003). Institutional and strategic barriers to public-private partnership: An analysis of Dutch cases. *Public Money & Management, 23*(3), 137–146.

Koppenjan, J. (2008). Creating a playing field for assessing the effectiveness of network collaboration by performance measures. *Public Management Review, 10*(6), 699–714.

Lægreid, P., Roness, P. G., & Verhoest, K. (2011). Explaining the innovative culture and activities of state agencies. *Organization Studies, 32*(10), 1321–1347.

Mandell, M., Keast, R., & Chamberlain, D. (2017). Collaborative networks and the need for a new management language. *Public Management Review, 19*(3), 326–341.

Meyer, R. E., Egger-Peitler, I., Höllerer, M. A., & Hammerschmid, G. (2014). Of bureaucrats and passionate public managers: Institutional logics, executive identities, and public service motivation. *Public Administration, 92*(4), 861–885.

Moynihan, D. P. (2012). Extra-network organizational reputation and blame avoidance in networks: The hurricane Katrina example. *Governance, 25*(4), 567–588.

Mulgan, G. (2012). The theoretical foundations of social innovation. In A. Nicholls & A. Murdock (Eds.), *Social innovation: Blurring boundaries to reconfigure markets* (pp. 33–65). Basingstoke: Palgrave Macmillan.

O'Toole, L. J. (1997). Treating networks seriously: Practical and research-based agendas in public administration. *Public Administration Review, 57*(1), 45–52.

Osborne, S. P., & Brown, L. (2011). Innovation in public services: Engaging with risk. *Public Money & Management, 31*(1), 4–6.

Osborne, S. P., & Flemig, S. (2015). Conceptualizing risk and social innovation: An integrated framework for risk governance. *Society and Economy in Central and Eastern Europe, 37*(2), 165–182.

Parker, D., & Hartley, K. (2003). Transaction costs, relational contracting and public private partnerships: A case study of UK defence. *Journal of Purchasing and Supply Management, 9*(3), 97–108.

Puttick, R., Baeck, P., & Colligan, P. (2014). *i-teams: The teams and funds making innovation happen in governments around the world*. London and New York: Nesta and Bloomberg Philanthropies.

Radnor, Z., & Osborne, S. P. (2013). Lean: A failed theory for public services? *Public Management Review, 15*(2), 265–287.

Rogers, E. M. (2010). *Diffusion of innovations* (4th ed.). New York: Simon & Schuster.

Sørensen, E., & Torfing, J. (2011). Enhancing collaborative innovation in the public sector. *Administration & Society, 43*(8), 842–868.

Tidd, J., & Bessant, J. (2013). *Managing innovation: Integrating technological, market and organizational change* (5th ed.). Chichester: Wiley.

Torfing, J., & Triantafillou, P. (2016). *Enhancing public innovation by transforming public governance*. Cambridge: Cambridge University Press.

Vangen, S., Hayes, J. P., & Cornforth, C. (2015). Governing cross-sector, inter-organizational collaborations. *Public Management Review, 17*(9), 1237–1260.

Vangen, S., & Winchester, N. (2014). Managing cultural diversity in collaborations: A focus on management tensions. *Public Management Review, 16*(5), 686–707.

Viladecans-Marsal, E., & Arauzo-Carod, J. (2012). Can a knowledge-based cluster be created? The case of the Barcelona 22@ district. *Papers in Regional Science, 91*(2), 377–400.

Walker, R. M. (2014). Internal and external antecedents of process innovation. *Public Management Review, 16*(1), 21–44.

Willem, A., & Lucidarme, S. (2014). Pitfalls and challenges for trust and effectiveness in collaborative networks. *Public Management Review, 16*(5), 733–760.

Wilson, J. Q. (1989). *Bureaucracy: What government agencies do and why they do it*. New York: Basic Books.

Wise, R., Wegrich, K., & Lodge, M. (2014). Governance innovations. In Hertie School of Governance (Ed.), *The governance report 2014* (pp. 77–109). Oxford: Oxford University Press.

Wynen, J., Verhoest, K., Ongaro, E., & Van Thiel, S. (2014). Innovation-oriented culture in the public sector: Do managerial autonomy and result control lead to innovation? *Public Management Review, 16*(1), 45–66.

Yin, R. K. (2013). *Case study research* (5th ed.). London: Sage.

Ysa, T., Esteve, M., & Longo, F. (2013). Enhancing innovation in public organizations through public-private partnerships: The role of public managers. In C. Greve & G. A. Hodge (Eds.), *Rethinking public-private partnerships: Strategies for turbulent times* (pp. 98–113). London: Routledge.

CHAPTER 9

Media and Bureaucratic Reputation: Exploring Media Biases in the Coverage of Public Agencies

Jan Boon, Heidi Houlberg Salomonsen, Koen Verhoest, and Mette Østergaard Pedersen

INTRODUCTION

Different theoretical perspectives on organizational reputation have been developed in several research traditions (for an overview, see Wæraas & Maor, 2015). This chapter can be situated in the political science approach to bureaucratic reputation theory (BRT), characterized by its empirical focus on government agencies and their standing within political-administrative systems (Carpenter, 2010).

Within the BRT framework, a bureaucratic reputation is defined as 'a set of symbolic beliefs about the unique or separable capacities, intentions,

J. Boon (✉) • K. Verhoest
Department of Political Science, University of Antwerp, Antwerp, Belgium
e-mail: jan.boon@uantwerpen.be; koen.verhoest@uantwerpen.be

H. H. Salomonsen • M. Ø. Pedersen
Department of Management, Aarhus University, Aarhus, Denmark
e-mail: hhs@mgmt.au.dk; mpedersen@mgmt.au.dk

© The Author(s) 2019   171
T. Bach, K. Wegrich (eds.), *The Blind Spots of Public Bureaucracy and the Politics of Non-Coordination*, Executive Politics and Governance, https://doi.org/10.1007/978-3-319-76672-0_9

roles, obligations, history and mission of an organization that are embedded in a network of multiple audiences' (Carpenter, 2010, p. 33). Today's knowledge society and blame culture have increased organizational concerns with reputational risk. According to Daniel Carpenter (2004), reputation-cultivating and/or -protective behaviour is the most powerful dynamic governing organizational behaviour. BRT scholars are interested in how agencies identify and respond to threats to their reputation. A series of studies demonstrate how agencies respond to reputational threats by changing the timing of their decisions (Carpenter, 2002), the public observability of decisions (Maor, 2011; Moffitt, 2010), their outputs (Maor & Sulitzeanu-Kenan, 2016), or their strategic communication (Gilad, Maor, & Ben-Nun Bloom, 2015; Maor, Gilad, & Ben-Nun Bloom, 2013).

Carpenter (2010) has proposed a framework of four dimensions of an agency's reputation: (1) performative, the ability to execute its tasks effectively, with respect to both outcome and output; (2) moral, the ability to meet the normative expectations posed to public organizations, such as protecting citizens and ensuring transparency; (3) technical, which depends on the 'expertise' and professional qualifications of the organization; and (4) procedural, which refers to the extent that the organization conforms with set procedures and legislation (pp. 44–46). How agencies perceive, process, and prioritize multiple (and potentially conflicting) audiences' expectations of different components of their reputation is a core interest of reputation theorists. Agencies must choose which dimension to stress towards specific audiences. This process is referred to in the literature as 'prioritizing' (Maor, 2015, p. 32). The act of prioritizing assumes that government agencies are rational and politically conscious organizations with incentives to avoid reputational damages and ultimately political sanctions.

In this chapter, we challenge the alleged rationality that is often assumed to be part of the prioritization process. More specifically, we test the claim that agency behaviour is (at least to some extent) driven by the distinctive logic of the media rather than merely by assessments of the relative strength of different dimensions of their reputation that are subjected to threats, or by the nature of their task.

Before delving further into this claim, it is important to note that a focus on the media is not new in the BRT field. In general, the notion that agencies are open systems whose behaviour is explained through relations with their broader environment, rather than merely via their relation with political superiors, has been at the core of reputation-based studies (Maor, 2015). The media serve as crucial players in the reputational calculus of reputation-sensitive agencies. First, the media are rapidly gaining power as informal forums for political accountability (Bovens, 2007). They are the most important source of information about government performance for citizens (Arnold, 2004). Second, the media serve a dual role as audiences in their own right and as institutional intermediaries used by other audiences—and the agencies themselves—to make sense of agency performance. Therefore, BRT scholars recognize that for many agencies, the media will be an important channel through which they signal their reputation uniqueness to their manifold audiences.

However, we argue that most BRT studies do not take into account that the media work according to a logic of their own (Altheide, 2004), which might interfere with the reputation signals agencies seek to send. Existing scholarship tends to treat the role of the media as a black box. Studies have insufficiently looked at the independent effect of media reporting as a biased representation of reality, which is shaped by media-specific criteria of relevance. This chapter contributes to the field by theoretically developing and empirically testing biases in media reporting about agencies. The priorities of the media should be part of the equation when accounting for agencies' behaviour. The media may have their own biases in terms of their reporting, which in turn may affect what are considered to be important reputational dimensions, audiences, and so on for agencies to cultivate. More specifically, this chapter examines media biases in terms of negativity and the media-induced Velcro effect, related to the number of reputational dimensions that are reported about. This Velcro effect entails that organizations which faced intense negative media coverage in the past have much higher chances of being criticized on multiple aspects by negative media coverage and reputational threats by audiences in the future. In addition, we analyse whether agencies show a differential response to media reporting depending on newspaper article characteristics.

We find inspiration in the developing field of research on the mediatization of politics and bureaucracy (Fredriksson, Schillemans, & Pallas, 2015; Mazzoleni & Schulz, 1999; Strömbäck & Esser, 2014) and in the established literatures on news values (Galtung & Ruge, 1965; Van Aelst, Sheafer, & Stanyer, 2012) and agenda-setting (McCombs, 2014). The former field has illuminated that the media have established themselves as an important institution that increasingly influences other socio-political spheres, including government bureaucracies. The mediatization literature accentuates the general and increasing importance of the media as a force to which public agencies need to adapt and/or respond to in a strategic manner. The latter literatures provide insights into the criteria used by media outlets to determine whether and how to cover a story, and how definitions of issues set in the media influence the public and political agenda. These insights will be used to formulate some expectations for the news coverage of public agencies.

In connecting with literatures on the role of the media and its logic on different spheres in society, this chapter also makes a broader contribution to expanding the knowledge base of the nexus between media and the bureaucratic sphere. Since the turn of the century, the mediatization of politics has attracted significant scholarly attention (Mazzoleni & Schulz, 1999; Strömbäck & Esser, 2014). Because the media have developed into the most important source of information for people in advanced democracies, they hold the key to the public sphere. Virtually no political actor or institution can afford to ignore the media's role in contemporary politics (Strömbäck & Esser, 2014). Public agencies have long been neglected in mediatization research. Recent studies, however, show that agencies have tended to internalize the media logic in their everyday practices (Fredriksson, Schillemans, & Pallas, 2015; Thorbjørnsrud, 2015). The nexus between reputation and media has gained broader academic and societal relevance as public values, routines, and organizational work procedures are increasingly adapted to the demands of the media.

The following sections discuss prioritization as a theoretically central, though empirically underdeveloped, concept of BRT. Hereafter, we bring in the media and discuss prioritization against the backdrop of mediatization.

Prioritization as a Central Idea of Bureaucratic Reputation Theory

Public agencies operate in uncertain contexts characterized by dilemmas, trade-offs, and paradoxes (Pollitt & Bouckaert, 2011; Verhoest, Verschuere, & Bouckaert, 2007). Many of these dilemmas consist of opposing value systems that ultimately reflect broader societal debates about what we expect from governments and the organizations within them. Agencies face a number of contradictory values in their daily work.

For instance, values related to achieving political ends may conflict with values such as equality, fairness, and justice. Likewise, values related to morality may conflict with a strong market orientation (Goodsell, 1989; Wæraas & Byrkjeflot, 2012).

When cultivating their reputation, public managers must prioritize between potentially conflicting expectations. The core challenge that agencies face is that audiences have different (and potentially conflicting) expectations about the way the agency should exercise its tasks, which might change over time (Maor, 2016). As noted by Carpenter and Krause (2012), 'satisfying some audience subset often means upsetting others or projecting ambiguity' (p. 29). Furthermore, the effect of enhancing one reputational dimension implies that another dimension will likely suffer. Agencies, then, must choose which dimension to stress towards specific audiences, a process that is referred to as 'prioritizing' (Maor, 2015, p. 32).

The act of prioritizing assumes that government agencies are rational and politically conscious agencies with incentives to avoid reputational damages. In the words of leading BRT scholar Moshe Maor (2015):

> ... reputation-sensitive agencies are adaptive, strategic, and sometimes even opportunistic actors.... They have a repository of ideas, values, and strategies that they may combine in various ways, deploy them politically, and redeploy them between different audiences, thereby redefining relations with these audiences.... Specifically, reputation-sensitive agencies are able to adapt to in order to cope with criticism by external audiences—that is, to accommodate themselves to the preferences of their external audiences. They are able to manipulate external audiences' opinions and shape rather than simply accommodate external audiences' opinions, turning them into a component of agency behavior. (p. 25)

Prioritization can occur at several levels. First, prioritization exists at the level of reputational dimensions. To illustrate, Carpenter, Chattopadhyay, Moffitt, and Nall (2012) have examined whether administrative deadlines impact the Food and Drug Administration's (FDA) timing of decisions. They focus on the trade-off between the FDA's interest in producing accurate decisions and protecting its long-term reputation for expertise, on the one hand, and its interest in sufficient staff funding and short-term reputation for prompt action, on the other. Their results show that deadlines result in the piling of drug approvals right before the deadline, compromising the agency's long-term reputation and, ultimately, the safety of approved pharmaceuticals. Second, prioritization exists between areas of agencies' functioning. Agencies often perform different types of functions that might be prioritized in reputation management. Maor, Gilad, and Ben-Nun Bloom (2013) have demonstrated this for the case of the Israeli banking regulator, which performs tasks in the area of prudential regulation (where it enjoys a strong reputation) and in the area of consumer protection and competition (where it has a weak or evolving reputation). They show how this agency tends to remain silent on issues regarding which it generally enjoys a strong reputation and on issues that lie outside its distinct jurisdiction, while responding to opinions about core functional areas for which its reputation is weaker and areas wherein its reputation is still evolving. Third, prioritization exists at the level of stakeholder audiences. A reputational perspective suggests that not all audiences are equal in the eyes of reputation-sensitive agencies. For example, Busuioc and Lodge (2017) have argued that reputational concerns determine which audiences are prioritized by agencies and which competencies will be emphasized in the account-giving process.

What these different perspectives on prioritization have in common is an underlying assumption of a rational process during which politically conscious agencies strategically weigh the pros and cons of dedicating their limited time, energy, and resources towards specific audiences. Bureaucratic reputation theorists have so far primarily, and rather implicitly, suggested that prioritization is a precondition for an agency's ability to cultivate a favourable reputation which ultimately leads to autonomy in the relation with the political principal (Maggetti & Verhoest, 2014; Verhoest, Rommel, & Boon, 2015). However, we take the position that agencies are not only political actors able to read, adapt to, and even manipulate their environments but also open systems that are affected by their environments. In the subsequent part of the chapter, we provide some empirical insights into how media biases relate to how agencies appear in, and respond to, reputational threats (and praises) in the media.

How the Media Might Affect Prioritization

This chapter seeks to contribute to the BRT literature through a critical reflection on the central idea of prioritization, the underlying mechanisms of which are poorly understood in empirical terms. We do not claim to come up with any final answers. Yet through some empirical illustrations, we hope to commence a discussion for further theorizing on the basis of rationality that underpins the prioritization process of agencies. The overall question, we feel, that BRT studies need to reflect more on refers to the extent to which prioritization is a rational–intentional calculus of the relative strength of their reputations and the task subject for reputational threats. In this chapter, we begin with a very focused theoretical and empirical contribution on the role of the media in the prioritization process of agencies. The media as an institution works according to a logic of its own, which has been shown by mediatization scholars to increasingly affect other spheres of society (Hjarvard, 2013), including the public sector (Pallas, Fredriksson, & Wedlin, 2016; Schillemans, 2012).

Hence, we explore the idea of the news media as an institution in its own right with a potential to influence how agencies appear in, and respond to, coverage about their actions, building on the concept of news values and agenda-setting. First, news values are general guidelines or criteria used by media outlets, such as newspapers or broadcast media, to determine how much prominence to give to a story (Galtung & Ruge, 1965). The media work according to a distinct set of professional norms and values is emphasizing more or less universally accepted criteria for newsworthiness such as timeliness, proximity, surprise, negativity, elite involvement, conflict, and personalization (Strömbäck & Esser, 2014; Van Aelst et al., 2012).

Second, a vast agenda-setting literature has shown the news media's ability to influence the salience of (attributes of) issues on the public agenda (Carroll & McCombs, 2003; Deephouse, 2000; McCombs, 2014). News sources provide definitions of issues, and they frame problems in particular ways, thus providing the terms of future public discussion. This observation has obvious implications for agencies. As a result of news values and agenda-setting tendencies, it is important to stress that neither the image that is portrayed of agencies in the media, nor whether this image is picked up by the media and eventually ends up on the radar of political principals, are fully the result of agency strategizing. They are equally as much the result of journalists' and editors' decisions. This has led scholars to suggest the importance of an organization's 'media reputation', defined as the overall evaluation of an organization as presented in the media (Deephouse, 2000, p. 1091). On the one hand, BRT studies have been blind to the role of the journalist, treating the media as a black box. On the other hand, agencies themselves need to be conscious of the role of the media in the construction of their media reputation.

Following the media's inclination to report more about events or (aspects of) organizations that are more negative, more proximate, more conflictual, and involving elites, we formulate the following tentative hypotheses:

- First, we expect that the media will pay relatively more attention to reputational threats than reputational praises (H1), following the media's inclination to have a bias towards negative stories involving conflict.
- Second, we expect that the media will pay relatively more attention to organizations' performative reputations (H2), following the media's bias towards stories that have a more direct impact on their readers.
- Third, an agency's reputation is formed because of audiences' perception of an agency over time, meaning that organizations develop a 'relational history' with their audiences, formed by audience's past judgement of its performance and prior assessments of its reputation (Coombs & Holladay, 2001). Such relational histories form 'reputational histories', which matters as they serve as Velcro increasing the likelihood of exposure to future reputational threats (Coombs & Holladay, 2001). This Velcro effect, introduced by crisis communication scholars, suggests that a negative reputational history primes audiences to be more negative towards an organization facing a new crisis (Coombs & Holladay, 2001), as audiences are more likely to remember negative rather than positive past behaviour of the agency (Coombs & Holladay, 2006). As noted by Coombs and Holladay (2001), a negative reputational history 'attracts and snags additional reputational damage' (p. 335). This follows the idea that once a negative frame about the organization is in place in the media, it leads to a media Velcro effect across reputational dimensions. More aspects of the organization are placed under scrutiny by the media in their pursuit of more negative reporting on an agency that is already subject to negative media coverage. Hence, we expect that the media will scrutinize more reputational dimensions of organizations with a negative reputational history (H3).

Next, this chapter focuses on whether the media's biased attention is reflected in the organizations' communication responses to reputational threats in the media. BRT scholars have examined these communication strategies in some detail (Gilad, Maor, & Ben-Nun Bloom, 2015; Maor, Gilad, & Ben-Nun Bloom, 2013). These studies emphasize communication as a strategic exercise, driven by a motivation to protect the organization from reputational threats, depending on reputational profile of different tasks.

This chapter explores communication responses from a different angle pertaining to the question: to what extent, and how, are article characteristics related to communication responses of agencies? For each article in which one of the agencies under study was criticized (reputational threat) and/or praised (reputational praise), we coded whether the agency reacted to the threat or praise within the same article (see also Gilad, Maor, & Ben-Nun Bloom, 2015; Maor, Gilad, & Ben-Nun Bloom, 2013). In this chapter, we explore the role of article characteristics 'page in the newspaper' and 'number of words'. As noted by Carroll and McCombs (2003, p. 37), journalists communicate the salience of a given story in different ways, including through the placement in the newspaper and the length of the article. Longer stories and stories closer to the front page indicate high salience. Agencies might consider media logic in their decision-making by anticipating that certain issue characteristics (such as conflict or personalization) will provoke longer stories and/or stories that are closer to the front page. In these cases, a rational agency response would be to include their viewpoint on the matter in the article in the form of a reaction.

We formulate the following two additional hypotheses:

- We expect that longer articles will be more likely to contain a response from an agency to a threat or praise, compared to shorter articles (H4).
- We expect that articles closer to the front page will be more likely to contain a response from an agency to a reputational threat or praise, compared to articles further away from the front page (H5).

RESEARCH DESIGN AND METHODS

The data material consists of all news articles that mention one of the five most salient Danish agencies (Pollitt, Talbot, Caulfield, & Smullen, 2004; Verhoest, Van Thiel, Bouckaert, & Lægreid, 2012): the Danish Financial Supervisory Authority (Finanstilsynet), the Danish Health Authority (Sundhedsstyrelsen), the Danish Business Authority (Erhvervsstyrelsen), the Danish Customs and Tax Administration (SKAT), and the Danish Veterinary and Food Administration (Fødevarestyrelsen) in the Danish newspaper *Berlingske Tidende* in the time period 1 January 2006 to 31 December 2015. As the ambition of the empirical analysis is to take a first step towards illustrating the relevance of the hypotheses and the theoretical arguments, the choice of the agencies informing the hypotheses is crucial to ensure a high degree of salience in the media. The included agencies thus represent most likely cases.

To identify all relevant articles, we searched for the name of each agency in INFOMEDIA, a Danish database of all published articles in the newspaper. After excluding letters and non-relevant articles, 5960 articles were identified. The articles were then coded on the basis of whether they contain a reputational threat or reputational praise. A reputational threat was coded if the article contained an explicit threat that can be directly linked to the agency in some way, while a reputational praise was coded if the description of the agency, its action, or its non-action included positive framing. No threats or praises where coded if the agency or its actions were described in neutral terms.

For each threat or praise we then coded which reputational dimension was targeted and whether the article contained a response by the agency to the threat or praise. The coding was done on the basis of a codebook by trained student assistants. To assess inter-coder reliability, the coders were asked to code the same articles. Inter-coder reliability coefficients (Krippendorff's alpha) were later calculated. The alphas for the variables were in general satisfactory (>0.7), but for two of the reputational dimensions, procedural and processual, the alphas were low: 0.45 and 0.17, respectively. This led to a systematic re-evaluation and quality check of all the coding by two full-time research assistants. If the two of them were in doubt about the coding, they discussed the coding to reach 100 per cent agreement on the coding.

We use Daniel Carpenter's (2010, pp. 45–46) four-dimensional framework, and suggest the following operationalization of reputational dimensions:

- The performative dimension addresses judgements on the quality, efficiency, and/or effectiveness of the services that are considered an agency's outputs and outcomes. These services can be a set of activities or policy instruments, and also an initiative, programme, or a report, that is the final manifestation of the agency's core task that is delivered to society, politicians, or other public actors.

- The technical dimension refers to having the necessary resources in terms of capacities, expertise, and skills to perform its tasks. It is judged irrespective of the actual performance and is hence irrespective of any output or outcome.
- The procedural dimension is reflected in explicit references to procedures, standards, norms and rules, which can be internal but also external to the organization, such as the constitution.
- The moral dimension refers to an agency's well-meaning intentions (regardless of actual output). Moral praises relate to an agency's attentiveness and compassion to different client groups; honesty; integrity; fairness; ethical behaviour; openness and transparency; ability to prevent 'inequity, bias, and abuse of office'; trustworthiness; and attentiveness to democratic values (e.g. transparency, equal rights, legal rights, responsiveness to citizens in terms of their being heard in processes and procedures, and equal access to service delivery for different groups). Moral threats relate to a lack of these qualities, but they also include references to turf protection, scandals, and/or indecent behaviour.

An additional dimension that is not covered by Carpenter's categorization was defined to address some aspects of what agencies do. This dimension is defined as the processual dimension. Agencies perform different types of tasks broadly related to regulation, service delivery, or exercising other kinds of authority (Rolland & Roness, 2010). These tasks are composed of different processes, steps, and decisions which follow up on each other:

- The processual dimension captures the processes and steps that do not directly reflect the final manifestation of the agency's task delivered to society, politicians, or other public actors and/or the output or outcome of the organization, but which are merely serving as means (or preliminary steps) to realize those ends. For instance, the processual dimension involves a variety of internal processes and procedures such as the drafting of plans of action or internal reports, but also collaborations with external parties if there is no mentioning of outputs or outcomes.

If a reputational threat applied to more than one dimension (for instance, an agency that breaches formal rules about ethical behaviour), then each dimension to which the threat applied was coded (in the example here, both the procedural and the moral dimension). We constructed a variable that takes a value of 1 for multiple threats and 0 for single-dimension threats, for cases where several dimensions were threatened or praised in the article.

If an article contained an agency's response to a reputational threat or praise, we coded this as a dummy where 1 means the article contains a response and 0 means the article does not contain a response. Non-responses might refer to agencies refusing to respond even though they were given the opportunity to, or to agencies not given the opportunity to respond by the journalist.

We operationalized negative reputational history as the percentage of articles with negative threat(s) in the last 365 days prior to the case article per organization. For the five agencies, this varies substantially in the time period from 2005 to 2015, from 0.0 per cent to 38.7 per cent, with an overall mean of 11.9 per cent. We also computed the same variable for positive reputational history as the percentage of articles with positive praises. As with the negative history, this varies from 0.0 per cent positive articles in the last 365 days to a high of 16.7 per cent articles for one agency in the last 365 days. The mean for positive reputational history is 4.7 per cent.

EMPIRICAL ILLUSTRATIONS

In this section, we present some empirical illustrations related to the hypotheses formulated earlier in the text. A total of 5960 articles were coded, 5243 of which were coded as neutral (88.7 per cent). Of the remainder, 717 were coded to contain a reputational threat (12 per cent), and 282 were coded to contain a reputational praise (4.7 per cent). The percentages do not sum to 100 because it is possible for articles to contain both threats and praises, which was the case for 79 articles in this sample.

Supporting H1 and mirroring the findings of previous scholarship (Deacon & Monk, 2001; Schillemans, 2012), we found that, although the majority of coverage involving agencies is neutral, the share of articles that contain a reputational threat strongly outweighs the share of articles that contain a reputational praise. The media, thus, is more likely to cover an agency's mistakes than an agency's accomplishments.

Table 9.1 presents an overview of the reputational dimensions that are addressed in the articles that contain a reputational threat and those that contain a reputational praise.

Table 9.1 Reputational dimensions

	Performative	Technical	Moral	Procedural	Processual
Article with reputational threat	527 (73.5%)	164 (22.9%)	150 (20.9%)	93 (13.0%)	103 (14.4%)
Article with reputational praise	198 (70.2%)	75 (26.6%)	15 (5.3%)	5 (1.8%)	48 (17.0%)

Supporting the notion that the media has a bias towards covering stories that have a more direct impact on citizens (H2), we observe that the performative dimension (which includes assessments of the quality, effectiveness, or efficiency of an agency's final outputs towards society) attracts the most attention, both in the negatively and in the positively toned articles. We see little distinction between articles with a reputational threat (73.5 per cent) and those with a reputational praise (70.2 per cent) in terms of the frequency of referencing the performative dimension. In both cases, the technical dimension is the second most covered category, which might have something to do with the fact that references about the quality of personnel and leadership, which relate to the news value of personalization, belong to the technical dimension. We do, however, see a distinction between the tone of coverage of the moral and procedural dimensions, both of which are more often covered negatively than positively.

Table 9.2 presents the results of the logistic regression models. In model 1, we regress whether the article contains a threat (1) or no threat (0) on the negative and positive reputational history of the agency. As a robustness check, we also ran logistics models where multiple threats (1) were compared with single threat (0), thus only utilizing articles with reputational threats. The models with reputational history cover the years between 2007 and 2015. The year 2006 was removed as we need at least one preceding year to calculate the reputational history. In all models, we have included dummies for years and organization which are, however, not shown in Table 9.2.

To illustrate and simplify the relationship between the variables, we show figures with the predicted probabilities of the independent variable of interest only if the coefficient is significant in the regression models. The predicted probabilities were done as average predictions (as observed) across the five agencies (Long & Freese, 2014). We also show the distribution of the examined independent variable in the predicted probability figures (see Figs. 9.1 and 9.2).

Table 9.2   Logistic regressions models

	Model 1	Model 2
	Multiple dimensional threat (1)	
	No threat (0)	*Single threat (0)*
Negative reputational history	7.629*** (6.912)	4.601** (3.068)
Positive reputational history	0.080 (0.026)	−2.998 (−0.637)
Year dummies	Included but not shown	
Organization dummies	Included but not shown	
Constant	−4.589*** (−7.003)	−0.764 (−0.890)
N	5346	601
Pseudo R^2	0.084	0.094

Note: z statistics in parentheses. $^{\dagger}p < 0.10$, $^{*}p < 0.05$, $^{**}p < 0.01$, $^{***}p < 0.001$. Robust standard errors in parentheses

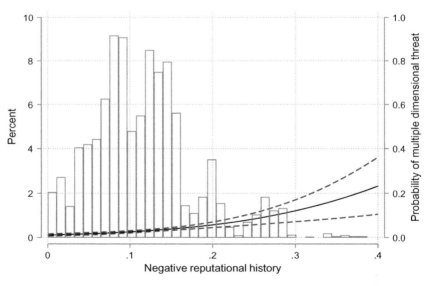

Fig. 9.1   Predicted probability of multiple threats as function of negative reputational history, based on model 1 (multiple threats (1) vs. no threats (0))

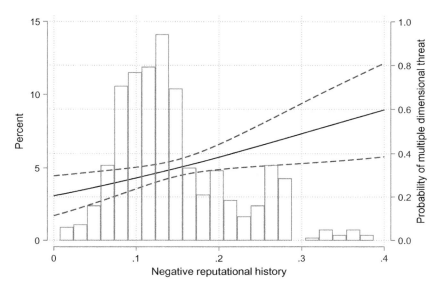

Fig. 9.2 Predicted probability of multiple threats as function of negative reputational history (only articles with threats), based on model 2 (multiple threats (1) vs. single threats (0))

In support of H3, the different analyses indicate the same trend: as negative reputational history increases, so does the likelihood that an article includes a threat on multiple dimensions. As hypothesized, we observe a Velcro effect across the dimensions that are reported in the media reports. Intense negative coverage leads to an increase in the possibility that multiple dimensions of an agency's functioning will be criticized at a later stage. This finding is in line with recent theorizing on crises as being dynamic, that is, potentially changing in subject during the course of the crisis (Frandsen & Johansen, 2017, pp. 47–48). Note that we do not observe the same pattern for positive reputational history, which has no significant effect on the presence of multiple dimensional threats.

Finally, Table 9.3 gives insight into the relation between article characteristics (length and page) and agencies' likelihood to respond within articles that contain a reputational threat. Figure 9.3 depicts this relation graphically.

The analyses find support for H4. The coefficient for article length is statistically significant and positive, thus indicating that articles are more

Table 9.3 Relationship between article characteristics and response likelihood

	Model 1	Model 2	Model 3
Length (log)	0.438** (2.871)		0.462** (2.973)
Page number (log)		−0.062 (−0.518)	−0.126 (−0.976)
Year dummies	Included but not shown		
Organization dummies	Included but not shown		
Constant	−2.903** (−2.822)	−0.051 (−0.116)	−2.795** (−2.680)
N	647	647	647
Pseudo R^2	0.066	0.055	0.067

Note: z statistics in parentheses. $^{+}p < 0.10$, $^{*}p < 0.05$, $^{**}p < 0.01$, $^{***}p < 0.001$. Robust standard errors in parentheses

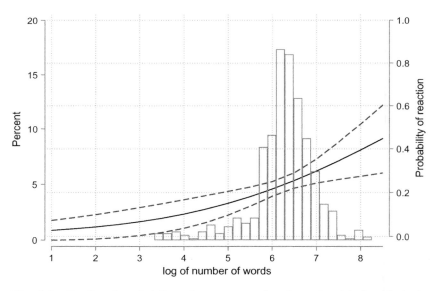

Fig. 9.3 Predicted probability of response as function of article length (only articles with threats)

likely to contain an agency's response to a reputational threat or praise as the length of the article increases. Figure 9.3 further illustrates this positive relation between article length and likelihood to contain a response. Most articles are distributed around 400–1100 words (between log(6) and log(7)). For an article of around 400 words, the probability that it contains an agency response is predicted to be 22 per cent. That probability increases to 30 per cent for an article of around 1100 words (different at $p < 0.01$).

Finally, the coefficient for the page number is negative, suggesting that articles are more likely to contain an agency's response as they appear closer to the first page. This finding offers preliminary support for H5, yet the observed relationship is not statistically significant.

DISCUSSION AND CONCLUSION

This chapter explored the mediatized context in which bureaucratic reputations are managed. We present a first explorative analysis on the extent to which newspaper coverage on public agencies is shaped by media-specific criteria of news values. Our analyses suggest the presence of a media logic to which reputation-conscious agencies respond. News articles are more likely to contain negative than positive stories (though the vast majority is neutral). Also, the media are more likely to report stories related to the performative dimension of reputation, which are more proximate to readers. We further find that more intense negative coverage is related to an increase in the probability that more dimensions of reputation will be criticized at a later point in time (suggesting a potential Velcro effect across the dimensions). Finally, articles are more likely to contain a response from the agency as their length (number of words) increases.

These findings have practical implications. Our results suggest that the media is more likely to cover an agency's mistakes than its accomplishments. Furthermore, agencies that enter into periods of more intense media coverage are more likely to be criticized on multiple aspects of their functioning. A clear implication for public agencies is to take the potential negative effects of media coverage seriously and to pay close attention to their media reputation. Studies on the mediatization of bureaucracy consistently show how (at least some) agencies increasingly anticipate and adopt news logic in their daily work (Fredriksson, Schillemans, & Pallas, 2015; Thorbjørnsrud, 2015). Anticipating negative coverage in a media setting that thrives on conflict, drama, and negativity is crucial for reputation-conscious agencies.

Our results also have implications for future studies that examine organizational reputation in the media. First, our findings can be interpreted as support for the benefits of a neutral reputation (Luoma-aho, 2007). Excellent reputations are risky in a public sector context. The better an agency's reputation, the higher its fall will be in case of a crisis. For public sector organizations, this risk may often be too high to take, as their functions require stakeholders' trust no matter the situation (Luoma-aho, 2007, p. 6). We find that media coverage is more often negative than positive (showing the risk that media attention carries), but that the overall majority of coverage is neutral. The mechanisms, however, remain unclear. Is neutral coverage the result of the media's tendency to report about agencies in a neutral manner (and if so, how does this relate to agencies' reputation management strategies)? Or is neutral coverage to some extent a reflection of agencies' own desire to maintain a neutral media profile? Either way, given the potential risks involved in cultivating an excellent reputation, one might also ask whether agencies can run the risks involved in having a neutral reputation in times when politicians are more than willing to regain political control, strengthen managerial accountability, and/or reduce agency autonomy if an agency faces reputational threats. We take the position that agencies are not only political actors able to read, adapt to, and even manipulate their environments, but also open systems that are affected by their environments.

Second, at the very least, we urge BRT scholars to no longer treat the media as a black box, but to recognize the media as an institution to which other institutions, including agencies, must respond. Current studies run the risk of overestimating the strategic nature of reputation management or the effects of these supposed strategies. Public organizations are not only biased in their attention themselves but also are facing attention biases among relevant stakeholders. This chapter focused on attention biases in the media's coverage of agencies as a result of news criteria (e.g. negativity, conflict and personalization). We urge future research to unravel the extent and conditions under which agencies are able to cultivate their reputation in a strategic manner through the media.

A main limitation of this chapter is its descriptive and decontextualized approach. Our aim is not to offer a concluding answer to the question of how media biases relate to reputation management. Rather, we sought to open up a discussion on how the distinct rationale of the media might provide fresh insights into a field that is dominated by agency-centred explanations for bureaucratic behaviour. We have been careful in stating that our results suggest certain effects that might be explained by media biases. Yet alternative explanations are also possible. Is the emphasis on the performative dimension of organizational reputations the result of media bias, or of strategic considerations of the agency that stress the performative dimension towards the media? Is the decreasing likelihood of including agency responses in shorter articles the result of the journalist's space restrictions, or are there other factors at play? Does the so-called Velcro effect we observed indeed signal a bias in audience and media attention, or are we by coincidence just witnessing periods of real-life malfunctioning across the reputational dimensions of the agencies included in this study? In order to explain the nexus between media and reputation management, we call upon future studies to look further into the mechanisms that underlie the relations we have observed in this chapter.

Acknowledgements We thank Stefan Boye for his help with the statistical analyses for this chapter. We also thank Martin Moos for collecting the data. The research is part of the Rep Gov project, funded by the Danish Reserach Council for Independent Reserach.

REFERENCES

Altheide, D. L. (2004). Media logic and political communication. *Political Communication, 21*(3), 293–296.

Arnold, R. D. (2004). *Congress, the press, and political accountability.* Princeton: Princeton University Press.

Bovens, M. A. P. (2007). Analysing and assessing accountability: A conceptual framework. *European Law Journal, 13*(4), 447–468.

Busuioc, M., & Lodge, M. (2017). Reputation and accountability relationships: Managing accountability expectations through reputation. *Public Administration Review, 77*(1), 91–100.

Carpenter, D. P. (2002). Groups, the media, agency waiting costs, and FDA drug approval. *American Journal of Political Science, 46*(3), 490–505.

Carpenter, D. P. (2004). Protection without capture: Product approval by a politically responsive, learning regulator. *American Political Science Review, 98*(4), 613–631.

Carpenter, D. P. (2010). *Reputation and power: Organizational image and pharmaceutical regulation at the FDA.* Princeton: Princeton University Press.

Carpenter, D. P., Chattopadhyay, J., Moffitt, S., & Nall, C. (2012). The complications of controlling agency time discretion: FDA review deadlines and postmarket drug safety. *American Journal of Political Science, 56*(1), 98–114.

Carpenter, D. P., & Krause, G. A. (2012). Reputation and public administration. *Public Administration Review, 72*(1), 26–32.

Carroll, C. E., & McCombs, M. (2003). Agenda-setting effects of business news on the public's images and opinions about major corporations. *Corporate Reputation Review, 6*(1), 36–46.

Coombs, W. T., & Holladay, S. J. (2001). An extended examination of the crisis situations: A fusion of the relational management and symbolic approaches. *Journal of Public Relations Research, 13*(4), 321–340.

Coombs, W. T., & Holladay, S. J. (2006). Unpacking the halo effect: Reputation and crisis management. *Journal of Communication Management, 10*(2), 123–137.

Deacon, D., & Monk, W. (2001). 'New managerialism' in the news: Media coverage of Quangos in Britain. *Journal of Public Affairs, 1*(2), 153–166.

Deephouse, D. L. (2000). Media reputation as a strategic resource: An integration of mass communication and resource-based theories. *Journal of Management, 26*(6), 1091–1112.

Frandsen, F., & Johansen, W. (2017). *Organizational crisis communication*. London: Sage.

Fredriksson, M., Schillemans, T., & Pallas, J. (2015). Determinants of organizational mediatization: An analysis of the adaptation of Swedish government agencies to news media. *Public Administration, 93*(4), 1049–1067.

Galtung, J., & Ruge, M. H. (1965). The structure of foreign news: The presentation of the Congo, Cuba and Cyprus crises in four Norwegian newspapers. *Journal of Peace Research, 2*(1), 64–90.

Gilad, S., Maor, M., & Ben-Nun Bloom, P. (2015). Organizational reputation, the content of public allegations, and regulatory communication. *Journal of Public Administration Research and Theory, 25*(2), 451–478.

Goodsell, C. T. (1989). Balancing competing values. In J. Perry (Ed.), *Handbook of public administration* (pp. 575–584). New York: Jossey-Bass.

Hjarvard, S. P. (2013). *The mediatization of society and culture*. London: Routledge.

Long, J. S., & Freese, J. (2014). *Regression models for categorical dependent variables using Stata* (3rd ed.). College Station, TX: Stata Press.

Luoma-aho, V. (2007). Neutral reputation and public sector organizations. *Corporate Reputation Review, 10*(2), 124–143.

Maggetti, M., & Verhoest, K. (2014). Unexplored aspects of bureaucratic autonomy: A state of the field and ways forward. *International Review of Administrative Sciences, 80*(2), 239–256.

Maor, M. (2011). Organizational reputations and the observability of public warnings in 10 pharmaceutical markets. *Governance, 24*(3), 557–582.

Maor, M. (2015). Theorizing bureaucratic reputation. In A. Wæraas & M. Maor (Eds.), *Organizational reputation in the public sector* (pp. 17–36). London: Routledge.

Maor, M. (2016). Missing areas in the bureaucratic reputation framework. *Politics and Governance, 4*(2), 80–90.

Maor, M., Gilad, S., & Ben-Nun Bloom, P. (2013). Organizational reputation, regulatory talk, and strategic silence. *Journal of Public Administration Research and Theory, 23*(3), 581–608.

Maor, M., & Sulitzeanu-Kenan, R. (2016). Responsive change: Agency output response to reputational threats. *Journal of Public Administration Research and Theory, 26*(1), 31–44.

Mazzoleni, G., & Schulz, W. (1999). 'Mediatization' of politics: A challenge for democracy? *Political Communication, 16*(3), 247–261.

McCombs, M. (2014). *Setting the agenda: Mass media and public opinion* (2nd ed.). Oxford: Polity Press.

Moffitt, S. L. (2010). Promoting agency reputation through public advice: Advisory committee use in the FDA. *Journal of Politics, 72*(3), 880–893.

Pallas, J., Fredriksson, M., & Wedlin, L. (2016). Translating institutional logics: When the media logic meets professions. *Organization Studies, 37*(11), 1661–1684.

Pollitt, C., & Bouckaert, G. (2011). *Public management reform, a comparative analysis: New public management, governance, and the neo-Weberian state* (3rd ed.). Oxford: Oxford University Press.

Pollitt, C., Talbot, C., Caulfield, J., & Smullen, A. (2004). *Agencies: How governments do things through semi-autonomous organization*. New York: Palgrave Macmillan.

Rolland, V. W., & Roness, P. G. (2010). Mapping organizational units in the state: Challenges and classifications. *International Journal of Public Administration, 33*(10), 463–473.

Schillemans, T. (2012). *Mediatization of public services: How organizations adapt to news media*. Frankfurt: Peter Lang.

Strömbäck, J., & Esser, F. (2014). Mediatization of politics: Towards a theoretical framework. In F. Esser & J. Strömbäck (Eds.), *Mediatization of politics: Understanding the transformation of Western democracies* (pp. 3–28). London: Palgrave Macmillan.

Thorbjørnsrud, K. (2015). Mediatization of public bureaucracies: Administrative versus political loyalty. *Scandinavian Political Studies, 38*(2), 179–197.

Van Aelst, P., Sheafer, T., & Stanyer, J. (2012). The personalization of mediated political communication: A review of concepts, operationalizations and key findings. *Journalism, 13*(2), 203–220.

Verhoest, K., Rommel, J., & Boon, J. (2015). How organizational reputation and trust may affect autonomy of independent regulators: The case of the Flemish energy regulator. In A. Wæraas & M. Maor (Eds.), *Organizational reputation in the public sector* (pp. 118–138). London: Routledge.

Verhoest, K., Van Thiel, S., Bouckaert, G., & Lægreid, P. (Eds.). (2012). *Government agencies: Practices and lessons from 30 countries*. Basingstoke: Palgrave Macmillan.

Verhoest, K., Verschuere, B., & Bouckaert, G. (2007). Pressure, legitimacy, and innovative behavior by public organizations. *Governance, 20*(3), 469–497.

Wæraas, A., & Byrkjeflot, H. (2012). Public sector organizations and reputation management: Five problems. *International Public Management Journal, 15*(2), 186–206.

Wæraas, A., & Maor, M. (2015). Understanding organizational reputation in a public sector context. In A. Wæraas & M. Maor (Eds.), *Organizational reputation in the public sector* (pp. 1–13). London: Routledge.

PART IV

Achilles' Heels and Selective Perception

Central Banks and Banking Regulation: Historical Legacies and Institutional Challenges

Jacint Jordana and Guillermo Rosas

INTRODUCTION

This chapter deals with an institutional singularity in the world of financial regulation that has multiple implications for the governance of finance, at both the domestic and global levels. On the one hand, we find central banks in charge of banking regulation; on the other hand, there are countries in which banking regulation is in the hands of separate regulatory agencies, without depending formally on central banks. Between these

J. Jordana (✉)
Institut Barcelona d'Estudis Internacionals, Barcelona, Spain

Department of Political and Social Sciences, Universitat Pompeu Fabra, Barcelona, Spain
e-mail: jacint.jordana@upf.edu

G. Rosas
Washington University in St. Louis, St. Louis, MO, USA
e-mail: grosas@wustl.edu

T. Bach, K. Wegrich (eds.), *The Blind Spots of Public Bureaucracy and the Politics of Non-Coordination*, Executive Politics and Governance, https://doi.org/10.1007/978-3-319-76672-0_10

195

extreme ideal types, there are also cases of hybrid configurations where responsibilities are shared or fragmented among different agencies (i.e. the central bank may be responsible for controlling systemic financial risks, while a separate regulatory agency controls everyday operations). Why do different institutional models for the regulation of banks and financial services persist worldwide nowadays? Why have these divergent models been adopted by different countries? Lengthy disputes have emerged about the pros and cons of different institutional configurations to better regulate and supervise financial sectors, but the policy implications of each model remain largely in dispute (Dincer & Eichengreen, 2012; Goodhart, 2002; Masciandaro, 2006; Melecky & Podpiera, 2013). More importantly, what are the economic consequences of different institutional designs? In particular, is it the case that some set-ups promote financial stability at the expense of limited or over-regulated credit flows? Is the pursuit of inflation control compromised by the pursuit of financial stability when banking regulation is housed within a country's central bank? Or are there institutional set-ups that promote better access to credit, financial stability, and price stability?

Here we explore the current divide and present an institutional portrait of the situation of banking regulation around the world. To this purpose, we will employ an original data set of regulatory agencies that includes yearly variations in their institutional design from the early 1970s to 2015 for over 100 countries. After detailing the characteristics of the data set and providing a descriptive overview of the institutional variety in banking regulation in the first two sections, in the third section, we will focus on the different institutional developments related to the central banks as supervisory authorities. After discussing the reasons for such institutional divergence in regulatory models, in the fourth part of the chapter, we will briefly consider some potential consequences of these alternative models and attempt to lay out an agenda for further research into these important questions. First, we will concentrate on arguments about their impact on domestic policies—monetary policy and banking policy, basically—and second, we will focus on the financial international architecture to discuss the implications of such institutional divergence for the global governance of finance. We conclude by raising a few open questions regarding this institutional puzzle in financial governance and claiming the need for a more focused and robust study of this issue and of its implications.

MEASURING INSTITUTIONAL MODELS IN BANKING REGULATION

In many countries, central banks have regulatory powers in finance. Not all cases are identical: while almost all powers are concentrated in central banks in some countries, elsewhere central banks share regulatory responsibilities with other regulatory agencies. There are also countries where central banks are scarcely involved in financial regulation, which is delegated to dedicated agencies—either a single, multi-area agency or a collection of specialized agencies.

We have gathered an original data set to obtain a better sense of the variety of institutional designs in financial regulation. Our sample of countries has a global focus, including about 100 cases. It includes all countries in the world with over 20 million inhabitants in the year 2000, plus other countries from four different regional entities: Latin America (Community of Latin American and Caribbean States), Africa (African Union), Europe (European Union) and Southeast Asia (Association of Southeast Asian Nations). However, we excluded countries with a gross domestic product below US$100 billion in the year 2000.

We consider in our analysis a period ranging from 1971 to 2015. In our data set, we identify who oversees banking regulation and define three institutional options: oversight by the executive (i.e. ministry and directly), the central bank, or a separate regulatory agency. For the latter two cases, we assess whether they have some level of formal independence from the government or not. We also track changes over time in these variables. Many changes have occurred during the period under examination, and our variables allow us to capture when the central bank or the regulatory agency becomes independent—a very common trend—but also when responsibilities have shifted from one institutional option to another.

Our main variable is simply the year of creation of a new banking regulatory authority in a specific country or the year in which an existing entity is tasked with banking regulation. For each country included in our dataset, we identify the major public institution responsible for banking regulation each year from 1971 to 2015, regardless of whether this institution had a broader regulatory scope or not (e.g. an integrated financial regulatory authority carries out banking regulation among other responsibilities). Then, we identify if this institution is a ministry, a central bank, or a separate regulatory agency.

When the central bank is responsible, we record the year since it assumed regulatory responsibilities for banking supervision, as opposed to the year of creation of the central bank. Similarly, when responsibilities for banking regulation are granted to a pre-existing agency, we record the year in which legislative action was taken to add these responsibilities. We consider that a banking regulatory agency exists when an organizational unit is clearly and formally separated from a departmental/ministerial structure, regardless of the prevalence or not of hierarchical links of the newly created organization to the executive or the legislative. Such organizations need to comply with four conditions for us to consider them regulatory agencies:

- The focus of the authority is devoted to regulatory tasks and activities (rule supervision, rule enhancement, rule definition, etc.).
- The organization is a public entity: it carries public tasks, their employees are public servants (tenured or not), and the budget is under public control.
- The organization is a stable institution of public nature regulated by public legal acts and ordinances.
- The organization has a national scope, covering all the territory of a country.

For our second variable, we define a simple dichotomous index based on the existence or not of a fixed term for the main person in charge of the regulatory agency. This is our indicator of delegation. We focus on the main person in charge of the agency with a full-time position—the chairperson, president, or director—without regard for how this person is named or elected. When there was not an identifiable head of the regulatory agency, but a board taking responsibility jointly, we took as a value for our indicator the year of introduction of a fixed term period for the board members. Relying on the existence of a fixed term strikes us as a more objective procedure to build an indicator of autonomy, at least more so than considering explicit declarations of independence, which are difficult to compare and evaluate across different administrative contexts. In fact, we exclude formal declarations of independence as a criterion for identifying the creation of an autonomous agency.

We do not purport to measure the relative degree of independence of agencies, but to check whether they have some formal capacity for autonomous decision-making. We chose to use the existence of a fixed term as a proxy for the introduction of delegation because the cost of removing the person in charge of the agency when there is a fixed term increases very intensively in most political environments. Furthermore, Hanretty and Koop (2012, p. 210) offer evidence that the existence and length of board member terms is the aspect that best predicts the overall independence of an agency, and Jordana, Fernández-i-Marín, and Bianculli (in press) shows that the introduction of fixed terms correlates with many other independence markers in regulatory agencies. The use of a single indicator of agency autonomy is undoubtedly a highly simplified procedure to talk about a complex issue, especially since scholars often point to the multiple dimensions of the concept of institutional independence. However, our aim is to isolate a key characteristic that might be found in very different settings—across sectors and countries—and that conveys a similar meaning regarding the connection between the agency and the political system. In doing so, we introduce a basic distinction in the role of regulatory agencies, identifying the moment in which the traditional hierarchical relationship to the executive vanishes. In many cases, a fixed term was introduced after the creation of the agency, often in the context of major reforms oriented to increase the credibility of the regulatory agency.

We coded a third indicator, separate regulation, as 1 for countries in which monetary policy decision-making structures are separate from financial policy decision-making structures, and 0 when both issues remain under the same institutional umbrella (Jordana & Rosas, 2014). This indicator identifies cases in which two separate agents have distinct responsibilities: one for monetary policy, the other for banking stability. When a non-independent central bank and a non-autonomous regulatory agency have distinct responsibilities, we still coded this configuration as 0, inferring that a single agent controls both institutions. We awarded the same code 0 to situations in which the executive has control over decisions of banking regulation and monetary policy, but also when both policies are under the responsibility of the central bank. This variable is very helpful in discussing the consequences of different institutional models of banking regulation, as we will show later.

We coded the degree of institutional fragmentation in financial regulation as a fourth indicator. We aim to observe if all areas of financial regulation are under the same institutional umbrella (the executive, the central bank, or a unified agency) or if different entities are responsible for different areas of financial regulation (e.g. we might find a central bank that is responsible for banking regulation, an independent agency devoted to capital markets regulation, and the executive as the direct regulatory authority for pensions, insurance, and other secondary financial markets). We elaborate a scale of fragmentation, from 1 (null fragmentation) to 4 (high fragmentation) that covers the 101 countries during the entire period under scrutiny. From these data, we prepared a very simple index of fragmentation; summing all country scores to have a single aggregate value for each year, and then dividing by the total number of countries in the dataset.

Finally, we acknowledge that the distribution of regulatory responsibilities on banking and other financial areas can overlap. In fact, there are many cases of hybrid configurations where responsibilities are shared or fragmented among different agencies (i.e. the central bank may be responsible for controlling systemic financial risks, while a separate regulatory agency controls everyday operations). There are various countries where central banks—which often focus on prudential regulation—share banking regulation responsibilities with independent agencies as well. At this point, our indicators do not capture overlap well, and we recognize this as an area for future improvement.

Evolution of Institutional Designs in Banking Regulation

In our sample, we found that a couple of large institutional transformations occurred in banking regulation from 1920 to 2015. First, a glance at Fig. 10.1 shows a gradual increase in the number of countries that transferred regulatory powers on banking from the executive to a separate public agency. By the 1970s, about half of the countries under consideration had already transferred these powers. For 30 countries, such responsibilities were transferred progressively to central banks—in many cases already existing institutions. However, for the remaining 20 countries, these responsibilities went to newly created regulatory agencies that were separate from central banks, a move that in fact occurred before World War II.

Then in the early 1990s, quite abruptly, many institutional changes occurred almost simultaneously reducing the direct regulatory role of the executive (and all but eliminated it since the 2000s). These sudden changes also moved in different directions: while 30 additional countries transferred regulatory powers to their central banks, more than 20 other countries decided to create new separate agencies for banking/financial

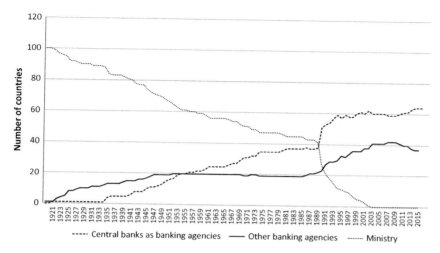

Fig. 10.1 Institutional separation between central banks, regulatory agencies, and ministries

regulation. Several contextual factors accelerated these changes, from the fall of the Soviet Union to the acceleration of worldwide agency diffusion during the 1990s or the popularization of new economic monetary policy doctrines. All these moves, in sum, consolidated the separation of banking regulation away from conventional ministries in the executive but also led to two new regulatory governance models in this sector.

How did the creation of separate banking agencies occur across different regions in the world? Consider Fig. 10.2, which displays the establishment of banking regulatory agencies separate from the executive in different world regions. In this figure, we do not distinguish between central banks and regulatory agencies but focus only on the year in which a country decided to transfer regulatory powers from the (finance) ministry to an institution outside the executive.

Figure 10.2 shows that Africa and Europe contributed to the large explosion of changes in the early 1990s. In the first case, this is related to the transfer of banking regulatory powers to already existing supranational central banks in several parts of Africa in the late 1980s and early 1990s; as for Europe, the disintegration of communist regimes in 1990 triggered several new cases of regulatory delegation in Eastern Europe. In contrast, Latin America and Southeast Asia placed banking regulation out of the

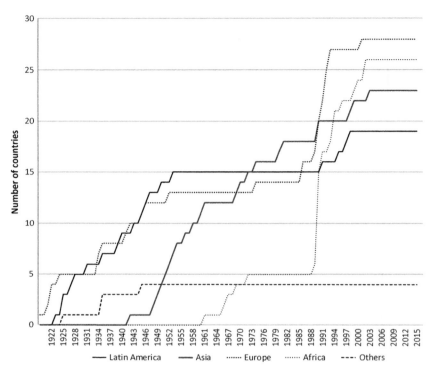

Fig. 10.2 Banking agencies: regional evolution (1920–2015)

hands of the executive at a steady pace. A few latecomers moved their regulatory structures to separate institutions, but not in a sudden move.

In any case, as can be observed in Fig. 10.2, all regions completed almost simultaneously the process of separation of banking regulation by the 2000s, ending a diffusion process that lasted almost a century. Regarding the territorial distribution of institutional models in the 2000s, there is also a clear pattern for each world region (see Fig. 10.3). Africa shows a monopoly of banking regulatory powers attached to the central bank, while in Latin America, in contrast, banking regulation is in most cases in the hands of a regulatory agency that is independent from the central bank. Asia has more countries in which banking regulation is based within central banks than in separate agencies. Among European countries, we find a more even distribution: 16 countries have a central bank

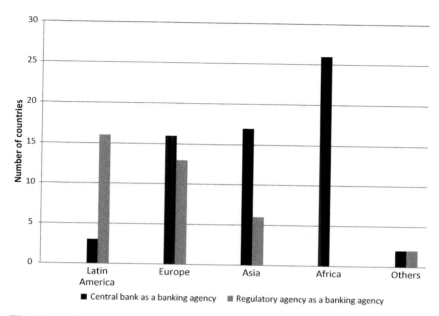

Fig. 10.3 Banking agencies: central banks versus regulatory agencies

with banking regulation responsibilities, while 13 have a separate regulatory agency. While many countries with separate regulatory agencies are in North and Central Europe, almost all Southern European countries adopted the central bank model.

Masciandaro and Romelli (2017) compiled a data set on central banking as regulatory authority that covers 105 countries and measured the level of unified financial regulation within the central bank. They found that large banking crises do trigger transformations in financial supervisory structures, moving financial supervision from the executive—or from separate agencies—to the central bank. They also found two other variables to be significant: the level of central bank independence, which exerts a positive effect on the likelihood that financial supervision is moved to the central bank, and the level of economic development, which exerts a negative influence (as more development, less probable to move regulation towards the central bank).

Beyond these propensities, we argue that the divide of institutional models in banking regulation is quite stable over time, a trait that reinforces the importance of path dependence effects in banking supervisory structures. During recent decades, the number of countries that have switched institutional models for banking regulation (once delegation was established to an agency or central bank) has been in fact quite small. From 1971 onwards, only 22 changes occurred, and 16 of them involved moving regulatory powers from the central bank to an independent regulatory agency. We identified only six cases in which the move was in the inverse direction, that is, from an independent regulatory agency to a central bank.

Most of these changes (60 per cent) have occurred in Europe, and there, most of them have been back and forth institutional switches. For example, both the United Kingdom and Ireland kept banking supervision in the hands of their central banks during many decades before switching in 1997 and 2002, respectively, to a separate financial regulator. However, these countries decided to transfer banking regulatory responsibilities back to their central banks after the 2008 global financial crisis (in 2013 and 2010, respectively). Hungary and Russia behaved similarly during the 2000s. In many other European countries, frequent debates arise as to the appropriate transformation of the existing institutional set-up (e.g. in Germany after the 2010 elections, see Engelen, 2010). In contrast, the switches in less-developed countries often occurred in the context of much larger institutional or political changes.

From these observations, we may infer that changes in institutional models of banking regulation are rare events. Deciding which actor is tasked with regulatory authority creates significant institutional path dependence. Subsequent grants of independence are not that relevant, as in many cases independence does not alter the institutional pattern previously adopted by each country. Thus, if independence over monetary policy was granted to the central bank, implicitly it was also granted over its banking regulation responsibilities. As for regulatory agencies, where these already existed, they were simply granted autonomy; where they were not in place, new agencies with fresh delegation of responsibilities were created, and were eventually entitled with independence. Diffusion effects may also be important in explaining why countries adopt one model over the other: Masciandaro and Romelli (2017) find that geographic proximity and trade linkages are relevant in determining institutional choice. Given the high concentration of institutional switches in Europe that we have uncovered, we can testify to the probable presence of diffusion effects in major institutional changes.

The turn towards independence in banking regulation is also an interesting phenomenon. Regardless of whether responsibilities for bank regulation are in a central bank or a separate agency, grants of independence are strongly clustered in a short period that started in the late 1980s. As can be observed in Fig. 10.4, before the 1980s, less than 10 countries had awarded independence to the authorities in charge of banking regulation, most of them central banks. However, from the late 1980s until the early 2000s, almost 70 more countries granted independence to their regulators. In a significant number of these cases, countries granted more autonomy to their central banks, an institutional requirement for monetary policy that became mainstream at that time (Marcussen, 2005), but also because of the strong diffusion mechanisms that were operating in this sector at that time (Polillo & Guillén, 2005). However, in many other countries in which regulation was assigned to separate agencies and not the central bank, a parallel diffusion mechanism occurred and formal independence protections were provided to them as well (Gilardi, 2005; Jordana, Levi-Faur, & Fernández-i-Marín, 2011).

In any case, as can be seen in Fig. 10.4, nowadays only about 20 per cent of the countries in our sample lack formally independent banking regulators, and this situation has become quite stable since the early 2000s. Most of the remaining cases of non-independent agencies or central banks

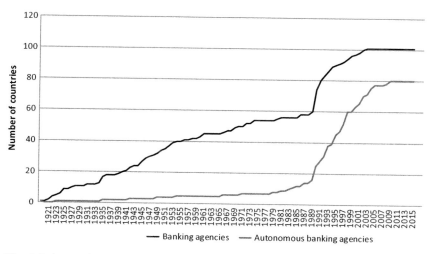

Fig. 10.4 Banking agencies: creation and autonomy year (1920–2015)

are linked to the persistence of authoritarian regimes, although there are a few cases of old separate banking regulatory agencies that have somehow resisted the turn towards independence. To conclude this section, we underscore that the large turn towards independence occurred in fact as a combination of granting independence to central banks—for reasons unrelated to banking regulation—and the simultaneous worldwide creation of many new regulatory agencies in finance that mimicked the pressure towards delegation to autonomous agencies that predominated at that time.

CENTRAL BANKS AS FINANCIAL REGULATORS: EXAMINING INSTITUTIONAL VARIATIONS

The new central banks established by public authorities that replaced private ones were pace-setters in shaping regulatory structures during the twentieth century. From a policy sector approach, it is essentially this sector that gave birth to the regulatory state (Levi-Faur, 2011). The first cases of publicly controlled central banks emerged in the late nineteenth and early twentieth centuries. Most of them were created initially as combined public–private institutions and only a few decades later were nationalized in the sense that the state took complete control over them. A third wave of institutional transformation for central banks started in the late 1980s, when they were granted formal independence, while those that did not receive formal independence were instead fully nationalized.

Since the early twentieth century, two options were open for banking regulation in parallel with the institutional development of central banks. The dominant Anglo-Saxon doctrine prescribed that regulation for financial services should remain separate from central banks, since some central banks included private bank owners in their board at that time. Specialized regulatory institutions in the financial sector were first introduced in Latin America in the 1920s. They were strongly influenced by North American designs, mostly a consequence of the missions of Edwin Walter Kemmerer, a Princeton University professor who acted as a consultant for many governments at that time (Drake, 1989). On the other hand, there are cases of central banks that were nationalized early in the twentieth century that were also awarded regulatory responsibility for the financial sector. This was the case, for example, in Spain, France, and Italy, but also in Argentina and Brazil, which were less susceptible to Anglo-Saxon influence.

Since the late 1980s, and in parallel with large transformations in global financial markets, a new architecture for financial regulatory supervision emerged that was based on the integration of different sector agencies (banking, insurance, securities, and pensions). Starting with Norway, Iceland, Sweden, and Denmark, the 1997 decision of the United Kingdom to transfer banking supervision from the Bank of England to a new agency with responsibility over all financial areas represented a turning point in the diffusion of this new institutional model (Kranke, 2005; Masciandaro, Quintyn, & Taylor, 2008; Taylor & Fleming, 1999). Later, the Scandinavian institutional model was followed by many other countries, particularly in Europe but also in other parts of the world, including developed and developing countries, as a response to the emergence of financial conglomerates and the experience of banking crises (Čihák & Podpiera, 2008).

The integration process did not always move towards the unified model for financial services, since national traditions were also very relevant in shaping new institutional developments (Lütz, 2004). In many countries, central banks remained responsible for financial supervision, defining a different institutional architecture. For example, the central bank took over regulation over the entire financial sector in countries like Ireland or Slovakia. We also find many other countries that decided to merge supervision over only two sectors, but not over the whole financial area, within a single agency (Herring & Carmassi, 2008). Masciandaro, Quintyn, and Taylor (2008) argue that the persistence of separate agencies for each sector is most likely when the central bank has a relevant role in financial supervision. To the contrary, when the central bank is not involved in supervisory tasks, the creation of a multi-sector agency charged with financial supervision is more feasible, and this allows these authors to talk about a 'central bank fragmentation effect' (Freytag & Masciandaro, 2007; Masciandaro, 2006).

We observe variations in both the Anglo-Saxon and Scandinavian models of institutional banking supervision design. When banking regulation is the responsibility of central banks, we find cases in which the central bank monitors a semi-autonomous department attached to the institution, but also cases in which supervision is carried out by a central unit within the bank under direct control of the governor. We also find a variety of institutional designs in cases in which central banks are not involved in banking regulation. There are countries in which a single regulatory agency supervises the whole financial area, while other countries have more focused regulatory institutions. For example, we see cases of regulatory institutions that combine banking regulation and insurance, or banking regulation and pensions, among many other possible combinations (Jordana & Levi-Faur, 2010).

More recently, an unconventional institutional architecture has emerged in which agencies are divided between those in care of economic risks of financial crisis—or macroprudential regulation—and those that conduct business supervision focused on the solvency of individual institutions—microprudential regulation. In several cases, central banks act as the agency responsible for preserving systemic stability throughout different financial sectors, while financial authorities outside the central bank take care of the operational risk of financial entities and of consumer protection. In a few cases, business regulation and consumer protection are also separated from banking supervision proper and carried out by a separate agency responsible for the whole financial area, as in Australia and the Netherlands (Herring & Carmassi, 2008). Masciandaro and Quintyn (2009) refer to this architecture as the 'horizontal (peaks) model', in which each regulatory goal is controlled by a different regulatory agency. In contrast, what they call the 'vertical (silos) model' corresponds to the more traditional regulatory architecture in which each financial sector is under full responsibility of a single regulatory agency. In between there are 'hybrid models', which integrate several sectors, and the 'unified model', in which a single regulatory agency oversees all financial sectors.

Among these recent institutional innovations, we find a similar novelty in the United States and the United Kingdom, where new agencies tasked with protecting the interests of financial consumers were created after 2008. The establishment of the Consumer Financial Protection Bureau in the United States as mandated by the Dodd–Frank Act represented a significant transformation in the regulatory governance of financial services, increasing fragmentation, but also providing additional strength to the regulatory system (Kastner, 2016).

A major consequence of the agencification processes that occurred intensively in the financial sector during the 1990s and early 2000s was an increase in the fragmentation index of this sector (see Fig. 10.5). As many new agencies were created in insurance, pensions, or securities and exchange, among other financial subsectors, fragmentation obviously increased. The creation of separate agencies in banking regulation, as well as the allocation of such responsibilities to the central bank, also pushed in

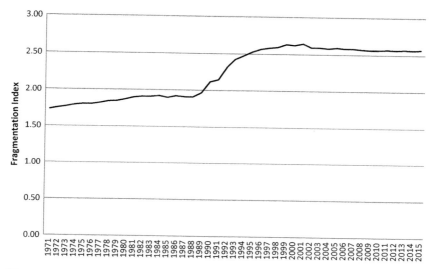

Fig. 10.5 Financial regulation Fragmentation Index (1971–2015)

the direction of large regulatory fragmentation in many countries. Thus, in 15 years, from 1986 to 2001, the index moved from 1.92 points to 2.64, an increase of 30 per cent.

In more recent years, this index has remained quite stable, and even slightly retreated. This is likely the result of the emergence of many multi-sector agencies, particularly in small- and medium-sized countries, that were eventually integrated into a single regulatory agency for all financial subsectors; we even find cases of central banks that agglutinated regulatory responsibilities for all financial subsectors (Jordana & Levi-Faur, 2010). This trend probably compensated during these years for the continuous and more visible pattern of new agency creation in different subsectors of finance that also continued during the 2000s, particularly in world regions like Africa and Asia where the executive had still retained responsibilities for some of these subsectors.

Consequences of Institutional Arrangements

Our data set allows ample opportunities to describe how the institutional structures to pursue financial regulation have changed over the past half-century; for several variables, we have been able to extend information back in time for a full century. This information will prove useful as we continue to explore what the consequences are of the process of agencification in banking regulation. As we discussed in previous sections, this process of agencification is unique among other areas where the state has developed regulatory capacity. The reason is that agencification in banking regulation has been characterized by two institutional models that vary according to different historical and economic circumstances. The effects of each institutional model on banking regulation performance are not completely clear. Consider the issue of fragmented versus unified regulatory authorities. Some authors argue that separate regulators also provide some advantages, for example, the ability to manage and compartmentalize sensible information, to accumulate experience within each sector, to limit risks of generalized inefficiency, or to provide more check and balances among public agencies (Monkiewicz, 2007). Also, some authors argue that institutional differences in the level of fragmentation are not very significant at all, and that the quality of supervisory personnel, or their independence, are more relevant characteristics (Herring & Carmassi, 2008). In addition, Goodhart (2002) argues that in developing countries, where qualified human resources are scarce and institutions tend to be weak, it is better to concentrate all capabilities within the central bank to make regulation stronger; in fact, Dincer and Eichengreen (2012) found some evidence supporting this pattern.

Such arguments about regulatory fragmentation and effectiveness are not very different to those in the field of utilities regulation (Jordana & Levi-Faur, 2010). However, the singular role that central banks play in financial regulation is not replicated by anything similar in utilities. Previous research has provided mixed results regarding the potential impact of financial supervisory architecture on the performance of a country's financial system. Arnone and Gambini (2007) and Čihák and Podpiera (2007) both found that integrated supervision and involvement of central banks correlated with better compliance with the Basel principles of banking supervision, but not necessarily with better performance. Dincer and Eichengreen (2012) found that banks are better capitalized when the central bank is the supervisory authority, but also that bank credit to the economy is appreciably inferior when the lead supervisor is the central bank. At this point, the database we have constructed can help us continue to explore correlational patterns in the distribution of fragmentation, on the one hand, and a panoply of economic outcomes such as financial stability, capitalization of financial intermediaries, and access to credit, on the other.

A related major discussion concerns potential conflicts between the goals of avoiding banking crises and promoting price stability when both goals are vested within the central bank. The debate concerns whether it is best to have separate agencies to pursue both goals or to have all authority over financial stability and price stability concentrated in the central bank (Copelovitch & Singer, 2008; Di Noia & Di Giorgio, 1999; Goodhart & Schoenmaker, 1995; Ioannidou, 2005). In the latter view, the central bank oversees inflation and supervises bank regulation within the same organization and under a single command but cannot necessarily avoid conflict between these goals. This is the so-called conflict of interest hypothesis; if this hypothesis is correct, we would expect a negative correlation between price stability and bank stability (in other words, a positive correlation between inflation and solvency) in countries with unified agencies. Countries with unified monetary-cum-banking authority would tend to carry out a more expansive monetary policy in the hope of reducing episodic instances of financial distress; alternatively, they could privilege price stability, but this comes at the expense of promoting financial instability.

In this chapter, we do not present evidence to confirm or discard the conflict of interest hypothesis. However, there is some evidence suggesting that regulatory central banks show a greater propensity to sacrifice some levels of banking stability in order to keep inflation under control (Rosas & Jordana, 2016), a finding consistent with Copelovitch and Singer's (2008) result that central banks with regulatory and supervisory responsibilities allow higher rates of inflation than central banks without these responsibilities. More generally, these findings show that institutional designs in regulation do matter and that the role of central bank in financial regulation is not neutral—and not only because of the fragmentation effect. These results also make sense from the logic of prioritizing goals, as far as monetary control appears to be a major goal in central banks, while banking stability is a goal pursued by a specific department or unit within the bank. Although these appear to be mere academic disputes about how to fine-tune central bank intervention in the economy, the underlying dilemma can be significant in cases where banking systems are unstable and no clear alternative is in sight. Separate agencies, with their specific objectives and multiple ways of implementing them, do not appear to suffer this trade-off directly, although they may experience difficulties related to institutional weakness and coordination under political tensions. Again, our data set provides an important resource with which to describe how the incidence of episodes of financial distress, systemic banking crises, inflationary crises, and so on varies among different institutional set-ups for bank regulation.

Finally, another consequence of central bank involvement in banking regulation is observable at the global governance level (cf. Singer, 2007). We argue that there is a collective action problem related to the heterogeneity of banking supervisors. On the one hand, there is a well-established and funded international organization involving all central banks in the world, the Bank of International Settlements (BIS), established in 1930. BIS is very active in support of global banking regulation, as can be clearly observed through the activity of the Basel Committee on Banking Supervision but does not easily integrate national agencies with supervisory responsibilities that remain separate from central banks. On the other hand, there is no formal international organization of banking regulators in the world, precisely because enormous institutional differences across countries have created very complex barriers to the establishment of a single association that are not easy to overcome. There are multiple international networks of banking regulatory authorities (Jordana, 2017), as well as informal international organizations, but not an integrated organization capable of distilling compromises and facilitating commitments among their members. Only the Financial Stability Board and their recent Regional Consultative Groups can be seen as an attempt to coordinate banking regulation that loosely integrates the two types of supervisory institutions.

Admittedly, our data set is not conducive to generate descriptive inferences about questions of global financial governance. However, the data set can help us advance the research agenda on the institutional causes of economic consequences to the extent that we develop a sound understanding of the processes that led to the adoption of different models. We think that processes of diffusion and emulation drove a large number of recent decisions to dramatically alter regulatory institutions, which suggests that indicators such as the number of neighbouring countries that have adopted a new institutional set-up can eventually be used as instruments for institutional change. This step is extremely important, as we lack in this literature opportunities to build credible causal inference designs.

CONCLUDING REMARKS

This chapter has analysed the process of agencification of banking regulation that expanded during the twentieth century and progressively reached almost all countries around the world. Undoubtedly, this was a vigorous diffusion process, probably one of the first among several similar processes that led to agencification in many other economic sectors during the final decades of the last century (Jordana et al., 2011). However, banking regulation has an institutional particularity, a singular characteristic not present in other sectors: the existence of two main options—central banks and separate banking agencies—gave policy makers a choice in how to delegate responsibility for banking regulation. The reasons why policy makers chose one option over the other are complex. Rather than providing a complete answer to the question of institutional choice, we considered several arguments about the reasons why institutional convergence has not occurred. Territorial proximity and historical path dependence are likely drivers behind each of these options, but the search for a country-specific optimal model was also a relevant factor in many countries' institutional decisions. It is also important to note, however, that the presence of two institutional options did not prevent the global diffusion of an independent agency model since the late 1980s.

A consequence of providing independence both to central banks and to banking regulatory agencies was the emergence of multiple principals in financial regulation, each one following autonomous decision procedures. Such fragmentation laid bare the emergence of divergent goals among regulators in the financial sector, especially when several agencies, among them the central bank, operated in different financial areas. This is an important problem that increased in recent years because of the universalization of agencification and the independence model.

To cope with the problem of fragmentation of financial markets' regulation, which has grown concomitantly with the sophistication of the banking sector and the fusion of different subsectors in the financial area, a tendency has appeared to create integrated financial agencies that oversee insurance, banking, pensions, security and exchange, and so on. Here, two options were also possible: to establish a separate and independent agency, or to attach an integrated regulatory unit within the central bank. The first option involved the risk of institutional weakness, predominantly in developing countries, but the second option raised another problem. When banking regulation is placed within the scope of the central bank, then a conflict of interest might emerge between the two different goals, monetary policy and banking regulation, ascribed to the central bank.

Considering these dilemmas, we observe that banking regulatory authorities operate under a variety of institutional configurations, where fragmentation represents a dimension in such variations and the presence of central bank as regulator another. It is difficult to argue which one is more effective. There is probably no optimal institutional design, and evidence in favour of the relative effectiveness of one institutional model over others is still scant. Here we have presented a picture of the vast amount of institutional variation around the world, and we have also provided a comprehensive view of the different institutional designs and how they have evolved throughout time.

REFERENCES

Arnone, M., & Gambini, A. (2007). Architectures of supervisory authorities and banking supervision. In D. Masciandaro & M. Quintyn (Eds.), *Designing financial supervision institutions: Independence, accountability and governance* (pp. 262–308). Cheltenham: Edward Elgar.

Čihák, M., & Podpiera, R. (2007). Experience with integrated supervisors: Governance and quality of supervision. In D. Masciandaro & M. Quintyn (Eds.), *Designing financial supervision institutions: Independence, accountability and governance* (pp. 309–341). Cheltenham: Edward Elgar.

Čihák, M., & Podpiera, R. (2008). Integrated financial supervision: Which model? *North American Journal of Economics and Finance, 19*(2), 135–152.

Copelovitch, M. S., & Singer, D. A. (2008). Financial regulation, monetary policy, and inflation in the industrialized world. *Journal of Politics, 70*(3), 663–680.

Di Noia, C., & Di Giorgio, G. (1999). Should banking supervision and monetary policy tasks be given to different agencies? *International Finance, 2*(3), 361–378.

Dincer, N. N., & Eichengreen, B. (2012). The architecture and governance of financial supervision: Sources and implications. *International Finance, 15*(3), 309–325.

Drake, P. W. (1989). *The money doctor in the Andes.* Durham, NC: Duke University Press.

Engelen, K. C. (2010). Germany's fight over BaFin: The ramifications of a Bundesbank takeover. *International Economy, 2010*, 54–72.

Freytag, A., & Masciandaro, D. (2007). Financial supervision architecture and central bank independence. In D. Masciandaro & M. Quintyn (Eds.), *Designing financial supervision institutions: Independence, accountability and governance* (pp. 213–264). Cheltenham: Edward Elgar.

Gilardi, F. (2005). The institutional foundations of regulatory capitalism: The diffusion of independent regulatory agencies in Western Europe. *Annals of the American Academy of Political and Social Science, 598*(1), 84–101.

Goodhart, C. A. E. (2002). The organizational structure of banking supervision. *Economic Notes, 31*(1), 1–32.

Goodhart, C. A. E., & Schoenmaker, D. (1995). Should the functions of monetary policy and banking supervision be separated? *Oxford Economic Papers, 47*(4), 539–560.

Hanretty, C., & Koop, C. (2012). Measuring the formal independence of regulatory agencies. *Journal of European Public Policy, 19*(2), 198–216.

Herring, R. J., & Carmassi, J. (2008). The structure of cross-sector financial supervision. *Financial Markets, Institutions and Instruments, 17*(1), 51–76.

Ioannidou, V. P. (2005). Does monetary policy affect the central bank's role in bank supervision? *Journal of Financial Intermediation, 14*(1), 58–85.

Jordana, J. (2017). Transgovernmental networks as regulatory intermediaries. *The ANNALS of the American Academy of Political and Social Science, 670*(1), 245–262.

Jordana, J., Fernández-i-Marín, X., & Bianculli, A. C. (in press). Agency proliferation and the globalization of the regulatory state: Introducing a data set on the institutional features of regulatory agencies. *Regulation & Governance.* https://doi.org/10.1111/rego.12189

Jordana, J., & Levi-Faur, D. (2010). Exploring trends and variations in agency scope. *Competition and Regulation in Network Industries, 11*(4), 342–360.

Jordana, J., Levi-Faur, D., & Fernández-i-Marín, X. (2011). The global diffusion of regulatory agencies: Channels of transfer and stages of diffusion. *Comparative Political Studies, 44*(10), 1343–1369.

Jordana, J., & Rosas, G. (2014). When do autonomous banking regulators promote stability? *European Journal of Political Research, 53*(4), 672–691.

Kastner, L. (2016). *The power of weak interests in financial reforms: Explaining the creation of a US consumer agency* (MaxPo Discussion Paper No. 16/1). Paris: Max Planck Sciences Po Center on Coping with Instability in Market Societies.

Kranke, M. (2005). *Financial market regulation in Sweden: Finansinspektionen—A toothless paper tiger?* (REGEM Analysis No. 14). Trier: Trier University.

Levi-Faur, D. (2011). Regulatory networks and regulatory agencification: Towards a single European regulatory space. *Journal of European Public Policy, 18*(6), 810–829.

Lütz, S. (2004). Convergence within national diversity: The regulatory state in finance. *Journal of Public Policy, 24*(2), 169–197.

Marcussen, M. (2005). Central banks on the move. *Journal of European Public Policy, 12*(5), 903–923.

Masciandaro, D. (2006). E pluribus unum? Authorities' design in financial supervision: Trends and determinants. *Open Economies Review, 17*(1), 73–102.

Masciandaro, D., & Quintyn, M. (2009). *Reforming financial supervision and the role of the central banks: A review of global trends, causes and effects (1998–2008)* (CEPR Policy Insight No. 30). London: Centre for Economic Policy Research.

Masciandaro, D., Quintyn, M., & Taylor, M. W. (2008). Inside and outside the central bank: Independence and accountability in financial supervision, trends and determinants. *European Journal of Political Economy, 24*(4), 833–848.

Masciandaro, D., & Romelli, D. (2018). Central bankers as supervisors: Do crisis matter? *European Journal of Political Economy, 52,* 120–140.

Melecky, M., & Podpiera, A. M. (2013). Institutional structures of financial sector supervision, their drivers and historical benchmarks. *Journal of Financial Stability, 9*(3), 428–444.

Monkiewicz, J. (2007). Integrated, consolidated or specialized financial markets supervisors: Is there an optimal solution? *Geneva Papers on Risk and Insurance: Issues and Practice, 32*(1), 151–162.

Polillo, S., & Guillén, M. F. (2005). Globalization pressures and the state: The worldwide spread of central bank independence. *American Journal of Sociology, 110*(6), 1764–1802.

Rosas, G., & Jordana, J. (2016). 'The conflict of interest hypothesis': Is there a trade-off between price stability and bank stability? Paper presented at the 24th IPSA Conference, Poznań.

Singer, D. A. (2007). *Regulating capital: Setting standards for the international financial system.* Ithaca: Cornell University Press.

Taylor, M., & Fleming, A. (1999). *Integrated financial supervision: Lessons from northern European Experience* (World Bank Policy Research Working Paper No. 2223). Washington, DC: The World Bank.

CHAPTER 11

Why Do Bureaucrats Consider Public Consultation Statements (or Not)? Information Processing in Public Organizations

Simon Fink and Eva Ruffing

Introduction

Public participation in administrative decision-making is becoming an increasingly common practice in modern liberal democracies (Rasmussen, 2015). The goal behind these consultation practices is to improve the legitimacy or the knowledge base of administrative decision-making (or both) (Kohler-Koch, 2007). In the last few decades, empirical research has produced a large number of studies that investigate whether public participation impacts administrative decision-making (see, e.g., Balla, 1998;

S. Fink (✉)
Department of Political Science, University of Göttingen, Göttingen, Germany
e-mail: simon.fink@sowi.uni-goettingen.de

E. Ruffing
Department of Political Science, University of Hannover, Hannover, Germany
e-mail: e.ruffing@ipw.uni-hannover.de

T. Bach, K. Wegrich (eds.), *The Blind Spots of Public Bureaucracy and the Politics of Non-Coordination*, Executive Politics and Governance, https://doi.org/10.1007/978-3-319-76672-0_11

Carpenter, 2010; Edelenbos, 2005; Klüver, 2012; Yackee, 2006). Although some studies find that public participation matters for administrative decision-making, the larger picture reveals that its effects are moderate at best. In other words, public organizations seem to have selective perception when it comes to taking public participation statements into account.

Most attempts to explain the variation in the effectiveness of public participation focus on the 'success factors' or 'quality criteria' of consultation procedures, such as the early onset of consultations, expectation management, and mobilization to ensure inclusiveness (for an overview, see Bryson, Quick, Slotterback, & Crosby, 2013). However, it is questionable whether these lists of success factors have explanatory power with regard to the impact that public participation has on bureaucratic decision-making. Furthermore, this approach is often under-theorized and leaves causal mechanisms in the dark.

To illustrate this problem, we discuss a comprehensive public participation procedure recently introduced in German electric grid planning. We demonstrate that although the procedure is in line with many of the discussed success factors, public participation has almost no effect on bureaucratic decision-making. Using this empirical puzzle as a starting point, we sketch out a positive theoretical approach for the effectiveness of public participation. As the consideration of public participation statements by public organizations is the *conditio sine qua non* of the participation's effectiveness, we shift the focus to these organizations and to the question of why and under what conditions they take consultation statements into account. We thereby focus on the *processing of participation participants' statements within public organizations*, a point that has been largely ignored by public participation research up to now (Moynihan, 2003).

To theorize these questions of information processing, we begin with the often neglected fact that consultations not only benefit public organizations but also create *problems* for them: first, consultations can induce an informational overflow for public organizations, particularly if organized civil society as well as other kinds of actors (especially citizens) contributes to the consultation. The organization has to somehow distinguish between relevant and irrelevant pieces of information; however, the question of what information can be considered relevant or irrelevant is far from trivial. Second, consultation statements might be contradictory, based on incorrect factual assumptions, and biased. How can these diverse statements be aggregated into administrative decisions? As Pfeffer and Salancik

(1978) put it: '... organizations cannot survive by responding completely to every environmental demand. The interesting issue then becomes the extent to which organizations can and should respond to various environmental demands, or the conditions under which one social unit is able to obtain compliance with its demands' (pp. 43–44).

Our contribution argues that public organizations follow a *resource dependence* logic to cope with the information processing problems of overflow and aggregation. The core idea of resource dependence is that public organizations are not able to attain their goals by relying on their intra-organizational resources alone and instead need resources, such as expertise, legitimacy, or staff from their environment. This idea of public organizations' resource dependence—especially in its initial version, which was developed by Pfeffer and Salancik (1978)—is developed further by two prominent approaches of public organization research: exchange theory (Bouwen, 2002, 2004; Klüver, 2012, 2013) and reputation theory (Carpenter & Krause, 2012). By building on both approaches, we argue that public organizations include only the consultation statements (with the pieces of information) that they need for their organizational survival into their decisions. If we follow exchange theory, this means that the resources needed for organizational survival are rigidly defined by the organization's environment. If we follow reputation theory, there is more room for strategic action by an organization, as it can—within limitations—decide what audience and reputation it wants to cultivate (Carpenter & Krause, 2012).

However, both the reputation and the exchange logics postulate that public organizations react only to specific kinds of information, to information from specific actors, or—an interaction argument—to specific kinds of information provided by specific actors. On the positive side, this built-in attention-directing logic allows public organizations to act on consultation statements at all. Without internal heuristics that structure the processing of consultation statements, public organizations would be paralysed by the number and ambiguity of statements. It is therefore rational for public organizations to institutionalize selective perception to cope with the problems of bounded rationality (see introductory chapter by Bach and Wegrich in this volume).

On the downside, this attention-directing logic creates blind spots in the information processing of public organizations. Some information—and some actors—are thereby neglected, which might lead to a situation in which the organization does not know what it is not knowing, and vital information is overlooked (see Lodge in this volume). This problem is all the more pertinent if no other actor in the political-administrative system uses this information, and there have been situations of coordination underlap in which vital information was not processed simply because no department or organization was responsible for processing this kind of information (see introductory chapter by Bach and Wegrich in this volume). In addition, this ignorance may also have reputational consequences: expectations about the aims and primary audience of a public organization are necessarily multi-faceted. Emphasizing the contributions of one group of actors or one specific type of information will necessarily disappoint some of an agency's audience and create the impression that the agency is not fulfilling its 'true' or 'whole' mission (Carpenter & Krause, 2012). As Gilad (2012) puts it, public organizations 'can and will sometimes act in ways that are inconsistent with shifts in public and political demands, in order to protect their core reputation' (p. 160).

Thus, our argument is that selective perception is simultaneously *necessary* to ensure that organizations can process information and function at all, and *dangerous* as it may preclude the processing of new and vital information and may damage an organization's reputation. In sum, our contribution thus argues that selective perception must be constantly *managed* and *monitored* to find a balance between necessary heuristics and perilous ignorance.

This chapter is structured as follows: in the next section, we outline the German procedure of public participation in electric grid expansion and argue that it conforms to most postulated success factors of participation. However, we empirically demonstrate that there is very little impact of participation statements on the decision of the Federal Network Agency (FNA), the public organization that processes the public participation. In the third section, we outline our theoretical argument, namely that this lack of impact is due to the selective perception and internal information processing logic of the FNA, in particular, and of public organizations, in general. The final section concludes with an outlook on venues of further theory development.

PUBLIC PARTICIPATION IN BUREAUCRATIC DECISIONS

The normatively oriented consultation literature claims that public administration should take consultation statements into account to improve the democratic quality and problem-solving capacity of administrative decision-making (Fung, 2015; Miller & Fox, 2006). The idea is that input by citizens and organized interests can add legitimacy to administrative decision-making and increase the quality of decisions, for example, by supplying local knowledge useful for implementing decisions.

A large part of the literature is concerned with discussing success criteria to inform the design of participation procedures. First, *inclusiveness* is nearly universally seen as a crucial criterion (Quittkat, 2011; Smith, 2009). All citizens and stakeholders affected by a decision should have the right to voice their opinions to ensure that all vital information be included in the decision. Second, *transparency* is deemed to be important (Papadopoulos & Warin, 2007; Smith, 2009) and includes transparency about the procedure, its aims and scope, and the quality of information supplied (e.g. about the problem under discussion). On the one hand, transparency is a value in and of itself, as it is necessary to inform citizens about the problem at hand and their participation opportunities. On the other hand, transparency also ensures that 'better' and 'the right' information is supplied to the consulting organization. Third, many authors state that the *quality of deliberation* is important in that the discourse in public participation procedures should not be dominated by power positions but by the quality of the reasons given (Beetham, 2012; Geißel, 2012). In this way, normatively acceptable solutions can be found. This criterion is of particular concern in participation formats that go beyond consultation and include face-to-face interaction between the involved actors. Fourth, participation must begin *early* in the decision-making process so as to give participants real influence over alternatives (Renn et al., 2014).

Nearly all of these conditions are met in the German public participation procedure for grid planning. In 2011, the German legislature amended the Energy Industry Act (EnWG) and introduced the Grid Expansion Acceleration Act (NABEG), which obliges the German FNA and the four German Transmission System Operators (TSOs)—Amprion, TenneT, TransnetBW, and 50 Hertz—to conduct consultations when planning grid expansion projects. The FNA is the central decision-making actor within this administrative planning procedure and also one of most independent German agencies (Ruffing, 2014).

The new planning procedure determines—on a very large scale—which power lines are necessary and mandates three consultations when planning the demand for new grids (see Fig. 11.1). First, the TSOs develop *scenario frameworks* that predict the development of German energy demand and production. These scenarios are publicly consulted and approved by the

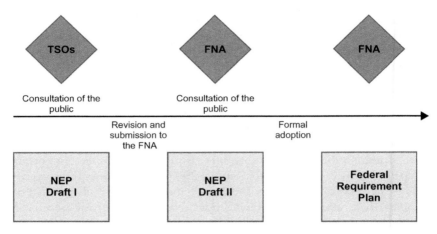

Fig. 11.1 Grid demand planning procedure in Germany (simplified overview, scenario framework consultation not shown)

FNA. Second, the TSOs develop a draft for the *network development plan* (*Netzentwicklungsplan Strom*, NEP) based on these scenarios. The NEP defines which places in Germany need to be connected with new power lines. The first draft of this plan is open for consultation, and the TSOs have to take the public's submissions into account when revising it. Third, this second draft is submitted to the FNA, which can approve it after a third round of public consultations and send it to both chambers of parliament, which adopt the plan as federal law. Thus, the TSOs and the FNA interact with the public, have to solicit their submissions, and take these submissions into account on three occasions when making their decisions.

The procedure is in principle *open and inclusive*. All citizens and organizations can submit their statements on three different occasions via email, a web form, or letters. Moreover, the procedure is also reasonably *transparent*. The documents under discussion are somewhat technical, but there is an extensive website (www.netzausbau.de) that explains the rationale of grid expansion and the purpose and functioning of the consultations. Concerning *deliberative quality*, the procedure cannot be as deliberative as face-to-face interactions (such as mini-publics); however, there is a certain amount of exchanging arguments since both the TSOs and the FNA have to substantiate their decisions in writing and discuss how they will react to the public's comments. However, the fourth success criterion is met nearly ideal-typically: the participation procedure begins with the *earliest* stages of grid planning, the scenario framework that forecasts the supply and demand of electricity in Germany. To summarize, when judged against ideal-typical deliberative institutions, the German participation procedure is clearly deficient; however, if we compare the procedure with examples of real-world participation procedures (Beetham, 2012; Smith, 2009), it scores reasonably well in terms of success criteria.

Nevertheless, the fulfilment of many of the postulated success criteria does not mean that the procedure will have a significant impact on the FNA's decision. To make this argument, we assessed how participant's input impacts the FNA in a quantitative study in which we measured the FNA's behaviour concerning the NEP as the dependent variable of our empirical analysis. The FNA's observable behaviour boils down to the decision of which electric grid projects to approve or reject. The binary dependent variable thus indicates whether the FNA will approve a given measure. In 2012, the FNA examined 81 grid measures and approved 47 of them, indicating that there is variation that is in need of explanation. The narrow structure of the planning process allows us to construct meaningful variables to assess the impact of the written consultations, as the policy only deals with the list of grid projects and there are no additional issues or multiple dimensions.

The *independent variables* were generated using 2905 submissions to the consultation of the FNA. We coded the submissions to assess (a) what kinds of arguments were made, (b) against which grid project, and (c) by what kind of actors. We used a combination of hand coding and dictionary coding approaches to code the submissions. To elucidate *which grid project a submission is directed against*, we used a dictionary approach. The dictionary contains the project code and the place names given in the description of the power line as keywords.[1] Moreover, using a newspaper analysis, we identified the places most likely affected by a grid project and added their names.[2] The *kind of arguments made* are coded using a dictionary indicating key words for legal, political, technical, economical, ecological, and medical arguments.[3] The *type of actor* was hand-coded by student assistants and the project leaders.[4] The categories are citizen, citizens' initiative, company, industry association, local government, regional government, federal government, science, parties, districts, and other. As the coding unit is the submission, a single submission could be directed against several grid projects and contain multiple kinds of arguments but could only come from one actor type.

The data generated from the submissions were then aggregated and combined with the data on grid projects and the behaviour of the FNA. The unit of analysis is the grid project, and we thus aggregated the submission data on the grid project. In the end, we have a dataset that contains (a) the list of grid projects in the NEP and their technical properties, (b) the number of submissions to the consultations of the FNA that criticized these grid projects, and (c) the reaction of the FNA to these submissions. The variables enter logit regression models. As control variables, we add the TSO responsible for planning, the length of the grid project, and whether the grid project is a new construction project or whether an existing power line is expanded.

Our first result is that the consultation mainly attracts citizens (see Table 11.1). Ninety-three per cent of the submissions to the consultation by the FNA came from citizens. This result is interesting in itself, for citizens obviously view the FNA as the public organization to address concerning grid expansion, and they invest resources in writing elaborate consultation statements. This finding supports the argument that the participation procedure is open in principle. Unlike many other participation forms, the participant pool has no bias towards organized interests (Rasmussen, 2015).

Table 11.1   Participants in the consultations

Actor type	Consultation of the FNA	
	Number of submissions	Percentage of submissions
Citizen	2720	93.63
Citizen's initiative	16	0.55
Company	21	0.72
Industry association	27	0.93
Environmental association	22	0.76
Local government	31	1.07
Länder government	19	0.65
Federal government	6	0.21
Science	0	0
Parties	9	0.31
Districts	12	0.41
Other	22	0.76
Total	2905	100

Table 11.2 Influence of submissions by actor type

	(1)	(2)	(3)	(4)	(5)	(6)
FNA: number of submissions	0.00 (0.002)					
Submissions to FNA by citizens		0.00 (0.002)				
Submissions to FNA by citizens' initiatives			0.14 (0.615)			
Submissions to FNA by local governments				−0.00 (0.239)		
Submissions to FNA by *Länder* governments					−0.05 (0.383)	
Submissions to FNA by districts						−0.05 (0.281)
New construction	−0.42 (0.852)	−0.54 (0.877)	−0.30 (0.854)	0.00 (0.883)	−0.36 (0.848)	−0.68 (0.854)
Length	0.00 (0.003)	0.00 (0.004)	0.01 (0.005)	0.00 (0.003)	−0.00 (0.002)	−0.00 (0.002)
Amprion	−1.17 (1.266)	−1.30 (1.302)	−1.26 (1.276)	−1.30 (1.302)	−0.94 (1.269)	−0.95 (1.251)
TenneT	−2.13* (1.289)	−2.32* (1.351)	−2.22* (1.310)	−2.64* (1.373)	−2.21* (1.277)	−2.33* (1.295)
50Hertz	−0.44 (1.462)	−0.89 (1.558)	−0.81 (1.477)	−0.46 (1.469)	−0.28 (1.468)	−0.37 (1.423)
Observations	69	69	69	69	69	69
Pseudo R^2	0.18	0.21	0.19	0.18	0.15	0.21
log-likelihood	−37.7	−36.6	−37.2	−37.8	−39.5	−36.3

Notes: Standard errors in parentheses; $***p < 0.01$, $**p < 0.05$, $*p < 0.1$. In the logit models, some actor types were dropped because of too few observations (~ too few contributions). The model also included submissions to the TSO consultation, but for reasons of simplicity, only the effects of the submissions to the FNA consultation are reported here

However, the interesting question is whether some actors are more 'listened to' by the FNA than others. Table 11.2 displays the results of logit regression models testing whether the number of submissions by certain types of actors increase or decrease the probability that the FNA will accept a grid measure. We can see that no actor group exerts special influence on the decision. Moreover (and somewhat surprisingly), no actor group exerts measurable influence on the decision at all.

The same holds if we categorize the submissions by the type of argument used. Table 11.3 reveals the results of logit regression models. There is no special impact of technical, legal, or environmental arguments.

Table 11.3 Determinants of FNA decision

	(1)	(2)	(3)	(4)	(5)	(6)	(7)
FNA: number of submissions	0.00 (0.002)						
FNA: submissions/ legal		0.00 (0.003)					
FNA: submissions/ political			0.08 (0.089)				
FNA: submissions/ technical				0.00 (0.004)			
FNA: submissions/ economy					0.00 (0.002)		
FNA: submissions/ ecology						−0.00 (0.006)	
FNA: submissions/ medical							0.00 (0.002)
New construction	−0.45 (0.856)	−0.34 (0.855)	−0.20 (0.877)	−0.51 (0.909)	−0.31 (0.856)	−0.09 (0.879)	−0.42 (0.842)
Length	0.00 (0.002)	0.00 (0.002)	0.00 (0.003)	0.01 (0.004)	0.00 (0.003)	0.00 (0.002)	0.00 (0.002)
Amprion	−1.11 (1.265)	−1.02 (1.253)	−1.14 (1.276)	−1.38 (1.331)	−0.99 (1.259)	−1.06 (1.274)	−1.07 (1.249)
TenneT	−1.95 (1.290)	−2.07 (1.263)	−2.46* (1.332)	−2.71* (1.420)	−2.05 (1.276)	−2.42* (1.280)	−1.99 (1.266)
50Hertz	−0.40 (1.460)	−0.14 (1.445)	−0.35 (1.467)	−0.87 (1.566)	−0.29 (1.444)	−0.03 (1.500)	−0.31 (1.431)
Observations	69	69	69	69	69	69	69
Pseudo R^2	0.19	0.16	0.19	0.22	0.18	0.19	0.18
log-likelihood	−37.5	−38.6	−37.6	−36	−37.8	−37.2	−37.9

Notes: Standard errors in parentheses; ***$p < 0.01$, **$p < 0.05$, *$p < 0.1$. Logit models. The model also included submissions to the TSO consultation, but for reasons of simplicity, only the effects of the submissions to the FNA consultation are reported here

To cross-check these results, we complemented the analysis with a qualitative approach. In its final decision, the FNA explains how the consultation statements were taken into account for each grid project.[5] The FNA's decision document first discusses whether each grid project fulfils the requirements of the EnWG and refers to two expert reports in particular that were commissioned by the FNA (one written by experts from the Graz University of Technology, one written by a consultancy agency). This first part of the FNA's decision document usually almost exclusively discusses load flows. On this basis, the FNA comes to a decision as to whether to approve a grid project. In the second part, the FNA discusses the consultation statements. This part only states that there were no specific issues and none related to the energy industry that were raised in the consultation regarding the specific grid project in two-thirds of all cases. This repeated reasoning indicates that such arguments are particularly relevant to the FNA's decision. In the remaining cases, the discussion refers to consultation statements; however, only in 2 (out of 81) cases did the FNA report that a decision had been made (also) in reaction to specific consultation statements.[6] In all other cases, the discussion only clarifies why the consultation submissions are *not* relevant to the FNA's decision (e.g. because they refer to possible line routings, which are only decided on much later in the planning process), or the critique is obsolete because the FNA rejected the grid project for *other* reasons (usually load flow issues).

We thus have a null finding that is puzzling to some extent. On the one hand, the participation procedure for German grid planning embodies most of the success criteria on participation procedures postulated in the literature. It is open, transparent, located early in the decision-making process, and—taking into account the fact that this is a difficult issue in written consultation procedures—deliberative to some extent. On the other hand, the participation procedure seems to have hardly any impact on the FNA's decision. Thus, the success factors do not have explanatory power regarding the question of whether public participation is effective in the sense that participants are able to influence bureaucratic decision-making. As these factors also provide no clues to causal mechanisms and do not allow for the definition of scope conditions, theory-building in the area of public participation is urgently needed.

ATTENTION IN PUBLIC CONSULTATION PROCEDURES: EXCHANGE AND REPUTATION LOGIC

We argue that public organizations face incentives and restrictions when processing information in consultation procedures, which influence their decision-making behaviour. Positive theoretical approaches for the analysis of organizational information processing are therefore necessary to explain variation regarding the influence of consultation statements, on the one hand, and to understand what happens 'inside bureaucracy', on the other hand.

The first restriction that public organizations face when processing information is some kind of *informational overflow*, which might be created by consultations. Therefore, organizations have to decide what information is relevant for the policy question at hand and the task of the agency, and what information is irrelevant for its task. For example, a policy question might contain legal, environmental, and political aspects, but the task of an agency—and the consultation—is only to assess the legal aspects of a problem.

The second restriction is that public organizations have to come to a *decision* at the end of the consultation process. That is, they need ways to attach weights to different kinds of information contributed in the consultation and to aggregate this information somehow. Some contributions may contain 'better' information or come from 'more important' stakeholders. The two restrictions are obviously interrelated as both stem from the logic of bounded rationality (Jones, 2017; Simon, 1964). We can think of the first restriction as attention costs (March, 1994) and the second as decision-making costs (Ostrom & Ostrom, 1971).

Our theoretical reasoning is concerned with the following two processes: what logic do public organizations use to filter the information they obtain during consultations, and how do they attach weights to the different pieces of information? Our argument is that public organizations process information according to a *resource dependence logic*, which we discuss in exchange and reputation logic versions. The core assumption of the resource dependence approach is that organizations' behaviour is influenced by the actors who control the resources they require for their organizational survival (Levine & White, 1961; Pfeffer & Salancik, 1978). In applying the resource-dependence approach to consultations, exchange theory argues that the consulting organization opens its decision-making processes in exchange for political or technical information provided by the public (Bouwen, 2002; Bunea, 2013; Bunea & Thomson, 2015; Klüver, 2013).

Scholars applying exchange theory assume that public organizations are dependent on *technical* information provided by consultation participants. Experts may take part in consultations and improve organizations' abilities to make technically good decisions. This argument is particularly prevalent in the literature on regulatory decision-making (Broscheid & Coen, 2007). Implementation research argues that public organizations need the technical knowledge of local communities to assess specific impediments to implementation (Hill & Hupe, 2002).

In addition, organizations might have to know the *preferences* of the wider public or specific stakeholders. In policymaking, this knowledge might strengthen their bargaining position vis-à-vis the other actors involved in the decision-making process (e.g. their political principals); in implementation, knowing whether a decision will be accepted by the wider public might be important for smooth implementation. The differentiation between technical information and preferences clearly resembles the classical differentiation made by Meyer and Rowan (1977) between effectiveness and legitimacy as two critical resources of organizational survival.

Resource dependence theory argues that the actors who are most important for organizational survival are also the most important for the behaviour of an organization. In this regard, the government and legislature (as the primary source of the agency's resources) constitute the organization's significant reference group (Levine & White, 1961). For most bureaucracies, the most important actors are the government and legislative actors as political principals, who are usually in a position to shrink or enlarge the task portfolio, budget, staff size, and so on of the organization, although there is certainly vast empirical variance in this regard, and some bureaucracies gain considerable autonomy in practice (Verhoest & Lægreid, 2010; Verhoest, Van Thiel, Bouckaert, & Lægreid, 2012). A default assumption is therefore that public organizations particularly need (informational) resources that are necessary to fulfil their mandate. Therefore, organizations will use their consultation procedures to find mandate-related information, which enables them to complete their mission successfully. Thus, concerning the heuristics used to filter and aggregate information, public organizations first determine which actor controls the vital resources for their survival. For most public organizations, this actor is its political principal. Second, the organization determines which mandate it is supposed to fulfil according to its most important stakeholder. Third, the organization structures its information processing heuristics in a way that privileges the information that is necessary to fulfil its mandate. For example, public organizations tasked with ensuring the safety of foodstuff might ignore information on animal maltreatment as long as consumer health is not endangered by these practices.

The results of empirical research that apply exchange theory suggest that actors are additionally particularly dependent on informational resources that nurture their influence in political bargaining processes, which might come from consultation participants. Bunea and Thomson

(2015), for example, demonstrate that the European Commission is more successful in translating its preferences into European law if a public consultation has been carried out prior to decision-making. Bouwen (2004) reveals that lobbying groups that are able to provide expertise gain access to the European Commission, whereas members of the Council of Ministers are more accessible to actors able to provide information on national interests.

In sum, exchange theory has a rather rigid concept of the informational needs of public organizations, which is mainly determined by their tasks and the necessity of influencing other actors in areas in which they are not entitled to make binding decisions by themselves. Obviously, an organization's mandate may include all kinds of aims, such as consumer protection, preserving effective market competition, and environmental protection as well as responsiveness to citizens or different stakeholders. (Informational) resources can be obtained in the organization's environment but are—as a default assumption—acquired only if they are necessary to satisfy the political principal. The public organization therefore grants influence to actors who are in possession of the most critical resources it needs to fulfil its mandate (Pfeffer & Salancik, 1978).

In contrast, reputation research is sensitive to the fact that public organizations are not completely at the mercy of their political principals but can strategically try to build a reputation (Carpenter, 2001; Gilad, 2012; Gilad, Maor, & Ben-Nun Bloom, 2015). According to the most well-known definition by Carpenter (2010), '[A]n organizational reputation is a set of symbolic beliefs about the unique or separable capacities, roles, and obligations of an organization, where these beliefs are embedded in audience networks' (p. 45).

This reputation might be a kind of protective shield for public organizations against accusations of neglect (which might *inter alia* come from their political principals) and is therefore an essential resource for public organizations, as well (Carpenter & Krause, 2012). The reputation approach is thus a special case of resource dependence theory that has a broader concept of resources and opens up more room for strategic considerations than exchange theory. Public organizations can choose particular audiences to build up their reputation (Carpenter & Krause, 2012) and may therefore be more sensitive to the information provided by members of this audience. Hence, a 'regulator's pursuit of a positive reputation … shapes their responsiveness to external signals as well as how they choose to respond'

(Gilad, 2012, p. 157), thereby explaining 'the interplay between external signals and intra-bureaucratic dynamics' (ibid.).

For example, Alon-Barkat and Gilad (2016) put forward the hypothesis that legally independent public organizations (which are subject to a low amount of political control) might be more in need of public legitimacy and might therefore be more responsive to bottom-up public demands. While the authors could not find empirical evidence supporting this argument for their sample of Israeli public organizations, they suggest that organizations might strive for a low political profile in order to 'decrease their risk of being targeted by protesters and of attracting concrete demands for policy change' (Alon-Barkat & Gilad, 2016, p. 54).

However, reputation considerations might not only shape public organizations' responsiveness vis-à-vis external actors but also influence internal decision-making. Bach (2015) has shown that the German Federal Institute for Risk Assessment pursued a strategy to establish itself as the one and only risk assessment agency, for example, by acquiring an ISO (International Organization for Standardization) certification for its decision-making procedures and later spreading them as the gold standard in summer schools for foreign risk assessment agency staff members. Their pursuit of reputation was therefore decisive in the agency's internal decision-making.

In terms of our argument about information processing, this means that public organizations do not necessarily consider the mandate envisioned by their political principal as the guiding principle for filtering and aggregating the information they obtain in consultations. Instead, they may try to cultivate a reputation of being particularly sensitive to public demands or fairness concerns, or of being technically competent. Thus, the organization (a) determines which reputation it wants to cultivate, (b) determines which stakeholders are most important to cultivate this reputation, and (c) structures its information processing processes accordingly.

All in all, from the exchange version of the resource dependence theory, we derive the assumption that public organizations filter information in public participation procedures according to their relevance to the task as spelled out by their political principals, in particular, because the political principals of public organizations usually control the most critical resources for their organizational survival. Even very independent public organizations that may enjoy financial autonomy from political principals depend on their political principals, which decide on agency's life or death.

From the reputation approach, we derive the assumption that public organizations might nevertheless enjoy some leeway in their strategic behaviour and might try to cultivate specific reputations vis-à-vis specific audiences. Predicting which reputational profile an agency will try to cultivate is difficult. The theoretical considerations by Alon-Barkat and Gilad (2016) are a first step in theorizing the strategic calculus of reputation management, but apart from that, there is very little theorizing. One promising area of theory-building might be the notion of path dependency. Building a reputation is a long-term process consisting of many small steps of living up to reputational demands. Thus, it is plausible that organizations try to nurture already existing (positive) reputations and only change their reputational strategy in times of crisis.

Returning to the big picture, both positive theoretical approaches suggest that public organizations will hardly satisfy the demands of 'the public' or 'the stakeholders' and will instead always prioritize particular arguments and stakeholders that provide them with the most critical resources for their organizational survival. This suggestion is hardly compatible with the expectation that public participation procedures will reconcile heterogeneous and ambiguous interests and thereby ensure the broad public acceptance of formerly contentious policies.

Comparative empirical research is necessary to test the explanatory power of the developed theoretical approach. The case of the German participation procedure in grid development presented in this chapter cannot serve as an empirical test; however, the approach spelled out in this chapter provides at least a plausible explanation for the ineffectiveness of participation. The FNA is not dependent on input to the public participation procedure for reasons of exchange (getting information to fulfil its mandate) or for reasons of reputation building (appearing as a responsive and citizen-friendly organization). Instead, its aim is to appear as a neutral and technically competent organization that conforms to its mandate. The FNA's mandate does not nurture expectations that it will consider larger parts of the submissions to be relevant. The very narrow and technical mandate instead gives the FNA little room to consider, for example, political arguments against certain electric lines. The FNA thus stuck very close to its mandate and used it as a relevance filter in the consultation procedure. In fact, in assessing the grid projects, the FNA even commissioned a study by the Graz University of Technology to assess the technical properties of each grid project. This information is often cited in the approval document to justify the approval or rejection of specific grid projects.

Hence, the information-filtering and decision-making logic of the FNA seems to rely on one trusted source of information.

With regard to reputation theory, for its reputation, the FNA does not seem focused on civil society actors, non-governmental organizations, or companies, which are the usual clientele of the FNA in its day-to-day decision-making. However, the data are of course not suitable for checking whether the FNA aims to boost its reputation vis-à-vis its parent ministry, the German legislature, or other actors. All in all, however, the FNA has been very successful at getting its NEP converted into law by the German legislature. The 2012 NEP was adopted by the legislature without any changes.

In sum, disregarding public participation statements and basing its decision on technical criteria alone is a rational strategy of the FNA to fulfil its mandate. The strategy is therefore perfectly in line with the theoretical assumptions derived from resource dependence theory. However, this strategy risks alienating all the actors that contribute to the consultation in the hope of influencing German grid planning. This is all the more problematic as most of these statements likely 'fall between the cracks of organizational attention' (see introductory chapter by Bach and Wegrich in this volume). Although our research is still ongoing, there is little empirical evidence that the statements made in the public consultation resurface in other parts of the demand planning process (e.g. in the Bundestag) (see Fink & Ruffing, in press).

Conclusion and Discussion

This chapter began with the observation that public participation research usually ignores how public organizations process information provided by consultation participants and is therefore not able to explain which consultation statements are considered by public organizations and why.

To illustrate our argument, we analysed the German electric grid planning procedure, which entails large-scale public participation. The participation procedure corresponds reasonably well to most normative prescriptions given in the participation literature: it is inclusive, transparent, and occurs early in the decision-making process. Its deliberative quality is not as high as that of a face-to-face participation forum; nevertheless, the participation process includes giving-reason requirements. However, there is no systematic relation between submissions from the public and the decisions of the bureaucratic actor that is supposed to be influenced by these submissions, namely the FNA. Thus, in light of most theories of participation procedures, a procedure that should in theory make an impact did not make one here. The FNA seems to have a blind spot concerning public participation statements.

We sketched a theoretical approach able to explain this blind spot that begins with two basic assumptions: first, public organizations' most fundamental interest is ensuring their organizational survival, and second, consultation procedures might provide resources for organizational survival, on the one hand, but cause problems for the organization, on the other hand, particularly regarding informational overflow and aggregation problems. A public organization interested in ensuring its survival therefore has to filter the information provided by consultation participants. We suggested that the public organization would take into account the information relevant either for fulfilling its mandate or for building up a specific reputation vis-à-vis particular actors. We hypothesized that all information not relevant according to these two filters would be ignored.

When this approach was applied to the German grid development participation procedure, we saw that public organizations are confronted with large amounts of information—in our example, almost 3000 consultation statements—that have to be processed. The example also illustrates that the agency was dependent on external technical information. This finding is in itself hardly surprising; however, if the agency is truly dependent on particular types of information, it is also reasonable to expect that it will acquire this information from the most reliable sources. For technical information, this source is typically not citizens who participate in consultation statements, even if they often have a remarkable understanding of technical problems. If anything can be expected to be influential in these circumstances, it is organizations able to claim an expert status.

Our specific case reveals very little hope for citizens' ability to influence bureaucratic decision-making; however, different filters can be applied in different procedures. For example, if a public organization is more dependent on local acceptance than on technical soundness, citizen initiatives might be more influential. However, the resource dependence of a public organization is highly contingent upon its task and mandate as well as upon the reputational fora it is able to address. Keeping both factors in mind, the theoretical approach sketched out in this chapter allows us to develop expectations on public organizations' information processing in specific consultation procedures, on who will be influenced by what arguments in public consultation procedures, and on the 'location' of blind spots in public organizations' decision-making.

In light of the typology developed in this volume (see introductory chapter by Bach and Wegrich), we theorize the intentional institutionalization of selective perception. According to our argument, this strategy is necessary but problematic. It is necessary because without selective perception, the organization would not be able to function; it is problematic because many stakeholders have broad notions of an organization's task and mission and will be disappointed if the agency does not react to their specific concerns. Moreover, with this strategy, organizations might miss out on vital information (see Lodge in this volume). For organizations, the crucial question is therefore how to manage their selective perception—that is, they need to be aware of this perception and its consequences and regularly probe whether selective perception is still functional or has caused major blind spots to emerge.

NOTES

1. For example, for the power line P33: Trassenneubau: Netzausbau Wolmirstedt—Helmstedt—Wahle, the key words are P33 Wolmirstedt Helmstedt Wahle. As some power lines have the same starting point or end point, the condition was that both the starting point and the end point (or the intermediate point) needed to appear in the submission (e.g. Wolmirstedt AND Wahle).
2. For example, if project P25 Barlt-Heide had been especially contentious in Prasdorf, we added that location as a keyword to identify this project in a submission. Or if a project was called Südwestkuppelleitung, we added that keyword.
3. For example, keywords for legal arguments were as follows: *gesetz verordnung richtlinie raumverträglichkeit rauminanspruchnahme raumwiderstand anwalt '§' rechtlich grundrecht raumordnung planfeststellung regelwerke absatz* EnWG Enwg NABEG EnLAG Enlag GG EEG. If any one of those terms occurred in the submission, it was coded as containing legal arguments. A single submission may contain multiple kinds of arguments, but the overall coding is binary: submission contains legal arguments, yes or no; contains political arguments, yes or no; and so on.
4. Krippendorff's alpha is 0.9.
5. The 'Bestätigung Netzentwicklungsplan Strom 2012' of the FNA, available at https://data.netzausbau.de/2022/NEP/NEP2022_Bestaetigung.pdf [accessed 30.10.2017].

6. The rejection of measure 69 and the approval of measure 61. With regard to measure 69, the report states that the necessity of the grid measure was doubted by the consultation participants. In addition, the TSOs were not able to present conclusive data on the necessity of grid measure 69, which is why the FNA rejected the measure. Measure 61 entails an upgrade of an existing electric line. In its decision document, the FNA reported that the content of the submissions regarding this measure is reflected in the decision. Looking into the submissions, only one submission addressed measure 61 and welcomed the proposal to include this upgrade project in the network development plan.

References

Alon-Barkat, S., & Gilad, S. (2016). Political control or legitimacy deficit? Bureaucracies' symbolic responses to bottom-up public pressures. *Policy & Politics, 44*(1), 41–58.

Bach, T. (2015). Wie "tickt" die öffentliche Verwaltung? Autonomie, Reputation und Responsivität von Regulierungsbehörden am Beispiel des Bundesinstituts für Risikobewertung. In M. Döhler, J. Franzke, & K. Wegrich (Eds.), *Der gut organizierte Staat, Festschrift für Werner Jann zum 65. Geburtstag* (pp. 162–181). Baden-Baden: Nomos.

Balla, S. J. (1998). Administrative procedures and political control of the bureaucracy. *American Political Science Review, 92*(3), 663–673.

Beetham, D. (2012). Evaluating new vs. old forms of citizens engagement and participation. In B. Geißel & K. Newton (Eds.), *Evaluating democratic innovations: Curing the democratic malaise* (pp. 56–67). London: Routledge.

Bouwen, P. (2002). Corporate lobbying in the European Union: The logic of access. *Journal of European Public Policy, 9*(3), 365–390.

Bouwen, P. (2004). Exchanging access goods for access: A comparative study of business lobbying in the European Union institutions. *European Journal of Political Research, 43*(3), 337–369.

Broscheid, A., & Coen, D. (2007). Lobbying activity and fora creation in the EU: Empirically exploring the nature of the policy good. *Journal of European Public Policy, 14*(3), 346–365.

Bryson, J. M., Quick, K. S., Slotterback, C. S., & Crosby, B. C. (2013). Designing public participation processes. *Public Administration Review, 73*(1), 23–34.

Bunea, A. (2013). Issues, preferences and ties: Determinants of interest groups' preference attainment in the EU environmental policy. *Journal of European Public Policy, 20*(4), 552–570.

Bunea, A., & Thomson, R. (2015). Consultations with interest groups and the empowerment of executives: Evidence from the European Union. *Governance, 28*(4), 517–531.

Carpenter, D. P. (2001). *The forging of bureaucratic autonomy: Reputations, networks, and policy innovation in executive agencies, 1862–1928*. Princeton: Princeton University Press.

Carpenter, D. P. (2010). *Reputation and power: Organizational image and pharmaceutical regulation at the FDA*. Princeton: Princeton University Press.

Carpenter, D. P., & Krause, G. A. (2012). Reputation and public administration. *Public Administration Review, 72*(1), 26–32.

Edelenbos, J. (2005). Institutional implications of interactive governance: Insights from Dutch practice. *Governance, 18*(1), 111–134.

Fink, S., & Ruffing, E. (in press). Legitimation durch Kopplung legitimatorischer Arenen. In A. Thiele (Ed.), *Legitimität in unsicheren Zeiten: Der demokratische Verfassungsstaat in der Krise?* Tübingen: Mohr Siebeck.

Fung, A. (2015). Putting the public back into governance: The challenges of citizen participation and its future. *Public Administration Review, 75*(4), 513–522.

Geißel, B. (2012). Impacts of democratic innovations in Europe. In B. Geißel & K. Newton (Eds.), *Evaluating democratic innovations: Curing the democratic malaise?* (pp. 209–214). London: Routledge.

Gilad, S. (2012). Attention and reputation: Linking regulators' internal and external worlds. In M. Lodge & K. Wegrich (Eds.), *Executive politics in times of crisis* (pp. 157–175). Basingstoke: Palgrave Macmillan.

Gilad, S., Maor, M., & Ben-Nun Bloom, P. (2015). Organizational reputation, the content of public allegations, and regulatory communication. *Journal of Public Administration Research and Theory, 25*(2), 451–478.

Hill, M., & Hupe, P. (2002). *Implementing public policy: Governance in theory and practice*. London: Sage.

Jones, B. D. (2017). Behavioral rationality as a foundation for public policy studies. *Cognitive Systems Research, 43*, 63–75.

Klüver, H. (2012). Biasing politics? Interest group participation in EU policy-making. *West European Politics, 35*(5), 1114–1133.

Klüver, H. (2013). Lobbying as a collective enterprise: Winners and losers of policy formulation in the European Union. *Journal of European Public Policy, 20*(1), 59–76.

Kohler-Koch, B. (2007). The organization of interests and democracy in the European Union. In B. Kohler-Koch & B. Rittberger (Eds.), *Debating the democratic legitimacy of the European Union* (pp. 255–277). Plymouth, UK: Rowman & Littlefield.

Levine, S., & White, P. E. (1961). Exchange as a conceptual framework for the study of interorganizational relationships. *Administrative Science Quarterly, 5*(4), 583–601.

March, J. G. (1994). *A primer in decision making*. New York: Free Press.

Meyer, J. W., & Rowan, B. (1977). Institutionalized organizations: Formal structure as myth and ceremony. *American Journal of Sociology, 83*(2), 340–363.

Miller, H. T., & Fox, C. J. (2006). *Postmodern public administration*. Armonk, NY: Sharpe.

Moynihan, D. P. (2003). Normative and instrumental perspectives on public participation: Citizen summits in Washington, DC. *The American Review of Public Administration, 33*(2), 164–188.

Ostrom, V., & Ostrom, E. (1971). Public choice: A different approach to the study of public administration. *Public Administration Review, 31*(2), 203–216.

Papadopoulos, Y., & Warin, P. (2007). Are innovative, participatory and deliberative procedures in policy making democratic and effective? *European Journal of Political Research, 46*(4), 445–472.

Pfeffer, J., & Salancik, G. R. (1978). *The external control of organizations: A resource dependence perspective*. New York: Harper & Row.

Quittkat, C. (2011). The European Commission's online consultations. *Journal of Common Market Studies, 49*(3), 653–674.

Rasmussen, A. (2015). Participation in written government consultations in Denmark and the UK: System and actor-level effects. *Government and Opposition, 50*(2), 271–299.

Renn, O., Köck, W., Schweizer, P., Bovet, J., Benighaus, C., Scheel, O., & Schröter, R. (2014). Öffentlichkeitsbeteiligung bei Vorhaben der Energiewende: Neun Thesen zum Einsatz und zur Gestaltung der Öffentlichkeitsbeteiligung. *Zeitschrift für Umweltrecht, 2014*(5), 281–287.

Ruffing, E. (2014). How to become an independent agency: The creation of the German Federal Network Agency. *German Politics, 23*(1–2), 43–58.

Simon, H. A. (1964). *Models of man*. London: Wiley.

Smith, G. (2009). *Democratic innovations: Designing institutions for citizen participation*. Cambridge: Cambridge University Press.

Verhoest, K., & Lægreid, P. (2010). Organizing public sector agencies: Challenges and reflections. In P. Lægreid & K. Verhoest (Eds.), *Governance of public sector organizations: Proliferation, autonomy and performance* (pp. 276–297). Basingstoke: Palgrave Macmillan.

Verhoest, K., Van Thiel, S., Bouckaert, G., & Lægreid, P. (Eds.). (2012). *Government agencies: Practices and lessons from 30 countries*. Basingstoke: Palgrave Macmillan.

Yackee, S. W. (2006). Sweet-talking the fourth branch: The influence of interest group comments on federal agency rulemaking. *Journal of Public Administration Research and Theory, 16*(1), 103–124.

PART V

Implications

CHAPTER 12

How to Deal with the Blind Spots of Public Bureaucracies

Tobias Bach and Kai Wegrich

INTRODUCTION

If blind spots, attention biases, and patterns of non-coordination present recurring but understudied phenomena of organizational behaviour in the executive domain, as the contributions to this volume show, 'what can be done about them?' is the obvious question. Can reform measures and institutional designs be adopted to avoid these attention biases leading to tendencies of non-coordination? And are some government systems better or worse at avoiding such tendencies? This concluding chapter addresses these 'so what?' questions in two main ways. First, we engage with three major approaches for public sector reform that—in different ways—seek to address the attention biases and coordination problems explored in this

T. Bach (✉)
Department of Political Science, University of Oslo, Oslo, Norway
e-mail: tobias.bach@stv.uio.no

K. Wegrich
Hertie School of Governance, Berlin, Germany
e-mail: wegrich@hertie-school.org

© The Author(s) 2019
T. Bach, K. Wegrich (eds.), *The Blind Spots of Public Bureaucracy and the Politics of Non-Coordination*, Executive Politics and Governance, https://doi.org/10.1007/978-3-319-76672-0_12

volume: (1) 'whole of government' and related approaches aiming at better coordination within government and between government and non-for-profit organizations, (2) 'better regulation' reforms, and (3) the 'behavioural insights' approach to policy design. For each of these three reform approaches, we question to what extent they seek to correct for blind spots and other attention biases—since this is obviously not written in the instruction leaflet for reforms—and how successful they are in doing so. Second, we probe whether and how our analytical perspective, developed in the introductory chapter, could be used to compare institutions in terms of their susceptibility to attention bias. This is meant as a first step towards exploring scoping conditions for the prevalence and intensity of different organizational attention biases in different jurisdictions. Taken together, these two themes sketch out an agenda for future research that explores the issues raised in this volume and applies the conceptual tools developed.

Before moving on to these issues, which are embedded in the more fundamental question of whether we can generate some general expectations regarding the possibility of correcting for attention biases and blinds spots, we address whether biases and blind spots can actually be identified and labelled as such, given that the attention bias of one organization might just be the right priority for another.

Can We See the Bias?

As we pointed out in the introduction to this volume, we consider blind spots and related phenomena of attention biases as instances of intentionally rational organizational behaviour in political contexts. In doing so, we inhabit the theoretical space of bounded rationality in public administration, which has continued to develop since Herbert Simon's (1947) seminal work in the late 1940s. When applied to organizations, bounded rationality comes with different expectations concerning the potential to identify biases than those provided by behavioural economics, which could be considered the first port of call for such questions: as opposed to individual decision-makers, it is much more difficult to clearly establish a bias as a deviation from 'objectively' rational behaviour in an organizational context.

The underlying assumption in behavioural economics is that biases resulting from bounded rationality are essentially deviations from rational behaviour that can be objectively identified by research. This claim is substantiated by virtually endless evidence of biases and blunders in the behaviour of *individuals* (Tversky & Kahneman, 1974). While bounded rationality is seen as inevitable in general, behavioural economists suggest it can be overcome and corrected for through smart design of the choice architecture in *individual instances*, which Thaler and Sunstein (2008) refer to as 'nudges'.

Matters are more complicated when it comes to *organizational behaviour* in political settings. Similarly to at the individual level, bounded rationality in organizational settings is also a coping strategy to deal with potentially unlimited amounts of information. Limiting the intake of information via clues or codes of communication reduces the complexity of the environment for organizations. As Luhmann (2000) stresses in his theory of social systems, organizations and systems deploy 'operational closure', that is, limiting the intake of new information, as they otherwise would be unable to take decisions at all (see Edeling, 2015, for a review of Luhmann's analysis of 'blind spots').

Hence, limiting attention to some pieces of information rather than others cannot be reduced to a bias in the sense of deviations from rational behavioural that can be identified objectively from the outside. On the one hand, division of labour combined with selective attention from subunits is how organizations expand the limited information processing capacity of humans; the selective perception of the individual subunit is the price to be paid for the overall higher level of rationality achieved by specialization (Simon, 1947). There are multiple local rationalities in formal organizations, which implies the existence of multiple standards of rational behaviour that do not easily lend themselves to an analysis of systematic deviations. On the other hand, in a political context characterized by multiple and often competing values and preferences, the assumption of the existence of some higher level of rationality to be identified from an external point of view is often problematic. First, many public organizations represent legitimate societal interests, which have conflicting views on pertinent societal issues. For instance, an environmental protection agency is likely to take a different perspective on the use of pesticides than an agency in charge of subsidizing agriculture. Second, public organizations are characterized by ambiguous objectives and multiple criteria of performance (Allison, 1997). In this context, Bovens and 't Hart (2016) argue that there is no such thing as an objective yardstick for assessing success and failure in the public sector, where organizations and policy programmes are assessed according to criteria of performance (such as goal achievement) and the more volatile criteria of reputation among key stake-holders. As emphasized by bureaucratic reputation theory, different stakeholders may value different aspects of public organizations' activities such as the quality of their services, but also their technical capacities or the moral quality of their activities (Carpenter & Krause, 2012; Boon et al., this volume).

To be clear: biases and blind spots in government behaviour can lead to serious blunders. And when things go wrong, like in financial regulation, police work, or detecting low-quality plastic surgery implants, it is easy to relate these blunders to blind spots or other attention biases of the responsible organization(s). But this will become more difficult for less extreme blundering, which stays below the radar of academic or journalistic observers. And even in cases where 'everyone' agrees that something has gone wrong, finding out precisely what has happened and who has failed to act or has taken a wrong decision is often almost impossible (Bach & Wegrich, 2016). Moreover, it is very difficult to establish ex ante whether some kind of attention bias is problematic or simply an expression of the normality of the politics of policymaking, which is shaped by conflicting views of different actors and organizations. This holds for more complex policy issues in particular. For example, in infrastructure governance, questions about where and how many resources to invest are becoming increasingly complex (see Wegrich & Hammerschmid, 2017) and difficult to solve by analytical means. Calculating the direct costs of building a road is simple, assessing the benefits doable but more contested. But basing decisions about building roads versus railways or between investing in hard (roads, trains), soft (education), or digital infrastructure on the results of cost-benefit analyses is meaningless. Differences between actors with different stakes in the infrastructure investment game will prevail, as analysis cannot resolve the issue; counter analysis will easily lead to divergent results and implications. Paradoxically, more analysis might lead to more, not less, conflict. A clear understanding of what counts as a rational decision from which deviations could be identified as biases is impossible to establish at that level of complexity.

What this implies for the identification of biases and their effects is that there is a grey zone between clearly identifiable strong biases and blind spots, on the one hand, and the necessarily diverging, similarly selective perspectives of different organizational units, on the other hand. Attention will always be selective, and particular organizational positions such as different ranks in a hierarchical system will always come with attention biases

(Egeberg, Gornitzka, & Trondal, 2016). From where we stand, there is no meaningful way to identify optimal decisions below the level of the most general statements of welfare economics (see also Bovens & 't Hart, 2016). However, as the contributions to this volume show, there is a way to empirically identify not only strong biases but also the negative consequences of organizational biases, such as patterns of deliberate non-coordination and the shifting of problems between different government entities. In short, the aim cannot be to come up with a general definition of what unbiased and blind spot-free organizational behaviour in political settings would be. Rather, the aim is to analyse clear instances of biases and in particular non-coordination. This will leave us with a more complex, but also a more realistic, picture of organizational decision-making in political contexts. We consider the comparison of similar policy or administrative domains with varying degrees of coordination and cooperation (see Heims, this volume; Busuioc, 2016) or over-time comparisons (see Lodge & Wegrich, 2014, on the politics of the 'switching yards' in Germany's welfare sector) as useful strategies to deal with this problem that cannot be solved on the definitional level.

De-biasing Political Organizations: An (Im)possible Job?

We now turn to the question of whether organizational biases can be corrected for by means of reforms and organizational (re)structuring. Since we have identified (in the introductory chapter) organizational mechanisms as being at the core of biases and blind spots, options for their manipulation to address blind spots should be available—so the answer should be 'yes'. For example, when particular organizational structures come with Achilles' heels (weaknesses in performance that directly follow from certain structures), then the trade-offs between different options should be subject to analysis and can inform reform efforts (Egeberg, 2012). Addressing problems of organizational bias and the politics of non-coordination would hence be part of the wider issue of administrative reform and organizational change.

We suggest that the perspectives offered in this book do indeed offer some analytical mileage for the analysis of administrative reform more generally. But we also suggest that biases, blind spots, and problems of non-coordination present particular challenges, both practical and analytical, and that the contributions in this volume offer relevant clues and heuristics for addressing these challenges. As many observers of administrative reform have pointed out, particular reforms might also come with the risk of reintroducing certain attention biases while trying to deal with entirely different ones. Hood (1991) made this point in possibly the most convincing way: reforms addressing particular problems and fostering particular administrative 'values' (efficiency, procedural fairness, and resilience) often shift attention to the type of value that is considered to be in short supply, only to realize later that this shift comes at the expense of one of the other values, leading to another cycle of reforms (see also Bach, van Thiel, Hammerschmid, & Steiner, 2017). Another approach towards understanding the (side) effects of reforms is grid–group cultural theory, which considers how different ways of organizing correspond to competing worldviews (hierarchical, egalitarian, individualist, and fatalist) that offer distinct solutions to administrative dilemmas (Hood, 1998; Lodge, Wegrich, & McElroy, 2010; Lodge, this volume).

Table 12.1 illustrates this kind of thinking in terms of 'antidotes' to organizational attention biases and exemplifies their side effects and limitations. In the following paragraphs, we discuss joined-up government reforms as a prominent antidote to public organizations' selective perception, better regulation and '(regulatory) impact assessments' as responses to blind spots, and behavioural insights as an approach to tackle bureaucratic politics. As to Achilles' heels, finding an unbiased solution to address a given policy problem can be considered elusive (see also Lodge, this volume). All organizational structures have an inbuilt bias, which might, for instance, lead to 'pendulum swing' types of reforms when dissatisfaction with the present structure's bias leads to the choice of an alternative structure. A new structure might promise a brighter future, and a heavy dose of optimism (or 'overselling') is typical for administrative reforms (Brunsson & Olsen, 1993). However, choosing alternative structures also entails uncertainty about their actual impact on solving perceived problems linked to the status quo. This uncertainty is one of the main reasons for the significance of organizational fashions and copying from supposedly successful organizations, as using 'modern' structures confers legitimacy (DiMaggio & Powell, 1983). Although we have no solution to these administrative dilemmas, sound knowledge about the effects of different ways of organizing can be an important contribution to making those dilemmas and trade-offs visible and moving them out of decision-makers' blind spots (Egeberg, 2012).

Table 12.1 Mechanisms, antidotes, and limitations of de-biasing organizations

	Achilles' heel	Selective perception	Blind spots	Bureaucratic politics
Mechanism	Organizational solutions come with inherent weaknesses	Prioritizing information on the basis of organizational position	Unawareness of incomplete information resulting from organizational frames and classification	Decision-making driven by protection of organizational interests and policy views
Antidote	Search for balance and the 'right' trade-off	(Forced) coordination across organizational boundaries	Procedural devices and detection tools	Institutional design avoiding destructive turf protection
Reforms (examples)	Re-organization	Joined-up government, organizational mergers	Better regulation (impact assessment)	Behavioural insights
Side effects/ limitation	Hunting around between organizational solutions	More complex decision-making, capacity problems in addressing multiple issues	Coping strategies and bias against complex policy options	Politics of policymaking

Variations of 'De-biasing': Three Reform Approaches

We now turn to the discussion of public sector reform approaches seen through the lens of organizational attention biases. The three reform approaches discussed further have been selected because they are prominent exhibits of reforms that have been tried and tested in a range of OECD (Organization for Economic Co-operation and Development) countries and beyond over the past two decades or so. But these reforms are also particularly interesting for our attempts to theorize about organizational attention and blind spots, because they can be considered as addressing three of the four biases we identified in the introductory chapter to this volume. The first reform approach, joined-up government, seeks to strengthen coordination across ministerial departments, and in doing so, it aims at overcoming the *selective perception* of the different policy specialists dominating departmental takes on cross-cutting issues.

The second approach discussed further, regulatory impact assessment, seeks to strengthen the evidence base of policy development in executive departments by prescribing procedural rules that policymakers have to follow when formulating policies and regulations. But as we argue, at the core of this approach is the idea of correcting for *blind spots* of policymakers, that is, aspects of the impact of the policy under consideration that are below the radar of these policymakers. The third (and most recent) approach, the so-called behavioural insights agenda, is also about strengthening the evidence basis of policymaking, but it addresses in particular an issue related to the biases we discussed as *bureaucratic politics* in the introduction, and specifically a variation of the confirmation bias in policymaking.

In the following, we will discuss the three reform approaches, in turn, focusing on how they seek to address organizational biases, how successful they are in doing so, and which new biases and limitations might be introduced by way of implementing these reform approaches.

Overcoming Selective Perception Through Joined-up Government

Among the perennial concerns of government reform policies is the coordination problem. Since the 1970s at the latest, the challenge of aligning the activities of a growing number of relevant organizational units within the executive, across different levels of government, and also with private and non-profit organizations has been subject to recurring reform waves (Bouckaert, Peters, & Verhoest, 2010). In particular, since the late 1990s, approaches such as joined-up government or whole of government reforms have proliferated across OECD countries and beyond (Pollitt, 2003). The direct and stated goal of these reforms is a less fragmented, more integrated, and better coordinated system of service delivery and policymaking—one that is able to address the wicked problems of today that are said to cut across the boundaries of departmental 'silos'. Hence, the central bias that joined-up government addresses is the selective perception of departmental policymakers who attend to information and signals from the specialized perspective of their issue area. As we discussed in the introductory chapter, such selective perception is deliberative in so far as it is about sorting what is relevant and what is not for achieving the policy and administrative aims and objectives for which a particular policy bureaucrat is responsible. Selective perception leads to disagreement between policy departments when problems overlap, that is, two or more departments seek engagement in an issue, and to inattention towards issues that are not a priority of any department (underlap) (Wegrich & Štimac, 2014).

Since the early 2000s, various approaches (and combinations) have been tried and tested to 'join up' government. This includes approaches that had already been tried in the 1970s, such as facilitating joined problem-solving perspectives across organizational (departmental) boundaries by establishing interdepartmental working groups dealing with cross-cutting issues (egalitarian), to the strengthening of the central coordination capacity of the core executive department, for example, by way of establishing 'strategic' units to push cross-cutting issues (hierarchical) (Dahlström, Peters, & Pierre, 2011) and the usage of cross-departmental targets as a variation of performance management (individualistic) (James, 2004).

Research on all three approaches report some measure of success. In particular, the combination of egalitarian approaches to horizontal self-coordination in joint task forces with the shadow of hierarchical intervention provided by some central coordination unit helps to push policy development on issues of overlap. Similarly, central units can help to establish some continuous attention to underlap issues when they are defined as priorities (Jann & Wegrich, 2018).

At the same time, such approaches have also seen many limitations and problems. With respect to overcoming selective perception as the main objective of de-biasing, all three approaches to strengthen coordination run into problems of complexity and capacity: only a finite number of cross-cutting issues can be addressed this way. Departments can only engage in very few interdepartmental task forces, central units can only address selective issues, and shared targets must be limited to a few issues to be meaningful. All three approaches continue to depend on the input, cooperation, and expertise of specialized units—and hence require selective perception as an administrative precondition to develop specialized expertise. That also implies that complete de-biasing is neither feasible nor desirable. It is not feasible because departmental actors will continue to be accountable for their core business and hence will put priority on achieving this (see also James, 2004, on this point); it is not desirable because cross-cutting coordination without department expertise resulting from specialists is meaningless.

In short, overcoming selective perception for better coordination of executive government is not impossible, but it will not be automatized

once one of the variations of joined-up government has been implemented. The task for the proverbial institutional designer is to balance
sustained attention to specialized issues with adaptability to new and
emerging cross-cutting issues.

Correcting Blind Spots Through Impact Assessment

A second reform area with implications for organizational attention is
known as better regulation or regulatory reform within the professional
circles advocating these reforms (Radaelli & Meuwese, 2009). A brain-
child of the wider policy analysis movement, better regulation has become
a major reform activity in a number of countries since the mid-1990s. This
reform field rests on the perception that regulation and policymaking are
characterized by systemic rather than incidental shortcomings and failures.
In particular, a bias with regard to the consideration of evidence concerning costs and benefits of policy/regulatory proposals has been identified as
the main problem. A key assumption was that policymakers lacked the
analytical tools and skills to assess the full range of impact of policies or
regulations under considerations.

The policy response was therefore to offer departmental policymakers
these tools and the training for applying these tools in a coherent way. In
our words, the problem of a lack of information about benefits and costs
of policy alternatives was considered a blind spot type of organizational
attention bias, which could (easily) be corrected by offering policymakers
new tools functioning as 'mirrors' to show them what they have not seen
so far. The tools included cost-benefit analysis and related approaches of
economic policy analysis, but also guidance to structure policy development according to the rational model of the policy cycle (from problem
definition, to the formulation of a select few options, etc.). Other
approaches put the emphasis on the measurement of regulatory costs,
such as compliance cost assessment in countries such as Germany and the
Netherlands. In other words, the approach was influenced by hierarchical
thinking in terms of rationalizing (and de-politicizing) the policymaking
process and the assessment of regulatory options. However, engagement
with policymaking departments and regulatory agencies long remained
advisory (and in that sense egalitarian).

However, raising awareness to consider the full range of impacts, costs,
benefits, and unintended side effects of policies and regulations under
consideration alone had rather limited effects on the practice of

departmental policymaking. Available research points at the sporadic, selective, and superficial application of impact assessment procedures ('box ticking exercises') (Radaelli, 2005, 2010). At the same time, correcting blind spots through analytical tools comes with its own biases: measurement exercises aimed at limiting the compliance costs of government rules and regulations mentioned above have been criticized for their own 'bias' towards the cost side of regulations. But our own empirical research has shown that these exercises have pointed policymakers to the number of target actors actually affected by a regulation (e.g. the number of affected companies), something that obviously was a blind spot before the measurement exercise was introduced (Wegrich, 2013).

The response to the observed lack of compliance with advisory impact assessment guidelines was a gradual hierarchization of the approaches. While there is substantial cross-national variation, available studies show how departmental compliance levels increase when impact assessment procedures are made mandatory and compliance is monitored by some kind of watchdog situated in a core executive department (such as a prime minister's office or the European Commission's secretariat general) (Jann & Wegrich, 2018; Radaelli, 2010). And whereas more hierarchical control leads to higher levels of compliance, it also leads to a range of coping strategies of departmental actors that allows them to fulfil impact assessment guidelines while sticking to their preferred policy option. This includes, for example, developing a set of policy options in a way that makes the preferred option unlikely to be taken off the table in the process (the 'straw man' approach) and leveraging 'presentational strategies' (Hood, 2011) in dealing with the assessment and evaluation of different options.

These observations question the initial assumption of 'simple' blind spots as the root cause of the limited consideration of evidence and policy options. Future research could consider two not necessarily mutually exclusive options for explaining the limited enthusiasm in the uptake of impact assessment procedures. One, departmental policy styles that consist of deeply ingrained normative values and worldviews of how policies and regulation should be done in that department could lead to 'hard' blind spots. For example, it is widely known among German federal policymakers, but not systematically explored in empirical research, that the Federal Ministry for the Environment favours regulatory options to non-regulatory ones, whereas the Federal Ministry of Economic Affairs is hesitant of regulatory approaches. Second, a bureaucratic politics game of the following variation could be at play: since policy development requires building support within a key actor network at early stages of decision-making, executive politicians and policy bureaucrats would rather game impact assessment procedures than allow them to derail the investment of political and bureaucratic capital invested. In essence, deviating from the original proposal would damage the reputations of the actors, who are essentially assessed against successful policy initiatives and not for the diligent application of impact assessment rules. One could call this sub-type of bureaucratic politics a variation of the confirmation bias of policymaking organizations (see also next section).

So far we have argued that overcoming blind spots in policymaking through better regulation has to contend with the coping strategies of policy bureaucrats. These coping strategies aim at preserving departmental autonomy and control (or 'turf') in policy development, that is, avoiding that findings from an impact assessment exercise nullify the political and bureaucratic capital invested during earlier stages of the process. However, Baldwin (2010) argues that what we refer to as coping strategies could also work very differently, namely by altering the policy development process in another way and introducing a new bias. He suggests that if measurement requirements are strengthened, policy bureaucrats will be incentivized to limit policy design to options that can be easily measured (see Hinterleitner and Sager, this volume, for a similar argument related to avoiding blame for policy operations). In particular, complex combinations of policy measures, which Baldwin (2010) considers to be in line with the 'smart regulation' playbook, would be avoided. Again, empirical evidence with which to test this claim is largely absent, but this argument serves as a warning that better regulation reforms could introduce new biases in pursuing the aim of overcoming existing ones.

Overcoming Bureaucratic Politics Through Behavioural Insights

Behavioural insights can be broadly understood as the deployment of methods and theoretical models from behavioural economics for policy design (Dolan, Hallsworth, Halpern, King, & Vlaev, 2010). While advocates of behavioural insights claim that those policy designs are not limited to nudges, there is a strong inclination towards testing and using nudges, commonly understood as ways to influence the choices of individuals without using substantive material incentives or enforcing regulatory standards (Thaler & Sunstein, 2008). In particular, nudges seek to correct for biases in individual decision-making that result in choices that those individuals themselves might consider problematic, such as eating too much junk food, avoiding regular visits to the dentist, and failing to enrol in pension plans. Such behaviour patterns are considered to be the result of the cognitive biases of individual decision-making that Kahneman and Tversky have uncovered in their seminal work since the 1960s—including confirmation bias, status quo bias, and availability bias (e.g. see Tversky & Kahneman, 1974).

The idea that similar biases riddle policymakers and organizational decision-making is one of the rationales of this volume and has been recently picked up within the professional community promoting this agenda. The Behavioural Insights Team (BIT), originally a unit in the UK Cabinet Office charged with promoting policymaking based on behavioural insights (and since 2013 a mutual company owned by the UK government, the charity Nesta, and BIT's employees), for example, has published a report on infrastructure governance that identifies optimism bias, planning fallacy, and groupthink as recurring biases in project planning and organizational decision-making (Behavioural Insights Team, 2016). But identifying problems is different from addressing them, and the application of behavioural insights to organizational decision-making is still under construction. There is, however, something along the lines of a proto-theory of how biases in decision-making could be overcome. David Halpern (2015), the director of BIT, calls this approach 'radical incrementalism' (pp. 291f.). At the core of this approach is the systematic testing of policy instruments using randomized controlled trials (RCTs). In line with behavioural economics more widely, RCTs are considered to provide the best possible evidence concerning the effectiveness of policy interventions. Radical incrementalism conceives of policy development as a sequence of small steps (the incremental aspect) aiming for feasible changes and quick wins. The radical aspect is the extensive usage of experimental methods for testing the effectiveness of policy interventions.

The way such radical incrementalism is supposed to settle in departmental policymaking is by cooperation between central 'nudge units' (e.g. BIT, which has provided the model for many others) and policymaking departments. From the underlying ideology of good policies ('libertarian paternalism', see Thaler & Sunstein, 2008) and the model of governance, radical incrementalism has a stronger individualist inclination than impact assessment, discussed earlier.

While analytical tools also play an important role—experimental policy trials, in the case of behavioural insights—reliance on decentralized production of knowledge features strongly in this approach. Hence the relation between nudge units and policy departments, so far, remains on the basis of voluntary cooperation. The implicit theory of how departmental policymaking will eventually change and overcome confirmation biases rests on demonstrating the capacity of trials to lead to policies that work. BIT, for one, has focused on quick wins producing efficiency gains that have gone beyond the initial set-up costs of the original nudge unit.

According to the proto-theory of radical incrementalism, relying on hard evidence provided by experiments could help to overcome confirmation biases in policy development, that is, the tendency of policymakers to select evidence supporting a pre-selected policy option to address a particular problem. However, as mentioned earlier in this chapter, this confirmation bias has its foundation in the politics of policymaking, hence we consider this confirmation bias a sub-type of bureaucratic politics biases. At the point of a formal, public launch of a policy initiative by a policy department, a substantial amount of political and bureaucratic capital has already been used to build support and forge coalitions in favour of the policy, as we discussed earlier in the context of better regulation and impact assessment.

The crucial question is whether policymakers will readily submit to following the results of experimental trials even if doing so would lead to the adoption of different policy options. The answer to that questions depends in part on how substantially different alternative policy options are from the original policy option. Different options for the design of forms for taxpayers might not be subject to strong political preferences, and hence Halpern (2015) stresses the importance of these low-hanging fruits to which anyone could subscribe. But if the approach of radical incrementalism is extended beyond this level of micro changes, the prospects for success might be similar to those discussed earlier in the context of regulatory impact assessment. In particular, the design of complex combinations of policy instruments will not be malleable to experimental trials. The same holds for changing implementation practices within and across organizations. As we know from a large body of scholarship, the success of any policy, either 'good' or 'bad', critically depends on its implementation (Pressman & Wildavsky, 1973; see Wegrich, 2015, for a recent review of this research tradition).

In short, we are sceptical that behavioural insights will substantially change the way policies are developed and designed, given the strong political incentives and organizational mechanisms (rather than just bounded rationality) underlying the confirmation bias of policymakers (Lodge & Wegrich, 2016). However, if behavioural insights were to have a deeper impact on how policies are conceived during policy formation, that is, if individual biases and heuristics would shift into the centre of how policy problems are conceived, this would come with other unintended effects. In particular, policy designs comprising complex combinations of policy instruments and organizational change could shift out of focus because they do not lend themselves easily to experimental testing or to the kind of behavioural interventions in the nudge family. Advocates of behavioural insights would probably not see why behavioural interventions should be incompatible with other policy tools and would stress that the systematic testing of interventions acts as an effective antidote against policy fads and fashions that 'do not work'. And while we would agree that these are not logically incompatible, we see different styles of policymaking at work that require different (and possibly conflicting) ways of thinking about how to design and implement policies.

*   *   *

This quick run-through of three important reform approaches that could be said to address biases in organizational decision-making shows that deliberate institutional change can indeed address biases and blind spots. But it also shows that de-biasing strategies can easily follow a limited or wrong 'implicit theory' of what the sources of biased behaviour are. Moreover, we have simplified our discussion and have not explored the interaction effects between different biases that we differentiate for analytical purposes. Any attempt to de-bias comes with the risk of introducing new biases. And finally, how a particular de-biasing strategy works and what its limitations are depend heavily on the political and institutional context. Different institutional contexts might be susceptible to different types of bias, an issue to which we now turn.

Towards Comparing Institutions

As we stressed in the introductory chapter, the focus of the blind spots perspective is on organizational behaviour. And while there is a clear link between the bounded rationality of individuals and the attention biases of organizations (Jones, 2017), we have stressed the organizational logics and (political) context factors that drive organizational (or administrative) behaviour. To further develop this research agenda, we suggest studying the drivers of variation in public organizations' attention biases. At the end of the day, we are more interested in how institutional and political contexts shape organizational patterns of attention biases and how to deal with or avoid coordination problems, rather than 'stamp collecting' different kinds of attention biases. Hence, a critical item on the agenda for further research is the question of whether some institutional systems are more susceptible to certain types of attention biases than others, and whether some institutional systems are better at dealing with biases than others. In this section, we take a first step towards such a contextual analysis by theorizing on organizational attention biases and possible antidotes in hierarchical and negotiated systems.

Much has been written on the different strengths and weaknesses of various institutional systems. In particular, the debate about different institutional modes of coordination (or decision-making) can be connected to our perspective of organizational attention biases. In his exploration of the merits and demerits of hierarchical and negotiated forms of coordination, Scharpf (1994) argues that one key problem of hierarchical forms of coordination is the 'information problem'. Hierarchical coordination has to rely on information from subordinated units (be they organizations or levels of government). But since bounded rationality also applies to hierarchical decision-makers and since subordinated units also have an interest in strategically presenting (limiting, exaggerating) information, this information will decline in quality or 'richness' while being transposed upwards. However, whether limited information processing capacity at the top just leads to a lower quality of decisions or whether there is systematic bias (as in selective perception) to particular pieces of information rather than others is not explored in Scharpf's (1994) analysis. But one can easily conjure up how political and social context factors could drive selective or biased attention. For example, Davis and Walsh (2016) show how financialization of the British economy was facilitated by the combination of the strengthening of the Treasury's position within the UK government and the eventual dominance of a frame of the financial market industry that saw financialization as more beneficial than reliance on the production sector. The latter view was represented by the Department of Trade and Industry (in existence until 2007) but was eventually crowded out by the weakening of this ministry.

With all the downsides to negotiated forms of coordination—such as their dependence on agreement with all involved actors and hence incapacity to take decisions that would enhance overall welfare but infringe on the interest of at least one player—typical problems of hierarchical coordination, such as bypassing a particular view of the problem, would be more unlikely. And negotiated systems are also more likely to display 'constructive rivalry' (Wilensky, 1967, p. 50) or the idea that bringing multiple perspectives into the policymaking process will lead to better policies and prevent failures (Bovens & 't Hart, 2016). However, the analysis of Seibel (this volume) in particular shows that such blind spots are not unknown to negotiated institutional systems, either. The failure of the German police authorities to critically review and eventually update their working theories for investigating the series of murders of citizens with immigrant backgrounds, and to consider violent neo-Nazism as a hypothesis, did not result from some central imposition of a frame. Instead, we see two mechanisms of organizational attention biases at work here. The framing of the police investigation following the theory of 'organized crime in the immigrant community' presented a blind spot, since this frame resulted in ignorance concerning information that would have substantiated the competing hypothesis (neo-Nazi terrorism). This was not about 'structural racism' in the police force, as Seibel (this volume) argues, but a result of the victims' ethnic profiles, which created a disincentive to push for centralization of the case(s). Likewise, bureaucratic politics played a role in preventing a correction of this blind spot, since this would have implied a centralization of the investigation to the federal level and hence touched all kinds of turf protection issues in the administrative federalism of Germany.

To conclude, we suggest that neither hierarchical nor more decentralized (or fragmented) institutional systems are free from the risks of biases and blind spots. Decentralized systems might suffer more from selective perception bias, and we would assume that hierarchical systems are generally more prone to blind spots as a result of the imposition of a particular frame (as in the UK financialization example). However, Seibel's case study shows that bureaucratic politics in decentralized systems can also lead to the persistence of shared frames among organizations at different government levels, instead of a diversity of organizations allowing different frames and views to challenge and monitor one another (see Gieve & Provost, 2012, for an analysis of shared frames among economic regulators prior to the financial crisis in the US).

In short, the link between institutional forms and particular types of attention biases is not deterministic, which has important implications for the development of a research agenda that moves towards the comparison of institutional systems. Even whether such a relation is one of probability, that is, hierarchical systems being more susceptible to blind spots than fragmented or egalitarian systems, is an open question. In developing (comparative) research designs, we have to be mindful of interactions between different mechanisms of organizational attention bias, such as the one just discussed.

CONCLUSION

The primary aim of the volume was to explore a related set of organizational behavioural patterns for which we used the umbrella term 'attention biases'. We identified four of them—selective perception, Achilles' heels, bureaucratic politics, and blind spots—and related them to coordination problems as unintended consequences. Building on seminal work from the bounded rationality lineage, the aim was to provide empirical illustrations of an understudied set of phenomena, to elaborate on commonalities and differences between those mechanisms, and to engage in concept development and theorizing. Hence, most of the chapters in the volume are conceptual, that is, using empirical material for illustrating theoretical arguments, single case studies, or comparative case studies. As this concluding chapter, focusing on questions of the 'what to do about this?' variety, has tried to point out, many important questions raised in this volume call for further empirical analysis and concept development. For example, the prospects and limits of de-biasing public organizations, policymakers, and bureaucrats remains a critical question to be addressed in future research. Likewise, several contributions to this volume highlighted the relevance of institutional contexts for different types of attention biases. While we could only provide a rough sketch of how such a contextual analysis might look, we consider this to be a promising area for further research. As elaborated in the introductory chapter to this volume, public organizations operate in political contexts, and any theory of administrative behaviour will be incomplete without considering how those contexts shape organizational decision-making.

References

Allison, G. T. (1997). Public and private management: Are they fundamentally alike in all unimportant respects? (1980). In J. M. Shafritz & A. C. Hyde (Eds.), *Classics of public administration* (4th ed., pp. 383–400). Fort Worth: Harcourt Brace College Publishers.

Bach, T., van Thiel, S., Hammerschmid, G., & Steiner, R. (2017). Administrative tradition and management reforms: A comparison of agency chief executive accountability in four continental Rechtsstaat countries. *Public Management Review, 19*(6), 765–784.

Bach, T., & Wegrich, K. (2016). Regulatory reform, accountability and blame in public service delivery: The public transport crisis in Berlin. In T. Christensen & P. Lægreid (Eds.), *The Routledge handbook to accountability and welfare state reforms in Europe* (pp. 223–235). London: Routledge.

Baldwin, R. (2010). Better regulation: The search and the struggle. In R. Baldwin, M. Cave, & M. Lodge (Eds.), *The Oxford handbook of regulation* (pp. 259–278). Oxford: Oxford University Press.

Behavioural Insights Team. (2016). *A review of optimism bias, planning fallacy, sunk cost bias and groupthink in project delivery and organisational decision making.* London: Behavioural Insights Ltd.

Bouckaert, G., Peters, B. G., & Verhoest, K. (2010). *The coordination of public sector organizations: Shifting patterns of public management.* Basingstoke: Palgrave Macmillan.

Bovens, M., & 't Hart, P. (2016). Revisiting the study of policy failures. *Journal of European Public Policy, 23*(5), 653–666.

Brunsson, N., & Olsen, J. P. (1993). *The reforming organization.* London: Routledge.

Busuioc, E. M. (2016). Friend or foe? Inter-agency cooperation, organizational reputation, and turf. *Public Administration, 94*(1), 40–56.

Carpenter, D. P., & Krause, G. A. (2012). Reputation and public administration. *Public Administration Review, 72*(1), 26–32.

Dahlström, C., Peters, B. G., & Pierre, J. (2011). Steering from the centre: Strengthening political control in Western democracies. In C. Dahlström, B. G. Peters, & J. Pierre (Eds.), *Steering from the centre: Strengthening political control in Western democracies* (pp. 3–21). Toronto: University of Toronto Press.

Davis, A., & Walsh, C. (2016). The role of the state in the financialisation of the UK economy. *Political Studies, 64*(3), 666–682.

DiMaggio, P. J., & Powell, W. W. (1983). The iron cage revisited: Institutional isomorphism and collective rationality in organizational fields. *American Sociological Review, 48*(2), 147–160.

Dolan, P., Hallsworth, M., Halpern, D., King, D., & Vlaev, I. (2010). *MINDSPACE: Influencing behaviour for public policy*. London: Institute of Government.

Edeling, T. (2015). Die bürokratische Verwaltung: Weder Paragrafenautomat noch triviale Maschine. In M. Döhler, J. Franzke, & K. Wegrich (Eds.), *Der gut organisierte Staat* (pp. 145–160). Baden-Baden: Nomos.

Egeberg, M. (2012). How bureaucratic structure matters: An organizational perspective. In J. Pierre & B. G. Peters (Eds.), *The Sage handbook of public administration* (2nd ed., pp. 157–167). Los Angeles: Sage.

Egeberg, M., Gornitzka, Å., & Trondal, J. (2016). Organization theory. In J. Torfing & C. K. Ansell (Eds.), *Handbook on theories of governance* (pp. 32–45). Cheltenham: Edward Elgar.

Gieve, J., & Provost, C. (2012). Ideas and coordination in policymaking: The financial crisis of 2007–2009. *Governance, 25*(1), 61–77.

Halpern, D. (2015). *Inside the nudge unit: How small changes can make a big difference*. London: WH Allen.

Hood, C. (1991). A public management for all seasons? *Public Administration, 69*(1), 3–19.

Hood, C. (1998). *The art of the state: Culture, rhetoric, and public management*. Oxford: Oxford University Press.

Hood, C. (2011). *The blame game: Spin, bureaucracy, and self-preservation in government*. Princeton: Princeton University Press.

James, O. (2004). The UK core executive's use of public service agreements as a tool of governance. *Public Administration, 82*(2), 397–419.

Jann, W., & Wegrich, K. (2018). *Generalists and specialists in executive politics: Why ambitious meta-policies so often fail*. Unpublished manuscript, Hertie School of Governance, Berlin; University of Potsdam, Potsdam.

Jones, B. D. (2017). Behavioral rationality as a foundation for public policy studies. *Cognitive Systems Research, 43*, 63–75.

Lodge, M., & Wegrich, K. (2014). Fiscal consolidation in Germany: Drifting away from the politics of the switching yard? In C. Hood, D. Heald, & R. Himaz (Eds.), *When the party's over: The politics of fiscal squeeze in perspective* (pp. 161–183). Oxford: Oxford University Press.

Lodge, M., & Wegrich, K. (2016). The rationality paradox of nudge: Rational tools of government in a world of bounded rationality. *Law & Policy, 38*(3), 250–267.

Lodge, M., Wegrich, K., & McElroy, G. (2010). Dodgy kebabs everywhere? Variety of worldviews and regulatory change. *Public Administration, 88*(1), 247–266.

Luhmann, N. (2000). *Organisation und Entscheidung*. Wiesbaden: Westdeutscher Verlag.

Pollitt, C. (2003). Joined-up government: A survey. *Political Studies Review, 1*(1), 34–49.

Pressman, J. L., & Wildavsky, A. (1973). *Implementation: How great expectations in Washington are dashed in Oakland, or, why it's amazing that federal programs work at all*. Berkeley: California University Press.

Radaelli, C. M. (2005). Diffusion without convergence: How political context shapes the adoption of regulatory impact assessment. *Journal of European Public Policy, 12*(5), 924–943.

Radaelli, C. M. (2010). Rationality, power, management and symbols: Four images of regulatory impact assessment. *Scandinavian Political Studies, 33*(2), 164–188.

Radaelli, C. M., & Meuwese, A. C. M. (2009). Better regulation in Europe: Between public management and regulatory reform. *Public Administration, 87*(3), 639–654.

Scharpf, F. W. (1994). Games real actors could play: Positive and negative coordination in embedded negotiations. *Journal of Theoretical Politics, 6*(1), 27–53.

Simon, H. A. (1947). *Administrative behavior: A study of decision-making processes in administrative organizations*. New York: Macmillan.

Thaler, R. H., & Sunstein, C. R. (2008). *Nudge: Improving decisions about health, wealth, and happiness*. New Haven: Yale University Press.

Tversky, A., & Kahneman, D. (1974). Judgment under uncertainty: Heuristics and biases. *Science, 185*(4157), 1124–1131.

Wegrich, K. (2013). Expertengremien und Reputation: Die Institutionalisierung regulativer Kontrolle in der bundesdeutschen Regierungsorganisation. In S. Kropp & S. Kuhlmann (Eds.), *Wissen und Expertise in Politik und Verwaltung* (pp. 285–304). Leverkusen: Barbara Budrich.

Wegrich, K. (2015). Jeffrey L. Pressman and Aaron B. Wildavsky, implementation. In M. Lodge, E. C. Page, & S. J. Balla (Eds.), *The Oxford handbook of classics in public policy and administration* (pp. 342–358). Oxford: Oxford University Press.

Wegrich, K., & Hammerschmid, G. (2017). Infrastructure governance as political choice. In K. Wegrich, G. Kostka, & G. Hammerschmid (Eds.), *The governance of infrastructure* (pp. 21–42). Oxford: Oxford University Press.

Wegrich, K., & Štimac, V. (2014). Coordination capacity. In M. Lodge & K. Wegrich (Eds.), *The problem-solving capacity of the modern state* (pp. 41–62). Oxford: Oxford University Press.

Wilensky, H. L. (1967). *Organizational intelligence: Knowledge and policy in government and industry*. New York: Basic Books.

Index[1]

A

Achilles' heel, 13–14, 23, 33, 40, 44, 45n2, 245, 246, 258
Administrative reform, 15, 25, 136, 245, 246
Agencification, 136, 208, 210, 213
Agency/agencies, 4, 13, 16–18, 23, 24, 72, 73, 75, 77–79, 81–83, 88, 89, 91, 94, 97–100, 106n6, 113–129, 134, 140, 144, 145, 152, 171, 195–213, 220, 221, 226, 228, 229, 231, 232, 234, 243, 250
Agenda-setting, 91, 173, 177
Agent, 39, 76, 82, 199
Ambiguity, 7, 21, 31, 45n1, 46n2, 53, 175, 219
Anticipatory blame avoidance, 138, 139
Antidotes, 246, 255, 256
Attention bias, 4, 10, 11, 13, 17, 18, 24, 49, 62, 87, 89, 91–104, 122, 127, 128, 178, 188, 241, 242, 244, 246, 247, 250, 255–258
Audiences, 17, 34, 58, 137, 140, 146, 172, 173, 175, 176, 178, 189, 219, 220, 230, 232

B

Banking regulation, 195, 197–201, 203, 204, 206–213
Behavioural insights, 242, 246, 248, 252–255
Better regulation, 242, 246, 250, 252, 254
Bias, 5–7, 9–11, 13, 15, 17–20, 23, 24, 25n1, 25n3, 29, 37, 39, 42, 44, 49, 88, 91, 93–95, 123, 171, 218, 224, 242–248, 250–257
Biased attention, 4, 49, 62, 63, 87, 89, 91–104, 122, 127, 128, 178, 188, 241, 242, 244, 246, 247, 250, 255–258

[1] Note: Page numbers followed by 'n' refer to notes.

Blame, 12, 15, 18, 24, 45, 115,
    133–146, 155–157, 160, 162,
    164, 172, 252
  avoidance, 6, 15, 17, 138, 144, 164
  deflection, 135, 145, 161
Blind spots, 3–25, 29–45, 49–65, 72,
    84, 88, 89, 91, 103, 104, 123,
    219, 234, 235, 241–258
Blunders of government, 4, 5, 244
Bounded rationality, 7–10, 49, 51, 62,
    219, 228, 242, 243, 255, 256,
    258
Bureaucracies, 4, 5, 9–11, 15, 17, 21,
    24, 43, 71, 72, 113–116, 121,
    123, 136, 154, 155, 158, 167,
    173, 174, 187, 227, 229, 241
Bureaucratic, 3–6, 9, 16–18, 21, 23,
    24, 113–117, 120, 121, 125,
    127, 154, 155, 167, 171, 218,
    220, 227, 233, 234, 244, 246,
    252, 254
Bureaucratic politics, 6, 7, 12, 15–18,
    25n1, 118, 124, 127, 128, 246,
    248, 251–255, 257, 258

C

Capacity, 7, 8, 36, 40, 41, 45, 50, 51,
    58, 92–97, 123, 128, 137, 139,
    143, 151, 153, 154, 156, 159,
    162, 163, 165, 171, 181, 198,
    210, 220, 230, 243, 244, 249,
    254, 256
Central banks, 14, 20, 24, 195,
    197–201, 203, 204, 206–213
Centralization, 52, 75, 78, 79, 257
Choice architecture, 243
Citizens, 3, 4, 13, 57, 71, 159,
    162–164, 172, 173, 181, 183,
    218, 221–224, 230, 234, 257
Collaboration, 6, 17, 24, 65, 94, 98,
    127, 151–154, 156–167, 181

Collaborative innovation, 17, 151,
    153–166
Communication, 21, 31, 93, 97, 104,
    153, 162, 172, 178, 179, 243
Competences, 9, 12, 15, 17, 18, 58,
    75, 78–80, 96, 103, 115
Complementarity, 16, 114, 115, 117,
    119–122, 125, 127–129
Complexity, 50, 52, 151, 164, 166,
    244, 249
Complexity reduction, 243
Conflict of interest, 211, 214
Consultation, 13, 217–235, 236n6
Context, 3, 8, 12, 17, 18, 20, 33, 36,
    38, 40, 49, 88–90, 94, 97, 114,
    118, 124, 127, 136, 139, 141,
    143, 154–158, 160, 162, 174,
    187, 198, 199, 204, 242, 243,
    245, 254–256, 258
Control, 13, 14, 31, 33, 38, 39, 41,
    59, 75, 76, 87, 89, 95, 102,
    103, 106n5, 115, 125–127, 136,
    141, 156, 157, 161, 164–166,
    188, 196, 198–200, 206–208,
    211, 224, 228, 229, 231, 251,
    252
Cooperation, 15, 16, 40, 74, 76, 78,
    80, 83, 84, 113–129, 139, 245,
    249, 253, 254
Coordination, 3–7, 9, 11–14, 16, 20,
    23, 25n1, 50–52, 64, 88, 92, 96,
    97, 101, 104, 113, 115–124,
    141, 160, 212, 220, 241, 245,
    247–249, 256–258
Coping strategies, 243, 251, 252
Crime, 20, 79, 80, 93, 94, 140, 144,
    257
Criminal, 12, 34, 44, 77–82
Crisis, 4, 19, 21, 22, 36, 59–61,
    88–90, 92–97, 104, 105, 136,
    137, 139, 178, 185, 188, 204,
    208, 232, 257

Cultural theory, 13, 23, 39, 49, 246
Culture, 21, 50, 54, 60, 65, 73, 94, 154, 156, 167, 172

D

Decision-making, 4–8, 10, 11, 13, 14, 17, 19, 31, 36, 37, 39, 42–44, 53, 58, 59, 72, 75, 80, 90, 91, 152, 179, 198, 199, 217, 218, 221, 227–231, 233–235, 245, 252, 253, 255, 256, 258
Decisions, 6, 9, 15, 21, 36, 37, 42, 44, 53–56, 61, 64, 74, 75, 79–81, 88, 91, 94, 99, 102, 104, 113, 138, 140, 152, 154, 155, 172, 175, 177, 181, 199, 207, 212, 218–220, 228–230, 233, 236n6, 243–245, 256, 257
Delegation, 60, 91, 95, 198, 199, 201, 204, 206
Delivery, 24, 133–136, 140, 141, 143–146, 181, 248
Dependence, 119, 204, 213, 219, 228–231, 233, 234, 257
Destructive turf protection, 16, 114, 117, 118, 120–122, 124–126

E

Elite polarization, 133–136, 145, 146
Enforcement, 38, 78–81, 83, 103, 127, 138
European Union (EU), 16, 61, 113–129, 197
Evaluation, 7, 95, 97, 98, 100, 102, 103, 106n6, 177, 251
Evidence, 20, 54, 82, 127, 199, 210, 211, 214, 231, 233, 243, 248, 250–254
Exchange theory, 219, 228–230
Executive politics, 32, 44, 45, 166

Expertise, 11, 21, 51, 53, 54, 60, 113, 115, 119, 129, 153, 157, 172, 175, 181, 219, 230, 249

F

Failure, 4–6, 11, 13, 16, 18, 19, 23, 24, 29, 30, 32–34, 37, 83, 84, 104, 113, 135, 136, 139, 142, 152, 154, 155, 160–162, 164, 243, 250, 257
Federal, 19, 21, 72, 78–82, 222, 223, 251, 257
Financial regulation, 14, 21, 22, 195, 197, 199–201, 203, 209–211, 213, 244
Formal organization, 4, 8, 51, 54, 243
Formal structure, 8–10, 19, 90
Fragmentation, 52, 63, 83, 123, 200, 207–211, 213, 214
Frames, 9, 18–20, 29, 177, 178, 256, 257
Framework, 10, 24, 25, 49, 115, 121, 122, 124–126, 128, 171, 172, 180, 221, 223

G

Goals, 5, 9–11, 14, 21, 51, 53, 57, 58, 72, 74–77, 91, 92, 94, 98, 102, 144, 146, 162, 208, 211, 214, 217, 219, 243, 248
Governance, 24, 32, 44, 45, 76–82, 84, 124, 126–128, 136, 195, 196, 201, 208, 212, 244, 253
Government, 4, 5, 11, 15, 18, 24, 31, 36, 40–43, 45, 52, 54, 62, 87, 95, 102–104, 105n2, 118, 124, 126, 128, 129, 134, 140–143, 156, 159, 160, 171–175, 197, 206, 223, 229, 241, 244, 245, 248–251, 253, 256, 257
Grid–group, 23, 39, 246

H

Hierarchical, 13, 23, 33, 51, 76, 102, 198, 199, 244, 246, 249–251, 256–258

Hierarchical coordination, 257

Horizontal specialization, 52–54, 93

Hybridity, 50, 52, 63

I

Image, 57–59, 141, 143, 157, 177

Implementation, 12, 18, 56, 76, 81, 88, 96, 101, 103–105, 153, 161, 163–166, 228, 229, 254

Independence, 95, 197–199, 203–206, 210, 213

Individual decision making, 91, 252

Influence, 63, 64, 128, 134, 138, 146, 158, 173, 174, 177, 203, 221, 225, 227, 229–231, 234, 252

Informal structure, 8, 10

Information processing, 4, 7, 14, 19, 20, 23, 36, 218–220, 227, 229, 231, 234, 243, 256

Inherent weakness, 6, 14, 25n2, 35, 93

Innovation, 17, 60, 151, 153–166, 208

Inspection, 36, 118, 119, 125–127

Institution, 8–10, 18, 37, 41, 54, 55, 64, 71, 72, 83, 90–92, 173, 174, 177, 188, 197–202, 206–208, 210, 212, 223, 242, 255–258

Institutional design, 10, 23, 74, 196, 197, 200–207, 211, 214, 241

Institutional fragmentation, 199

Institutionalization, 10, 18, 50, 54, 64, 235

Institutional systems, 256–258

Instrumental, 11, 49, 54, 55, 61–63

Interests, 8, 16, 17, 32, 33, 36, 37, 55, 62, 73, 90, 91, 101, 116, 122, 141, 156, 158, 172, 175, 183, 208, 211, 214, 221, 224, 230, 232, 234, 243, 256, 257

J

Joined-up government, 246–250

K

Knowledge, 30, 32, 51–54, 114, 151, 153, 158–160, 163, 172, 174, 217, 221, 228, 229, 246, 254

L

Leaders, 51, 52, 55, 61, 73, 74, 79, 97, 101, 103, 105, 106n6, 223

Leadership, 8, 10, 11, 16, 21, 51–53, 55–57, 59, 60, 65, 71–83, 102, 154, 157, 160, 163, 183

Limits of administration, 113

Local rationality, 5, 59, 89–91, 101–103, 243

Logic of appropriateness, 54, 56, 63, 72

M

Media, 18, 22, 25, 43, 104, 136, 137, 139–143, 154, 155, 162, 171–189

Mediatization, 173, 174, 177, 187

Mission, 16, 17, 41, 45, 58, 72, 114–128, 172, 206, 220, 229, 235

Mission-related, 114, 115, 117, 119–122, 125, 127, 128

Moral behaviour, 181

Multi-level administration, 77

Multiple stakeholders, 7

Myths, 49, 50, 57–59, 64, 90

N

Negative coordination, 25n1, 50, 52

Negotiated coordination, 256, 257

Networks, 24, 34, 58, 79, 126, 137, 151, 152, 156–159, 167, 172, 212, 222, 223, 230, 236n6, 252

News media, 18, 177

Non-coordination, 6, 7, 15–17, 24, 115, 241, 245

Norms, 6, 8, 10, 19, 38, 41, 54–56, 63–65, 93, 96, 116, 121, 124, 127, 154, 155, 177, 181

Nudge, 243, 252–255

O

Organization, 4, 29, 50, 72, 90, 113, 134, 153, 172, 198, 218

Organizational attention, 6–11, 13, 18, 22, 23, 39, 122, 127, 128, 233, 242, 246, 247, 250, 256–258

Organizational environment, 9

Organizational identity, 11, 15, 22, 146

Organizational maintenance, 7, 15, 24, 119, 121, 123

Organizational role, 6, 11, 52

Organizational structure, 8, 13, 19, 51, 80, 90, 103, 245, 246

Organizational survival, 34, 41, 115, 219, 228, 229, 231, 232, 234

Organization theory, 8, 49, 62, 63

Overlap, 12, 16, 34, 35, 50, 52, 114, 115, 117–122, 124–129, 200, 248, 249

P

Participation, 142, 218, 220, 221, 223, 224, 227, 232–234

Partnerships, 129, 158, 165, 166

Path dependency, 54–56, 62–65, 232

Pathologies, 4, 11, 20

Performance, 7, 21–23, 33, 38, 39, 59, 74–78, 94, 95, 98, 106n5, 117, 136, 138–140, 142, 155, 156, 173, 178, 181, 210, 243, 245

Performance management, 38, 88, 94, 249

Planning, 13, 218, 221, 223, 224, 227, 233, 253

Polarization, 17, 133

Police, 4, 34, 60, 77, 87, 244

Policymaking, 9, 13, 24, 32, 229, 244, 248, 250–255, 257

Political agenda, 88, 102, 174

Political context, 3–7, 17, 18, 20, 89, 90, 94, 154–156, 242, 243, 245, 256, 258

Positive coordination, 25n3

Power, 6, 14, 21, 42–44, 53, 61, 64, 90, 103, 137, 173, 197, 200–202, 204, 218, 221–224, 227, 232, 235n1

Pragmatism, 20, 72, 74, 82–84

Preparedness, 22, 88, 93–95, 104

Principal, 137, 141, 142, 176, 177, 213, 229–231

Prioritization, 17, 22, 73, 74, 82, 134, 138, 144–146, 172, 174–179

Prioritizing, 95, 172, 211

Procedural, 22, 30, 42, 43, 58, 59, 64, 154, 155, 172, 180–183, 246, 248

Professional integrity, 20, 71–83, 106n7

Professional standards, 37, 73, 75, 80, 83–84

Public management, 25n2, 38, 153

Public organization, 4–6, 9, 10, 12, 15–18, 21, 22, 24, 50–55, 57–59, 63, 64, 89, 116, 151, 152, 154–157, 159, 162, 164, 172, 188, 217, 243, 244, 246, 256, 258

Public participation, 217, 218, 220–227, 231–234

Public sector reform, 241, 247

R

Radical incrementalism, 253, 254
Rational behaviour, 5, 6, 10, 88, 242, 243
Rational decision, 91, 102, 244
Rationality, 7, 8, 51, 61, 122, 123, 172, 177, 243
Reactive blame avoidance, 139
Regulation, 22, 24, 36, 37, 75, 126, 134, 137, 142, 176, 181, 195, 197–201, 203, 204, 206–213, 248, 250–252
Regulatory agency, 13, 123, 134, 195–204, 206–209, 213, 250
Regulatory cooperation, 113–129
Regulatory impact assessment, 246, 248, 254
Reputation
    management, 50, 57–59, 64, 135–139, 142–146, 176, 188, 189, 232
    theory, 219, 233
Reputational dimensions, 173, 175, 178, 180, 182
Reputational threats, 15, 136–140, 144–146, 172, 173, 176–183, 185, 186, 188
Resource dependency theory, 119, 229–231, 233
Responsiveness, 73, 181, 230, 231
Risk
    attitudes, 151, 166
    avoidance, 164
Routine decision making, 55
Routines, 43, 77, 88–91, 101, 104, 117, 153, 174
Rules, 6, 9, 13, 44, 55, 56, 64, 72, 90, 123, 154, 181, 198, 248, 251, 252

S

Safety, 38, 75, 94, 95, 115, 124–126, 175, 229

Selective attention, 13, 15, 114, 117, 243
Selective perception, 6, 11–13, 19, 25n1, 35, 153, 218–220, 235, 243, 246–250, 256–258
Specialization, 4, 5, 8, 12, 14, 19, 51–53, 63, 64, 91, 93, 243
Stakeholders, 7, 8, 15, 16, 36, 57, 58, 61, 63, 65, 93, 152, 153, 166, 176, 188, 221, 228–232, 235, 244
Strategic decision, 172, 256
Strategy/strategies, 16, 23, 32, 34, 44, 72, 89, 99, 100, 134, 135, 138–143, 145, 152, 157, 159, 160, 163, 166, 175, 179, 188, 232, 233, 235, 243, 245, 251, 252, 255
Symbols, 49, 50, 57, 58, 61–64, 90
System maintenance, 74–84, 106n7

T

Tasks, 4, 15–17, 19, 20, 22, 50, 54, 55, 64, 73, 75, 76, 80, 83, 92, 94, 96–98, 100, 102, 105, 114–127, 134, 135, 138, 144–146, 172, 175–177, 179–181, 198, 207, 228–231, 234, 235, 249, 250
Threats, 16, 17, 31, 43, 76, 135, 136, 172, 179–183, 185
Transparency, 138, 141, 172, 181, 221
Turf protection, 15, 16, 20, 24, 113–129, 181, 257

U

Underlap, 12, 50, 52, 220, 249
Unintended consequences, 10, 18, 31–35, 45, 144, 154, 258

V

Values, 8, 10, 37, 39, 54–56, 64, 65,
72–74, 84, 90, 103, 114, 119,
120, 125, 127, 152, 154,
173–175, 177, 181–183, 187,
198, 200, 221, 243, 244, 246,
251

Velcro effect, 173, 178, 185, 187, 189
Vertical specialization, 8, 52, 92, 94

W

Worldviews, 14, 21–23, 35, 37,
39–41, 45, 246, 251